DINING IN
CATERING

THE NEW ART

OF MATCHING

WINE WITH FOOD

SIMON AND SCHUSTER

New York   London   Toronto   Sydney   Tokyo

red
Wine
with
fish

DAVID ROSENGARTEN

and JOSHUA WESSON

Simon and Schuster
SIMON & SCHUSTER BUILDING
ROCKEFELLER CENTER
1230 AVENUE OF THE AMERICAS
NEW YORK, NEW YORK 10020

MANUFACTURED IN THE UNITED STATES OF AMERICA

10 9 8 7 6 5 4 3 2 1

LIBRARY OF CONGRESS CATALOGING IN PUBLICATION DATA
ROSENGARTEN, DAVID.
    RED WINE WITH FISH : THE NEW ART OF MATCHING WINE WITH FOOD /
  DAVID ROSENGARTEN AND JOSHUA WESSON.
        P. CM.
    INCLUDES INDEX.
    1. GASTRONOMY. 2. WINE AND WINE MAKING. 3. DINNERS AND
DINING.
    I. WESSON, JOSHUA. II. TITLE.
    TX631.R67   1989
    641'.01'3—DC20   89-35751
                                                      CIP

ISBN 0-671-66208-2

THIS BOOK IS LOVINGLY DEDICATED
TO LORRY, LENNY, MICKI, HOWARD, CONNIE . . .
AND TO EVERYONE IN THE WINE INDUSTRY NAMED BOB.

A book is necessarily a collaborative effort. After World War II, they shot collaborators; we rather prefer to thank ours.

First of all, our deep appreciation goes to a group of people who were instrumental in various ways in the development of *Red Wine with Fish*. Thanks above all to our dynamic agent, Pam Bernstein of the William Morris Agency. Also playing key roles were Lou Broman, Michael Buller, Frank de Falco, Jerry Gross, Robert and Susan Lescher, Henry Morrison, and Amy Shapiro.

We owe a debt of gratitude to the wonderful team at Simon & Schuster that brought this project to life. First and foremost, thanks to Carole Lalli, our superb editor, whose sage counsel put the book on track over and over again. Thanks also go to Carole's indefatigable first-mate, Kerri Conan, as well as Lisa Kitei, Eve and Frank Metz, and Martha Reddington.

Along the way, a number of America's best food-and-wine editors permitted us to flex our food-and-wine muscles in their publications . . . and supplied invaluable guidance in the process. Thanks to Sally Belk, Stanley Dry, Barbara Fairchild, Liz Logan, Marvin Shanken, Ila Stanger, Harvey Steiman, and Jan Weimer.

A special thanks to that tiny band of visionaries who started writing about wine with food before we did, giving us inspiration and lots of wine and food for thought: Barbara Ensrud, Barbara Lang, and Shirley Sarvis.

We also owe great thanks to those cooking-school administrators who allowed us to ramble on about food and wine at their schools, and who helped shape our ideas on the subject. Thanks to Anne Brown, Dorothy Cann, Ruth Henderson, Peter Kump, Chris Toole, and Michael Weiss.

Another group of people was instrumental in our food-and-wine education, by helping us arrange our gastronomic pilgrimages to the world's "must-taste" locations; with many of these people, we shared marvelous food, wine, and conversation. Thanks to Lamar Elmore, Pat Iocca, Mary Lyons, Philippe Pascal, Doreen Schmid, and Jack Vincent.

Lastly, we never could have mounted this effort without the moral support of hundreds of friends, relatives, fellow writers, and fellow lovers of wine with food. They've sat through countless hours of our endless analysis, telling us we're nuts, when necessary—and telling us, when absolutely necessary, when to shut up. Thanks to the thousands of restaurateurs who allowed us to practice our art without throwing us out. And thanks, specifically, to Len Allison, Colman Andrews, Alexis Bespaloff, Betsy Blumenthal, Cathleen Burke, Rory Callahan, Bill Clifford, Fred Dame, Susy Davidson, Dani Effron (aka The Plum, Plummer, and/or Suwar Plum), Andy Feldman, Bruce Frankel, Howard Goldberg, Evan Goldstein, Karen Hubert, Frank Johnson, Hugh Johnson, Jean-Michel Lafond, Susan and David Liederman, Tom Lynch, Elin McCoy and John Walker, Cassandre McGowan, Jean-Michel Montagu, Roger Mummert, Philippe Nusswitz, Neil Rosen, Lewis Rosengarten, Anne Rosenzweig, Niki Singer, Joy Sterling, Kathleen Talbert, Tony Taylor, Danny Wesson, Rebecca Wesson, David Zatzkis, and, of course, the fabulous Winettes.

To become an expert on matching wine and food, there are only three things that you need to know:

1. The taste of every wine in the world, from every vintage.
2. The taste of every food in the world, from all producers.
3. How every wine and every food will taste together in every circumstance.

There are no experts on matching wine and food.

Despite a history of vivid claims to the contrary, this really is not a subject that lends itself to expertise. There are hundreds of thousands of wine labels in the world; who knows them well enough to be able to say which is the best one for a certain food? Beyond that, who knows them well enough in every vintage? And who can keep track of the progress of these wines from older vintages as they ready themselves for their moment at the table?

Food is no easier. Who can say that the leg of lamb the butcher offered today will be rich in lamb flavor or short on it? That it will be tender and silky or dry and tough? How about the oysters from the fishmonger: Mild? Briny? Coppery? What does "fricassee of escargots" on a restaurant menu mean precisely and what secret ingredients has the chef included? The wine-and-food "expert" will have to know the answers to these questions before making a selection.

Moreover, wine is not drunk in a vacuum. How will conservative Uncle Lou react to the coupling of red wine and fish that you're serving? Will the wintertime dinner that you've arranged for next Saturday—a hearty stew with a bottle of winter-weight Provençal red—have its character and reception changed completely by an unexpected February thaw? Will the Champagne that you've bought for an opening-night celebration dinner taste bitter after the critics have mauled the celebrant? Wine and food together is a sensory experience wrapped in layers of emotion, and the so-called expert has a great deal indeed to take into account.

The contemporary response to the quandary of matching wine and food differs greatly from the response of earlier generations. In fact, for much of the last few centuries the art was not viewed as a perilous one at all. The hundred-and-one subtleties that are really involved in the process were brushed aside, and sacrificed to the god known as

"The Rules"—which stated that you must drink red wine with red meats, Sauternes with Roquefort, white wine before red wine, and so on. The Rules were the frightened reaction of an earlier age to the possibility of great uncertainty. Rather than admitting that the pursuit of the perfect wine-food match might yield only frustration, the formulators of The Rules gave us a cocksure catalogue of perfection that stymied many a creative palate.

The modern age, of course, has engineered a palate revolt. We're apparently much more comfortable with uncertainty than our grandparents were, and this has had obvious ramifications at our table. We know that there's no single perfect choice . . . that what you think is the best wine to go with your chicken salad *is* the best wine to go with your chicken salad . . . that sometimes the most unlikely but intelligently made wine choice, one that you'd never find even in the footnotes of The Rules, is the most interesting wine choice. This reaction to the rigidity of another day has been a liberating force indeed for anyone interested in the pleasures of wine and food.

Unfortunately, it may have gone too far in some quarters. There are responses to absolutism other than anarchy. The belief that one wine selection is just as good as another deprives many people of gastronomic pleasure. Some wines really are better with some foods than other wines. Many meals really are improved by the selection of just the right wine. There really is an objective better-and-worse in matching wine-with-food. But in these heady days of gastronomic liberation, wine-and-food lovers are reluctant to admit that this can be so. Who wants to appear authoritarian?

The trick is to be decisive, clever, and insightful without being authoritarian. Rules—the favorite ploy of authoritarian types—are out of the question, since rules can't possibly cover the variables involved in a wine-and-food match. But something quite sensible, modern, and manageable can be substituted for rules: principles.

Principles never tell you exactly what you must drink with what, but they tell you how to think about wine and food together so that you can make the best choice in any given situation. Principles sensitize you to the subtleties of wine-and-food matching so that your understanding—and even your enjoyment—improves dramatically. Principles give you the ammunition to break the old rules creatively and wisely, because you've got something even greater on your side than rules.

In our collective desire to avoid the rigidity of the old order, we've all resisted formulating a sensible and congruous set of generalities. No rules seemed better, for a while, than strict rules. But no rules are not as good as good sense. And that is what this book represents—a search for the good sense that will create no experts, but will help more people derive more pleasure from the age-old art of wine and food together.

The only way to learn about combining wine and food is to taste wine and food together. The logic is flawless. Art students can't possibly understand Monet if they've never gazed at his paintings, and music students can't begin to explore the complexities of Mozart concerti if they haven't listened to any. Written guides to such subjects cry out for first-hand experience.

This guide is no different—except that you won't find the subject of our discussions in museums or concert halls. The first-hand experiences that supplement this book are to be found in your dining room and kitchen, and you'll get the most out of our work only if you actively approach it in those two rooms. All of the book's insights are bound up with foods, dishes, menus, and specific wines, all of which you can easily buy and prepare at home. By just reading through this book you'll certainly learn a good deal—but it won't compare to what you'll learn if you cook and taste along with it.

We are constantly amazed at the extent to which otherwise sensitive diners dutifully accept the terrifying tradition known as "food-with-wine rules." When told that a big Chardonnay is the best wine for salmon in cream sauce, for example, they often ignore the unpleasant bitterness

PART I

rediscovering your taste

on their palates, eager to fall in line with the conventional wisdom.

We say "Phooey!" to the conventional wisdom. There's nothing conventional about this section, which is respectfully dedicated to the liberation of your palate. First, we force you to taste a few interesting food-and-wine matches along with us to establish what we mean by good matches—and perhaps to jar your preconceived assumptions in the process. Then we tell you why the old rules should have gone the way of knickers and Model T Fords. Finally, we establish a modern way of matching wine with food that will enable you to exercise your own good taste.

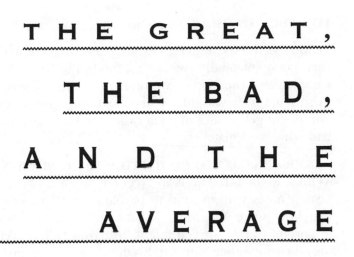

CHAPTER 1

THE GREAT,
THE BAD,
AND THE
AVERAGE

What makes a great food-and-wine match? It's surprising how seldom that question gets asked. There's no dearth of advice from "experts" on what cheese goes with what red wine, on what fish goes with what white wine, on what dessert goes with what dessert wine. But there are precious few words that attempt to explain *why* any of these things are so, *why* these matches are considered to be great.

You're told, for example, that soup is best with sherry. After you try ten soups with ten sherries—and every combination is vastly different—you'll still wonder what the experts are getting at. *Why* is soup best with sherry? What are we looking for? What bells will announce that gastronomic compatibility has been reached?

The first order of business, we feel, is to establish our criteria for great wine-and-food matches. We could spend six volumes telling you that this match is great, or that match is great—but if you don't have a sense of what we mean by "great," it will be an empty exercise.

Toward this end, this first chapter is a food-with-wine tasting that you conduct along with us. There are fifteen different "tastes" in this tasting, and by going through them with us you'll learn exactly what we mean by great matches, average matches, and bad matches.

Here's what you'll find:

FIVE FOOD ITEMS All are inexpensive, and easy to buy or prepare.

THREE WINE POSSIBILITIES FOR EACH FOOD ITEM The first is a wine that goes splendidly with the food; the second is a wine that complements the food in a humdrum, ordinary sort of way; and the third wine is downright awful. Taste through these matches so that you might get an idea of what others think of as great, ordinary, and bad wine-food matches.

A DISCUSSION OF WHY EACH MATCH MIGHT BE CONSIDERED GREAT, AVERAGE, OR BAD This is an excellent opportunity for you to compare tasting notes with us, and to perhaps develop a new perspective on matching wine and food. What you think is obviously the most important thing, but you might find your thinking changing, maturing, focusing, after you match your opinions against ours.

Each match is presented in the following format:

FOOD ITEM NUMBER The food item that will be tasted against the three wines.

LOOK FOR Read this category for a description of the food in question so the food you choose can come as close as possible to the food used in our original experiment. You must be careful, since small variations in the food can make big differences in the match.

A Great, Average, or Bad Match

THE WINE The wine that turned out to be great (or average or bad) with the food item under consideration.

LOOK FOR The details that you need to know in selecting the wine for this experiment. If we suggest a red Bordeaux, for example, you'll need to know what *kind* of red Bordeaux was used. Was it from the Médoc or from Pomerol? Was it from a vineyard that makes rich wine or light wine? Complex wine or simple wine? Was it old or young? All of these factors come into play in choosing wine for food, and in this section we'll guide you toward the best wines for the experiment. Make your own selection—or show the section to a trusted merchant, and have him guide you to the appropriate wine.

THE MATCH A careful analysis of what went right—or wrong—in each particular match-up. Remember, if you read these notes without simultaneously experiencing the match, you're missing a wonderful opportunity to bring words and wine closer together.

Even with these precautions, it's still quite possible that your response to a specific match will be quite different from the printed response. Good. This would be true if we were standing in the same room tasting these matches, and there's nothing wrong with that. Be skeptical as you work your way through these matches. Be positively ornery. Don't accept anything at face value. You must be an *active* participant in order to derive benefits from this exercise. These are not writ-in-stone-tablet prescriptions meant to endure for eternity; these are matches designed to get a dialogue rolling, and provoke thought.

From this chapter you will learn to sharpen your perceptions and to approach the subject differently, but you probably won't learn exactly what wine to serve with what food. We'll come closer to that in a later chapter. Remember that the best matchers of wine and food do not have lists memorized. What they do have is lots of tasting experience backed by lots of reflection, and a developed intuition as to why certain things might reasonably be expected to go well together.

How you work through this chapter is of prime importance. It would not be a good idea, for example, to tackle all fifteen matches at one sitting. You'll find that palate fatigue sets in very quickly; most tasters experience a dulling of their senses after about six to eight wines.

We recommend planning a party or a dinner around these matches. We have found events like these to be a great deal of fun for people at all levels of wine knowledge—seasoned experts as well as first-time curiosity-seekers. In addition, by including more people—and asking each to bring a bottle—you ensure that a merry evening will have an extremely reasonable price tag.

Here's one way to go about things. Select two food items from the chapter. Line up three glasses for each taster. Pour the three wines from the first food match. Taste them one by one, so that everyone can become familiar with the wines before the serious work begins. Group discussion always helps to focus your impressions. Then serve the first food item. Taste it, then try it with the wine designated as making a bad match. Move on to the average match. Conclude with the great match. See if there's a consensus. Follow the notes in the book and disagree violently if you want to—but keep thinking.

Rinse the glasses—and repeat the process with the second food item. For an extra thrill, include a wine with each food item—a fourth wine—that you've selected. See if the group can come to a conclusion as to whether the fourth wine is great, average, or bad with the food.

If the crowd is a dedicated one, you may move on to a third, a fourth, or even a fifth food item.

When you've finished, you'll probably have some wine left over. Great! Now it's time to serve dinner. Use the leftover experiment wines to accompany the food you serve to your guests.

As you progress through the experiments in this chapter, you'll no doubt discover that there are recurring ways in which wine and food can be good, bad, or ordinary together. Watch for the following patterns:

1. SYNERGISM. This is the most dynamic action of wine and food together. It doesn't happen often, but when it does it usually makes a match either great or bad. In a synergistic action, the wine and the food combine to create a total effect that is different from the effects of the two taken individually. Most often this takes the form of a third flavor that is not found in either the food or the wine. For example— as you'll see later—Port and Roquefort together usually create an impression of butterscotch or vanilla in the mouth. Where did it come from? No one knows, but it makes the match lovely. Conversely, some wines and foods together, like tannic, low-fruit reds with oily fish, create a completely unpleasant third flavor that renders the match a disaster. Always be on the alert for synergistic action.

2. REFRESHMENT. This is obviously a very simple way wine and food are good together. Cold white wines as well as red wines are often refreshing with food. Occasionally, a wine is so refreshing with a food that the match is elevated into the great category; more often, the refreshment is one of the elements in a match that is average— pleasant, but nothing special.

3. NEUTRALITY. This doesn't sound very attractive, but it's a great improvement over the plethora of matches that produce unpleasant additional tastes. In a match characterized by neutrality, nothing turns more acidic, or more harsh, or more bitter, or more sweet, or more anything; the wine and the food go their own ways, inflicting minimal damage on each other. Neutrality is found in matches described as average.

4. THE TRANSFORMATION OF WINE OR FOOD. Sometimes a match features an enormous change in either the wine or the food; one element holds its ground, while the other appears completely different. As you'll see, this is the case in the bad match of artichoke

hearts and red Bordeaux; the artichokes taste pretty much the same with the wine, but the wine is merely a ghost of its former self when drunk with the artichokes. Sometimes a transformation works for the better; a wine or a food can be improved by its marriage to a partner, e.g., an acidic wine with salad; its acidity is canceled out. Matches in which this phenomenon takes place can be characterized as great, average, or bad depending on the circumstances.

One last note before we begin: It's difficult indeed to write about the experience of tasting wine. Much of the literature on the subject is either too scientific (and therefore hard to understand), or too impressionistic to mean anything. We have tried to strike a balance. Our descriptions of the following matches are meant to be a faithful record—in specific but everyday language—of the sensations we experienced in tasting these wines and foods together. If you're not familiar with any of the terms that we use, consult the Glossary of Winemaking and Winetasting Terms, see page 213.

The descriptions are scientific insofar as we have tried to be objective, accurate, and complete—but it's hard to avoid emotion completely in a subject such as this. In any event, do not be put off by the welter of detail that you're about to see; all of these words merely represent an attempt to put down on paper what's in the matches. Try writing a few precise descriptions yourself, and you'll soon discover that we're all speaking exactly the same language.

FOOD ITEM 1 OYSTERS

LOOK FOR fresh, raw oysters—still in their tightly closed shells. Shuck them yourself, and eat them as soon after shucking as possible. It is important that no strong-tasting sauces interfere with the oyster flavor in this experiment; a squeeze of fresh lemon juice will have to suffice.

A GREAT MATCH

THE WINE Three-year-old Chablis (village level)

LOOK FOR a French Chablis with a village appellation. Wines from specially designated vineyards in the village of Chablis—Premier Cru Chablis and Grand Cru Chablis—are better wines, but not necessary for this match. It is important that you *do not use* the California wine known as Chablis as this is usually among the worst of California wines, and bears no relation to its French namesake. California Chablis is fruity and slightly sweet; French Chablis is dry, acidic, and steely.

THE MATCH An all-time great. One of those rare matches in which the wine works equally well as a vital partner to the food and as an exquisite refreshment. An oyster is a living pump, taking in and belching forth as much as one hundred gallons of water a day. To the oyster, this may be hard work or great refreshment but no matter—to us, it is how the oyster picks up its subtle taste of minerals. And therein lies the key to the match: The ground beneath the grapevines in the village of Chablis is also rich in minerals. You can smell it in the wine. The bouquet of Chablis is often called steely or flinty; these are hard qualities to identify, but if you smell a white wine grown on the calcium-rich limestone slopes of Chablis and then smell a wine made from the same grape—Chardonnay—but grown on different soil, you will certainly discern a trace of minerals in the Chablis.

In any case, make short work of the oyster—then swirl and sniff the wine. The flavor compatibility already announces itself. Taste the wine, and the mineral aspects of the two items rush together—the oyster taste predominates, then the Chablis taste, then they're indistinguishable, then the oyster reemerges, then the Chablis . . . and so on through an exhilarating aftertaste. Furthermore, the acidity of the Chablis cuts unerringly through the brininess of the oyster. You would not have thought that such quiet and simple items could create such furious energy. Not everything's dynamic, however; the marriage of similar textures—unctuous Chablis and slippery oyster— is the quiet anchor of the match, no less thrilling for its stillness.

AN AVERAGE MATCH

THE WINE One-year-old Vinho Verde

LOOK FOR the youngest Vinho Verde from Portugal that you can find; this is an exceptionally light, crisp, and neutral white wine that loses its charm within a year or two. Beyond the question of youth: Try to find a Vinho Verde that has a good deal of sparkle in it—some Vinho Verdes are practically still, but some are like sparkling wine. Try to find one that's very dry; many prepared for the American market have some sweetness. Also make sure that the acid level is high; some of these wines are a bit flabbier and less lively than others. Ask your wine merchant for help in selecting a dry, acidic wine.

THE MATCH The Chablis is hard to top, but were it not for the existence of Chablis, Vinho Verde might be the finest solution available. The wine's acid cuts the fishiness. Its light body creates an attractive texture contrast. Its bubbles dance around the slow-moving oyster. There is a long aftertaste that heightens the oyster flavor, but the Vinho Verde itself is not improved. It's only a light refreshment, and that's exactly what's wrong with the match. It's all oyster. Lovely, but it's always more fun to watch *two* good musicians in a duet.

A Bad Match

THE WINE Ten-year-old red Rioja (Reserva)

LOOK FOR a light-bodied red Rioja, designated Reserva, from a good vintage, with ten years of age. Experiments showed that red wines with heavier body and younger fruit work better with oysters than red wines—like this one—with considerable delicacy. Do not buy one of the most expensive Riojas from a good vintage; this is likely to have too much body for this experiment. A low-to-medium cost wine, just at or past its peak, is perfect.

THE MATCH This is a classic demonstration of the origins of the white wine with fish principle: The aftertaste of this Rioja-Oyster match is characterized by an intense, lingering fishiness that is most unattractive. This is exactly why you are always advised to steer clear of red wine with fish. In actuality, the fishy aftertaste does not materialize in all marriages between red wine and fish; in this experiment, many fruity, non-woody reds blended rather nicely with the raw oysters. But Rioja is a washout.

Food Item 2 Pizza

LOOK FOR a fresh-baked, store-bought pizza with plenty of spicy tomato sauce. The sauce is important here, because it offers the wine its greatest challenge. The dough and the cheese are relatively simple to match appropriately, but the tomato-based melange of herbs, acid, and sugar poses a few problems. To keep the experiment pure, do not get creative with toppings; plain pizza works best.

A GREAT MATCH

THE WINE Two-year-old Dolcetto d'Alba

LOOK FOR a Dolcetto from the Piedmont region in the northwest corner of Italy. The wine's name implies sweetness but, like a Beaujolais, it's really a dry red wine that sometimes creates an impression of sweetness through its buoyant fruitiness. It's also much richer than most Beaujolais. Try to find a Dolcetto from a rich Piedmont vintage, and try to find a wine from a producer noted for rich Dolcettos—like Vietti, Valentino, Ratti, Luciano Sandrone, or Aldo Conterno.

THE MATCH It's not as easy as you might imagine to match pizza perfectly. Many wines are turned harsh or sour by the sauce, many are turned insipid by the cheese, many are turned thin by the richness. The Dolcetto has safeguards against all of these problems.

To begin with, the Dolcetto is not without a good dose of its own acid, and one taste tells you that the acid of the tomato sauce is not going to be a problem: usually, two acids tend to smooth each other out. Tasting further, you find that the rich fruitiness of the wine handles the rich oiliness of the pizza very nicely. And the blend of flavors is superb; what was a whisper of spiciness in the Dolcetto before it met the pizza now becomes a statement.

AN AVERAGE MATCH

THE WINE Four-year-old Napa Valley Merlot

LOOK FOR a Napa Merlot with lively flavors, good body, and, at least, moderate tannin. A number of Napa Merlots would be perfect for this experiment (Newton, Duckhorn, Rutherford Hill, Stag's Leap). The Merlots being produced in the Santa Ynez Valley near Santa Barbara are very attractive as well. Avoid vintages known for lighter, thinner wines; medium richness helps in this match-up.

THE MATCH This is a quite pleasant match spoiled only by the fact that the Merlot is somewhat diminished by the pizza; it would do even better alongside a less busy dish. You'll be able to see this if you taste the wine first, then taste the pizza, then go back to the wine: nice, but diminished.

In any event, notice the fine blending of flavors between the food and wine: The herbal character of the Merlot is a lovely complement to the Italian tomato sauce. Notice the long finish after you've tasted the food and wine together; the flavors reverberate with neither the food nor the wine predominating. And there's very little development of bitterness or harshness. Though the Merlot is thinned out by the pizza, it makes a surprisingly appropriate and refreshing partner.

A BAD MATCH

THE WINE One-year-old Muscat de Beaumes de Venise

LOOK FOR a Muscat de Beaumes de Venise that's vintage-dated; not all of them are. If you buy a nonvintage one, it may be past its youth of minty, melony, honeyed flavors.

THE MATCH This is a silly match—the worst idea since Hawaiian Pizza (pizza with a pineapple topping). Beaumes de Venise is loaded with sweet apricot flavor, and if you try it with pizza you might feel as if you're at your fourth birthday party—guzzling sweet drinks with everything, appropriate or not. The situation is worsened by the fact that the "vin doux naturel" contains a light fortification—it's about 15 percent alcohol—and the wine's additional heat doesn't like the pizza any more than the sugar does. The cold wine is not even refreshing with the hot pizza—just cloying. Together, they produce a sweet aftertaste that seems to get sweeter and sweeter.

FOOD ITEM 3 MARINATED ARTICHOKE HEARTS

LOOK FOR artichoke hearts—the ones that come in little glass jars—marinated in oil, herbs, and garlic. Not much to choose from here; there are a number of suitable brands that are widely available.

A GREAT MATCH

THE WINE Nondosage Champagne, nonvintage

LOOK FOR a French Champagne that is dry as a bone—with no dosage, or sweetening agent, added. One such is Laurent-Perrier Ultra Brut, and another is Piper Heidsieck Brut Sauvage; either is what you want for this experiment. Artichokes are notoriously difficult to match with wine—in fact, the classic rule is to serve *no* wine with artichokes—because of a naturally occurring chemical that makes everything you taste after you've tasted an artichoke taste sweeter. This is obviously not desirable if you're drinking wines of great subtlety.

However, if you think of the wine that accompanies the artichoke as a good refreshment—if you sacrifice the wine to the artichoke, essentially—you will enjoy this match a great deal. And, if you choose an extremely dry nondosage Champagne, the sweet aftertaste may even seem like an improvement.

THE MATCH Taste an artichoke heart, then swirl and sniff the wine. There is no hint of a problem here; the yeastiness of the Champagne is a most appealing aroma next to the subtle but unmistakable flavor of artichoke. Taste the sparkling wine, and remember to drink freely and fast; the key to appreciating this match is as much in the cool sensation of bubbles running over viscous artichoke hearts as in any flavor impressions. The two are lovely together; there's a nice play back and forth in the subtle flavors, and a splendid marriage of textures.

But is the wine ruined—turned to artificially sweetened syrup? The nondosage Champagne is not; its high acid content has staved off, to a great extent, the offending chemical. Drink freely again—this is not a match designed for small sips and close scrutiny—and observe the smooth finish which features aftertastes of wine and artichoke in roughly equal proportions. The winner is neither the wine nor food—it is, by a knockout, the match.

AN AVERAGE MATCH

THE WINE Four-year-old red Châteauneuf-du-Pape

LOOK FOR a rich and concentrated Châteauneuf-du-Pape—still in its youth—from a moderate vintage.

There has been a great change in recent years in the style of Châteauneuf-du-Pape; only a handful of makers still produce the rich and vigorous wine of old. Many producers today are making a "modern" Châteauneuf-du-Pape: lighter, fruitier, more suitable for early consumption. Look for the former style here, from such wineries as Château de Beaucastel, Domaine de Chante Perdrix, Clos des Papes, and Domaine du Vieux Télégraphe. It is best that you choose a Châteauneuf-du-Pape of this ilk because thinner wines will get buried by the artichokes.

THE MATCH It is immediately apparent that this is a good flavor match-up; the spicy, peppery character of Châteauneuf-du-Pape marries well with the Provençal herbs and garlic of the artichokes. Some nice things also happen in the "feel" of the match. The wine is rich and the artichokes are oily; they feel right together.

The big problem, of course—as always with artichokes—is the sweetening of the food. It seems that the tannin and coarseness of the wine fend off the sweetening factor to some extent; the wine is certainly changed in an unnatural way by the artichokes—made a bit sweeter—but it's not at all unpleasant. And the wine is not complex or subtle enough to make us mourn excessively over the change.

A BAD MATCH

THE WINE Ten-year-old red Bordeaux from the Margaux appellation

LOOK FOR a Margaux from a château of moderate quality and from a vintage of moderate pedigree. There's no need to waste money on a great Bordeaux from a great year to see how bad this match can be; of course, the more you spend on the Bordeaux the more unpleasant this match becomes. But a nice wine from a nice château in a nice vintage—with 5–10 years of age—will make the point well.

THE MATCH Wine and food don't have to be positively awful together to make a bad match; it's enough, to our way of thinking, that either the wine or the food is completely ruined by the marriage.

This poor Bordeaux never had a chance. Taste it before you taste the artichokes; wines from the Margaux appellation are among the most delicate of red Bordeaux. You can feel in your mouth that there's not a great deal of weight—certainly not compared to a Cabernet Sauvignon from California—and yet the wine manages to be rich in flavor. Now try an artichoke. Go back to the wine. The beautiful balance that some vigneron struggled a whole summer to achieve is wiped away. The wine tastes thin, acidic, and sweet. It's not repulsive as a thirst-quencher after the artichokes, but it's a great waste of a lovely achievement.

FOOD ITEM 4 ROQUEFORT

LOOK FOR a ripe piece of French Roquefort—creamy and well-veined with blue; avoid Roquefort that is very white, very waxy, and very salty. Other kinds of blue cheese won't work as well for these experiments, which are all based on true Roquefort.

A GREAT MATCH

THE WINE Twenty-year-old Vintage Port

LOOK FOR a rich Port past the unattractive hardness and vigor of youth. Vintage Port from a great house such as Warre's or Graham's will supply the greatest thrills, but you can substitute less expensive wines—such as:

1. **LATE BOTTLED VINTAGE PORT** These can be drunk younger; Quinta do Noval made a good, moderately priced one in the 1975 vintage.

2. **TAWNY PORT WITH AN INDICATION OF AGE** These lovely, nutty wines say "ten-year-old," "twenty-year-old," etc., depending on their age. The Taylor thirty-year-old is fabulous.

THE MATCH One of the very best examples of synergistic action. Ports at all quality levels love Roquefort, and produce with the wine a third flavor that might strike you as butter, butterscotch, caramel, or vanilla. The wine's tannin (if you're using Vintage Port) counteracts the powerful salt and flavors of the cheese, taming it, making it gentle, increasing its appeal. The same can be said of the cheese's effect on the wine. A jigsaw puzzle match if there ever was one.

AN AVERAGE MATCH

THE WINE Two-year-old California Zinfandel

LOOK FOR a forceful young buck of a wine—loaded with alcohol and fruit. Zinfandel is produced in many styles in California; they include a fruity Beaujolais-style wine, and a more complex claret-style wine. Neither of these is called for here. What works best is a Zin of larger proportions—spicy, briary, peppery, and rich. The wine should have medium to full body, and at least 13 percent alcohol. Try to find a wine that is meant to be aged for several years, but drink it young for this experiment. A two-year-old wine that has three years to go until its peak would be perfect. Dry Creek Valley in Sonoma produces many Zins that would be appropriate for this experiment, as does Amador County.

THE MATCH We feel that red wine with cheese has an inflated reputation. Cheese—especially strong cheese—tends to mask the tannin of wine, and to make most reds seem pleasant but bland. The one style of red wine that works reasonably well with cheese, we believe, is young, alcoholic, and very flavorful.

Zinfandel can fit this bill perfectly. The taste of the cheese brings out a lively grapiness in the bouquet of the wine. In the mouth, one senses a heightening of the wine's alcohol and acid—not at all to the detriment of the match. It's a titanic struggle that—unlike some titanic struggles—is most interesting to watch. As always with red wine and cheese, some of the tannins of the Zinfandel get reduced—but there's enough going on in this match so that the tannin reduction does not spell out insipidity. We prefer the Port, of course—and Sauternes—but Zin is a reasonable alternative.

A Bad Match

THE WINE One-year-old Muscadet

LOOK FOR a fruity young Muscadet—which also will undoubtedly be light and fairly acidic.

THE MATCH Taste the cheese. Problems start with the wine's bouquet; what seemed pleasant before the cheese (apple-buttery hints reminiscent of a very light Chardonnay), now seems like a mere insipid jug wine.

The taste is worse. Any Muscadet flavor is removed by the overpowering flavor of the cheese; all that remains is a bitter harshness brought about by the response of the wine's alcohol to the cheese. (It's possible that the alcohol is emphasized because the wine has nothing else strong enough to stand up to the Roquefort.) What's especially remarkable is the obliteration—in one's perception—of the Muscadet's tremendously refreshing acidity.

Food Item 5 Roasted Almonds

LOOK FOR lightly roasted, moderately salty almonds. Even better, buy plain blanched almonds and roast them according to the following simple recipe.

ROASTED ALMONDS

⅓ pound blanched almonds

1 teaspoon peanut oil

1½ teaspoons coarse salt

Preheat oven to 300 degrees F. Spread almonds in one layer in a roasting pan, and roast in oven for 22 minutes. Remove, mix with oil, then mix with salt. Spread on a towel to cool, 15–20 minutes. These are best when eaten within a few hours.

Serve six as an appetizer

NOTE: Following this recipe assures a better experiment, and an even better bowl of almonds.

A GREAT MATCH

THE WINE Bual Madeira (nonvintage)

LOOK FOR a medium-rich, medium-sweet, type of Madeira known as Bual, with great acidity. Malmsey (even sweeter) could also work in this combination—as could the drier Madeiras (Sercial and Verdelho)—but Bual works best of all. There's no need to buy an expensive Vintage Madeira to conduct this experiment.

THE MATCH Madeira's cachet in the world of wine is that it's baked as it's being prepared for bottling—a practice that pays enormous dividends when the wine is drunk with roasted nuts. The roasted flavor of the wine reinforces the roasted flavor of the nuts, and the almond flavors bring out a nutty dimension in the wine. This action is most apparent in the long finish, where wine and food take turns in registering impressions; a third flavor seems always on the point of emergence. The Bual works better than other Madeira types because it has enough sweetness to override the potential bitterness in the almonds, but also has enough acid to cut their richness.

AN AVERAGE MATCH

THE WINE One-year-old White Zinfandel

LOOK FOR a fresh, young White Zinfandel with a pale orange or salmon color. (Though the wine is called white, it's actually a kind of rosé.) What's most important here is the wine's value as a refresher; it should be light, just slightly sweet, and with enough zingy acid to bring the package alive. This is a wine that goes downhill rapidly, so make sure that the bottle you buy is from this or last year's vintage.

THE MATCH The almonds are quite salty, and the first thing you notice is the cool relief offered by the White Zinfandel. It's a fairly neutral wine, but a subtle, new flavor dimension in the wine—a touch of nuttiness?—is created by the food and wine together. Noticeably absent, at any rate, are distasteful flavor clashes. Finally, the wine's acid cuts through the storehouse of fat, rendering the nuts a little less cloying than usual. This is not a dynamic match, but it's easy to imagine mindlessly eating and drinking more than you should if these items were served together on a summer afternoon.

A Bad Match

THE WINE White Retsina (nonvintage)

LOOK FOR a white Greek Retsina. Many of the Retsinas available in the American market are similar: light, dry, and with the unmistakable taste of pine resin—which in fact has been added to the wine. It's a fabulous taste with Greek food, but it's a taste that's not always appropriate.

THE MATCH Though refreshing, the match features a distasteful synergistic action. The pine resin coaxes a very powerful bitterness out of the nuts, a sensation that grows in intensity for several seconds after you've swallowed the wine.

If you have carried out these experiments along with us, you now have a first-hand understanding of what we mean by "great," "average," and "bad" matches. Let's now challenge the conventional wine and food wisdom.

CHAPTER 2

WHAT MOSES BROUGHT DOWN FROM THE MOUNT: THE CONVENTIONAL WISDOM

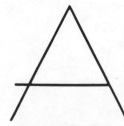

friend of ours recently called for some advice. He's a wine buff, and along with some like-minded friends, he was planning a wine-tasting dinner, designed to provide an evening of amusement and education. He wanted to know what lineup of foods would best show off a series of wines, and what wines should be chosen to accompany the foods.

Not anxious to impose our preferences on him, we asked him to come up with a list of foods and wines that he'd be interested in, and then we'd comment on the likelihood of compatibility. Keep in mind that this merry wine-tasting group had lined up an accomplished local chef to do the cooking, and had access to practically any wine in the world. The report came back:

Caviar   *Champagne*
Fillet of Sole with Lobster Sauce   *White Burgundy*
Rack of Lamb   *Red Bordeaux*
Salad   *No wine*
Cheese Course   *Red Burgundy*
Dessert   *Sauternes*

We hadn't realized until this moment that there could be a gastronomic equivalent of safe sex.

Oh, this group was probably headed for a reasonably successful dinner. But in choosing only what the books say you should choose, they were making three big mistakes:

1. They assumed that these classic combinations were guarantees of culinary compatibility. They're not, of course. It's easy to go wrong with them, as we shall see, unless you're aware of the things that are really important.
2. If they got it all to fit exactly right . . . so what? They'd be having their 497th rack of lamb with red Bordeaux since they recently discovered red Bordeaux. . . . Isn't it time to give something else a try?
3. They were trying to please someone . . . maybe us, maybe the chef they were working with, maybe even themselves. Rather than risk embarrassment before any of these parties, they chose the standard party line.

It was a perfect example of what's wrong today in the selection of wine with food.

Because a bunch of aristocratic types in France and England, somewhere deep in the nineteenth century, developed the habit of serving certain wines with certain foods in a certain order, many aspiring gourmands of our day have become devastatingly uncreative in their attempts to match wine with food. They continue to feel that there really are certain givens, the gastronomic equivalents of the Ten Commandments . . . and woe unto him who smasheth the tablets.

What makes the situation especially painful is the fact that many of these people have a dual concern: They don't want to serve the wrong wine because it won't taste very good with the food, and because, in the social crucible that wine-food matching has become, they don't want to lose respect.

For our money, nothing engenders respect more than an honest attempt to match wine creatively with food, without fear of "The Rules." And nothing can be more creative than ignoring a bunch of stale, age-encrusted admonitions that work less often than they fail.

REFUTING THE GREAT WINE COMMANDMENTS

Let's begin with the Rule of Rules, the Great Wine Commandment from the Omniscient Sommelier: WHITE WITH FISH, RED WITH MEAT.

Even people with no respect for rules put their faith in this one; anarchists in France dutifully quaff Muscadet with their broiled fish before throwing rocks at City Hall. And if you ask a neo-Prohibitionist what goes with lamb, he'll probably blurt out "red wine" before he remembers that the proper response should be "nothing."

Why does this formula hold such power? There is, historically and conceptually, some sense in it. Fish is oily, and sometimes . . . well . . . fishy. You squeeze lemon juice on fish to cut through the oil and the exaggerated fish taste. And an acidic glass of white wine serves admirably as a substitute for lemon juice. Furthermore, there are sometimes elements in red wines—like tannin, like the flavor of wood—that interfere with fish; they seem to emphasize and bring out the fishy aspects or to create a metallic taste in the finish.

Meat is heavier than fish and demands a heavier wine to stand up to it. What comes to mind first when you think of heavy wine, red or white? The former, of course. In this way, red wine with red meat was born.

So far, so good. And in the nineteenth century, these rules were fairly decent guidelines. There was only one commonly available dry white wine that was heavy: the best white Burgundy. Not many people could afford that, so most of the whites that were being drunk were fairly light. And reds were stout, often full of tannin and wood; rich Rhônes were prized as much as Bordeaux, Bordeaux itself was heavier than it is today, and Port was being drunk more widely at table. Even red Burgundy—a relatively light wine today, made as it is from 100 percent Pinot Noir—was being beefed up with the addition of heavier southern reds.

But times have changed. Many of the whites being drunk today are fairly heavy wines; some, from California, Australia, and other places, resemble rich white Burgundy and they flood the market. These wines are available at prices that most people can afford. You have to look pretty hard to find a really light, acidic white these days.

Conversely, reds have lightened considerably. Bordeaux wines are made to be lighter, as are the wines of Barolo, Châteauneuf-du-Pape, and many other traditional red-wine regions. Even Sonoma Zinfandel has lightened up. Furthermore, the world has discovered a range of light, heretofore regional red wines like Beaujolais, Chinon, and Rioja—wines that have changed forever the international game of matching wine with food.

So—in these oenologically androgynous times—it doesn't make sense to subscribe to formulations that were simplistic to begin with in a much simpler era.

Many reds today can supply the twist of acid that's necessary to cut through fish. Often, they're sufficiently low in tannin and wood flavors to work perfectly. And with the sometimes Baroque creativity of modern chefs, many a fish dish actually makes more sense with the additional complexity of a red.

At the same time, many of today's powerhouse whites can stand up to meat. There was never a reason why rich white couldn't stand up to chicken and veal, but lamb and even beef are possibilities today for white wine pairing. (Don't forget that our meat is often bred to be "lighter" in these health-conscious times.)

Many people perform an unconscious color-coding when choosing wine for food. Fish is white, so the wine must be white. There's a strong tradition of white wine with chicken, based on the fact that chicken is white. Blood-rare steak? Red wine, of course. Thankfully, well-done steak has not inspired anyone to create grey wine.

There's a kind of psychologically satisfying order in matching the colors—but if you confuse palate with palette you'll flunk more than art history.

So it's *flavor-matching* we're after. But keep in mind that, often, it's not the flavor of the main ingredient—the fish or meat in question— that makes or breaks a match. More important is the *way in which* the fish or meat has been prepared. Sauces, seasonings, cooking procedures—these are the elements that push basically neutral fish and meat toward one wine or another. Shakespeare said something like "the preparation is all," qualifying him as Stratford's first wine and food critic.

Here are two dishes—one made with fish, one made with meat— that help make the point.

Red Wine Works with Fish

Prepare this simple broiled trout dish, and open a few bottles of the suggested wines. The dish is tailored to support red wine, with the inclusion of bacon and a rich, brown sauce. Keep these ideas in mind when thinking about serving any fish with red wine; if you can brown it up in some way, it helps. And spanking fresh fish will always increase the probability of a good match with red wine.

Broiled Brook Trout with Bacon and Vinegar Sauce

Salt and freshly ground black pepper, to taste

1 14-ounce fresh brook trout, cleaned (head and tail left on)

6 slices thin bacon

Sweet butter for the baking pan, plus 2 tablespoons more

½ cup rich brown stock (or canned beef broth, low salt is best)

2 teaspoons red wine vinegar

Preheat broiler. Salt and pepper the cavity of the trout. Wrap completely in the bacon slices. Select an oval flame-proof baking pan that's just a bit larger than the fish; butter it well. Place the fish in the pan, and broil for 8 minutes. Turn the fish over and broil for an additional 5 minutes.

Remove the fish, and remove the bacon slices from the fish. Collect about a tablespoon of the crispest part of the bacon, and chop it finely. Discard the rest of the bacon, or reserve for another use.

Deglaze the pan with the stock and the vinegar. Add the bacon bits, and reduce the sauce over high heat for 2 minutes. Turn heat down, and whisk in the remaining 2 tablespoons of butter.

Fillet the fish, placing each fillet on a dinner plate. Pour the sauce over and around the fish and serve.

Serves 2

For an enjoyable experiment with some friends, prepare this dish, and serve four wines with it: a light white, a heavy white, a light red, and a heavy red. That's exactly what we did, and the tasting confirmed our beliefs.

A light, white wine, a one-year-old Muscadet (Château de la Chesnaie, Muscadet de Sèvre et Maine, *sur lie*) performed admirably with the dish, just as the old tradition indicates. It was dry and tart, cutting through just as lemon would. And it had just enough fruit to stand up to the richer elements of this dish, like the bacon and the brown stock.

But a few other whites in the tasting proved that white isn't always a good choice for fish. A four-year-old Napa Valley Chardonnay (Conn Creek Barrel Select) was awful with the dish. We liked the wine itself; full of fruit, in the classic California Chardonnay style. But it was low in acid, so it didn't cut through the fish; it was high in alcohol, which brought out the fishiness; and the impression of sweetness in the wine grew and grew when taken with the slightly acidic sauce. The same fate awaited similar white wines in our tasting.

Our favorite wine of the tasting was a light red, a one-year-old Beaujolais-Villages from Georges Duboeuf. Served with a little chill, it was an ideal accompaniment: Its high acid worked just like lemon, its exuberant fruit stood up to the bacon, and its sweetness emerged when taken with the sauce. The next time someone claims that red wines don't go with fish, tell them Georges sent you.

Of course, red wine doesn't *always* go with fish, either. A beautiful four-year-old Barolo (Vietti, localita Rocche), from Italy's Piedmont

Broiled Brook Trout with Bacon and Vinegar Sauce

GOOD CHOICES

One-year-old Château de la Chesnaie, Muscadet de Sèvre et Maine, *sur lie* (light, acidic, fruity white)

One-year-old Beaujolais-Villages, Georges Duboeuf (light, acidic, fruity red)

BAD CHOICES

Four-year-old Conn Creek Chardonnay, Barrel Select, Napa Valley (a rich, fruity, low-acid, slightly sweet, high-alcohol white wine)

Four-year-old Vietti Barolo, localita Rocche (a rich, tannic, high-alcohol red wine)

region, was tannic to begin with—but the tannin turned positively vicious with the fish, completely overpowering the finesse of the dish. This is a wine to drink ten years from now with game, not today with fish.

And this, of course, is the main guideline. Red works wonderfully with fish, just as long as you don't choose a tannic, oaky monster. Of course, many white wines these days can be tannic monsters, so avoid them too. Look for good acid, whether the wine is white or red. Choose reds with lots of young fruit. Don't expect very oily, fishy fish—like anchovies, mackerel, sardines, or herring to work well with red wine (though even these can work with red wine on occasion). And be especially careful about pairing red with shellfish; rich lobster, shrimp, and crab appear to be likely enough candidates for red wine—but, in practice, that fishy finish often comes through when shellfish is served with red, especially if the shellfish is served chilled.

Guidelines: Red or White for Fish?

❢ if serving red wine, choose a young, fruity red

❢ use a high-acid wine, whether red or white

❢ avoid oaky whites and tannic reds

❢ simple fish dishes are best with light whites and light reds

❢ if serving red wine with shellfish, use only the lightest reds

❢ for red wines, avoid fishy fish (anchovies, sardines)

❢ for red wines, something "brown" in the preparation, whether from ingredients or technique (like broiling, grilling, meat juices, etc.), helps

White Wine Works with Meat

It's obvious that white meat works well with white wine in the right context—veal and chicken in cream sauces, for example. And well-done red meat—like lamb stew—is absolutely fabulous with a rich white. But here's a dish that's medium-rare and works splendidly with white wine—crossing the color line with impunity.

DEEP-FRIED LAMB CHOPS WITH SPICY COATING

Salt and pepper the lamb chops well. Combine the white wine, the olive oil, the garlic, and ¼ teaspoon of the cumin. Spread the mixture over the lamb and marinate, refrigerated, for 6 hours.

When ready to serve, heat the oil to 375 degrees F. While heating, mix the bread crumbs with the paprika, the salt, and the remaining teaspoon of ground cumin. Break the egg in a flat bowl, and beat well. When the oil is hot, dip the chops in the egg, then coat them well with the seasoned bread crumb mixture. Immerse them in the hot oil for 2–3 minutes, or until the chops are golden on the outside and medium-rare on the inside.

Serves 2

Salt and freshly ground black pepper, to taste

4 rib lamb chops, each about ½-inch thick

1 tablespoon dry white wine

1 tablespoon olive oil

1 large garlic clove, sliced

1¼ teaspoons ground cumin

3 cups sunflower oil

¾ cup fresh bread crumbs

1 tablespoon hot paprika

1 teaspoon salt

1 large egg

Deep-Fried Lamb Chops with Spicy Coating
GOOD CHOICE
Two-year-old Meursault, Les Meix Chavaux, Domaine Guy Roulot (a fairly full white Burgundy with good acid and spicy wood flavors)
BAD CHOICES
Seven-year-old La Rioja Alta Viña Ardanza Reserva (a medium-bodied, complex red)

Three-year-old Cabernet Sauvignon, Carmenet Sonoma (a rich, herbal red)

Two-year-old Barton & Guestier St.-Julien (an exuberantly fruity young red Bordeaux)

Try this dish with a range of whites and reds, as we did. Our top performer was a two-year-old Meursault (Les Meix Chavaux from the Domaine Guy Roulot), a luscious, woody-tasting white Burgundy that also featured good acidity. That acid helped to cut through the richness of the deep-frying, and the lamb flavor brought out a range of spicy flavors in the wine that were truly exciting. There was absolutely no incongruity here between the flavors of rare lamb and the flavors of white wine.

Interestingly, most reds that we tried with this dish were not nearly as graceful as the white. A Rioja Reserva (a seven-year-old Viña Ardanza), a Sonoma Cabernet (a three-year-old Carmenet), and a red Bordeaux (a two-year-old Barton & Guestier St.-Julien)—good wines all—became more astringent, more tannic, more woody, and more bitter with the dish. Moreover, the dish seemed to require a kind of wash-it-down refresher, a challenge far better met by the cool white wine.

Guidelines: Red or White for Meat?

❦ white meats in cream sauces are generally good with white wine

❦ white meats with browned treatments are generally good with red wine

❦ red meats, cooked rare (grilling, broiling, sautéing), work nicely with red wines

❦ red meats, cooked rare but with certain spices or off-beat techniques (like deep-frying), can take white wine

❦ red meats, cooked a long time (like lamb stew), are good with red or white wines

THE DREADED DON'TS

White with fish and red with meat are the two commandments, as we've seen. But there are also a range of corollary commandments, which we'll call the Dutiful Do's and the Dreaded Don'ts.

Here are four of the most Dreaded Don'ts:

Don't serve wine with salad!
Don't serve wine with eggs!
Don't serve wine with artichokes!
Don't serve wine with chocolate!

To which we add: Don't pay attention to any of the above!

Why are hosts so intimidated by these injunctions? Obviously, they must feel that there's some sense in them—but the historical perspective shows us that what made sense for our great-grandparents makes little sense for us today.

Many of the old rules were formulated in the nineteenth century by influential hosts whose guests spent their evenings washing down Escoffier's specialties with Europe's best grape juice. Therefore, most of the hand-me-down rules were created for the very greatest of wines. The four foods listed in the Dreaded Don'ts above *do* change the taster's perception of the wine he or she is drinking. So if you're drinking perfect or near-perfect wine, it really is a bad idea to have it altered on the palate by an artichoke or a salad.

But how many of us drink Château Lafite-Rothschild every night? Or even every other night? Or alternate Sundays in May? Or leap years in which the Russians lose in hockey? Frankly, a lot of the wines we drink could use a little help from the food that they're served with to make up for their shortcomings.

And it is in this way that the Dreaded Don'ts become the Helpful Hints.

SALAD CAN WORK WITH WINE

Salad can be a problem for wine if the vinegar is too sharp; it makes subtle, well-balanced wines taste downright unpleasant. It makes slightly sweet, alcoholic wines taste coarse. But if you use small amounts of mild vinegar—or lemon juice!—wine can be delicious with a salad. A simple salad of mixed greens only works well enough with wine, but the odds improve when other ingredients, such as meats, cheese, nuts, or other vegetables are incorporated. This is especially true when wines with good acidity are served with the new generation of California-style composed salads such as this one.

SMOKED TURKEY AND FIG SALAD WITH ROASTED SUNFLOWER SEEDS

Preheat oven to 500 degrees F. Shell the sunflower seeds, place on a baking sheet, and sprinkle liberally with salt and pepper. Roast for 2 minutes and reserve.

Tear the Boston lettuce and the red leaf lettuce into large pieces. Rinse, along with the watercress, and dry well.

3 tablespoons sunflower seeds

Salt and freshly ground black pepper, to taste

(continued)

½ head Boston lettuce

4 large leaves of red leaf lettuce

8 sprigs watercress, heavy stems removed

1 large, ripe, fresh fig

¼ pound smoked turkey breast

2 tablespoons white wine vinegar

6 tablespoons walnut oil

Peel and slice the fig into twelve sections. Cut the turkey breast into thin, wide ribbons (about 2- x 1- x ⅛-inch thick). Steam over boiling water for about 30 seconds, just to moisten. Toss with the fig and set aside.

Prepare the dressing: Place the white wine vinegar in a small bowl. Slowly beat in the walnut oil with a wire whisk, until a light, creamy dressing is formed. Season well with salt and pepper.

Add 1 tablespoon of the dressing to the turkey-fig mixture. Toss well, then add to the greens. Toss well, adding the rest of the dressing. Divide among four serving plates. Garnish each plate with the sunflower seeds by placing four evenly spaced seeds on the rim of each plate. Top the salads with the remaining seeds.

Serves 4 as a first course or 2 as a main course

Smoked Turkey and Fig Salad with Roasted Sunflower Seeds

GOOD CHOICE

Two-year-old Glenora Johannisberg Riesling, Finger Lakes (a light, fruity, slightly sweet, high-acid white)

Probably the most crucial element for a salad-appropriate wine is good acidity; the acidity in the salad minimizes the acidity in the wine, and vice-versa. It's almost as if the acids cancel each other out. In fact, a wine that is flawed by too much acidity might be rescued by a salad! Make sure that the flavors of the wine are appropriate for the kind of salad you're serving.

We found an absolutely delightful wine to go with this salad—a two-year-old Glenora Johannisberg Riesling from the Finger Lakes region in New York State. It was very much like a semi-dry Riesling wine from the Mosel or the Rhine, though with a bit more body than most. Its acid matched perfectly with the salad dressing, and its bit of sweetness was a perfect match for the fresh fig in the salad. In addition, the smoky turkey and the nutty seeds were perfect foils for the fruit flavors of the wine.

~~~~~~

Guidelines: Salad with Wine

❦ use a high-acid wine

❦ if there's something sweet in the salad, use a wine with a little sweetness

❦ light wines are generally best

❦ complex and/or subtle wines are not a good idea

~~~~~~

EGGS CAN WORK WITH WINE

People have the mistaken notion that eggs pose serious problems for wine. Many sources repeat this myth, though none that we know of offers explanations. The fattiness of the egg may cause a problem or two for wines with high alcohol, making the wines taste even hotter. But—once again—by careful selection, you can actually improve some wines by serving them with "problem" foods. Lighter wines can be fattened up by a partnership with eggs. And, in the following dish, the many additional elements—sausage, pimiento, chick-peas— help to bring the eggs and the wine to a very happy understanding.

EGG GRATIN WITH CHICK-PEAS AND CHORIZO

Preheat broiler. Place 1 tablespoon of the olive oil in a heavy sauté pan over medium-high heat. Add the onion slices, and cook for 2–3 minutes, until softened but not browned. Add the chick-peas, and crush lightly with the back of a wooden spoon. Blend onions and chick-peas, and cook for 1 minute. Remove from heat, season well with salt and pepper, add two teaspoons of the parsley, remove mixture from pan, and set aside.

Place another tablespoon of olive oil in the sauté pan. Heat quickly, over medium-high

2 tablespoons plus 2 teaspoons olive oil

1 medium onion, thinly sliced

¼ cup cooked chick-peas (or canned)

Salt and freshly ground black pepper, to taste

(continued)

1 tablespoon very finely chopped fresh parsley

1 chorizo (or other spicy sausage), about 2 ounces, cut into 8 broad, diagonal slices

1 baguette

4 large eggs

2 pimientos, cut into 16 julienne strips

Egg Gratin with Chick-Peas and Chorizo

GOOD CHOICE

Three-year-old Lan Rioja (a light, fairly low-alcohol red with spicy flavors)

heat. Add the chorizo slices in a single layer, and cook them for 30 seconds on each side. Remove from pan and set aside.

Place the baguette in the hot oven. Heat for 5–6 minutes, or until the crust is toasted and the inside is still soft. Cut six slices (¼-inch-thick) of bread. Reserve the rest of the loaf for another use.

Place three slices of bread in each of two earthenware gratin dishes (oval shape, approximately 10 x 4 inches). Drizzle the remaining 2 teaspoons of olive oil over the bread. Divide the chick-pea mixture in half, and spread it evenly over the bread slices in each dish. Lay four slices of chorizo over all in each dish, leaving two slight depressions near the center of each dish for the egg yolks.

Break and separate the eggs. Divide the whites evenly between the two dishes, and scatter the pimiento strips over them. Place the dishes under the broiler, and broil for 3–4 minutes, or until the whites are just starting to set. Remove from the broiler and, with a spoon, make two definite depressions near the center of each dish. Slip the egg yolks into these depressions, and place the dishes in the oven for 3 minutes, or until the yolks are cooked but runny.

Remove from oven, sprinkle reserved parsley over all, and serve.

Serves 2 as a brunch or luncheon dish

The injunction against wine with eggs was smashed when we served a light, young red Rioja with this dish. A three-year-old Lan from a fair vintage was absolutely delicious: The pimiento accented the wine's fruit, the spicy sausage and the spicy wood flavors of the wine were synchronized, the light wine seemed more substantial, and the egg brought out an intriguing tobaccolike flavor in the wine.

As demonstrated here, a good way to improve the odds of wine success with eggs is to include other elements in the egg dish that you know will react favorably with wine. Cheese, meat, bread, vegetables—there's a wide range of ingredients to choose from.

Another possibility—as any Burgundian will tell you—is to use the wine, in some way, in the cooking process. *Oeufs en Meurette*, a great specialty of the Beaujolais region, features eggs poached in a bacon-and-Beaujolais sauce, then served with the thickened sauce. It's not hard to guess what wine appears at table with this dish.

Notably, Beaujolais features reasonably low alcohol—and it's a good idea to seek out wines of that type to serve with eggs.

Guidelines: Serving Eggs with Wine

❧ avoid high-alcohol wines

❧ prepare the eggs with other ingredients (like meats, cheeses, etc.) that you know to be wine-friendly

❧ use wine in the preparation of the dish, if possible

ARTICHOKES CAN WORK WITH WINE

Here's a classic example of a food changing the perception of a wine: There's a chemical in artichokes that makes anything you taste, after tasting an artichoke, taste sweeter. The solution is simple: Prepare artichokes with acidic ingredients, then serve the dish with a very dry, acidic wine that could use a little sweetening. In the following dish, you'll notice the effect most if you use fresh artichoke hearts—but you can substitute canned hearts.

NIÇOISE SAUTÉ OF ARTICHOKE HEARTS

Cut the artichoke hearts into quarters, and set aside.

In a heavy sauté pan, heat the regular olive oil over medium heat. Add the garlic, and sauté for 2 minutes. Make sure the garlic does not turn brown. Add the artichokes and the olives. Shred the basil, and add two-thirds of it to the pan. Cook, stirring frequently, for 5 minutes. Remove contents of pan and keep warm.

6 fresh artichoke hearts, cooked, with chokes removed

2 tablespoons regular olive oil

2 large garlic cloves, minced, about 4 teaspoons

(continued)

9 Niçoise olives, pitted
and coarsely
chopped

⅔ cup very firmly
packed basil leaves

½ cup white wine

2 tomatoes, peeled,
seeded, juiced, and
cut into strips or 2
canned tomatoes,
squeezed and cut
into strips

⅔ cup chicken stock

2 tablespoons extra-
virgin olive oil

Deglaze the pan with the white wine. Reduce over high heat for 2 minutes. Add the tomato strips and the chicken stock. Reduce over high heat for 2 minutes, until slightly thickened. Remove from heat and, with a wire whisk, beat in the extra-virgin olive oil.

Divide the reserved artichoke mixture among four plates. Strew the cooked tomatoes over the artichokes, then pour the liquid from the pan over all. Garnish with the remaining shredded leaves of basil.

Serves 4 as a first course

Niçoise Sauté of Artichoke Hearts

GOOD CHOICE

Two-year-old Oddero Barbera d'Alba (a high-acid, low-tannin, medium-bodied red)

With this dish, we served a wine that goes magically with many foods: Barbera d'Alba from the Piedmont region in Italy. Made from the Barbera grape in the vicinity of Alba, as the name indicates, this red wine always features low tannin and high acid, making it friendly to a wide range of foods. Along with these features, you also get a good deal of fruit flavor and, sometimes, a fairly rich texture.

The flavors of the two-year-old Oddero Barbera d'Alba that we used—all fruit and berries—were lovely with the artichoke sauté. But

Guidelines: Improving Wine with Artichokes

❡ serve high acid wines with artichokes to compensate for the extra sweetness

❡ unless you want a sweet-savory match between wine and food, make sure the wine you serve with artichokes is extremely dry

❡ avoid top-quality wines; if you want to enjoy the wine exactly as it is without altering its taste don't serve artichokes

❡ light reds with high acid will usually work best

❡ include something acidic in the dish (like tomatoes) to offset the sweetening effect

most important was the high acid in the wine. The sweetening effect of the artichokes was offset a bit by the tomatoes in the dish, but the artichokes still delivered: Everything we tasted after eating them seemed sweeter. Off-dry wines with low acid taste flabby and sweet with this dish, but the high-acid Barbera d'Alba is actually improved by the combination.

Do not try this with a venerable bottle of great Burgundy that you've been waiting to taste for twenty years. There's no point in altering the flavor of a wine if you're concentrating on it for some reason or other. But for 95 percent of dining situations, there's absolutely nothing wrong with wine and artichokes. Many an overly tart Beaujolais, Muscadet, village Chablis or dry Mosel wine could be improved by appropriate dishes made with artichokes.

Chocolate Can Work with Wine

Sweet chocolate desserts can clash with sweet wines. This has led some to suggest that the best bets with chocolate are rich, dry red wines—like Cabernets or Zinfandels from California. But we find that these wines turn thin and acidic with chocolate. The best strategy is to prepare a moderately sweet chocolate dish, cut in some way by an acidic ingredient . . . and to serve it with a blockbuster dessert wine.

Chocolate Cake with Fresh Raspberry Sauce

Preheat oven to 400 degrees F. Line a round 9-inch x 2-inch baking pan with buttered wax paper.

Chop the chocolate into ¼-inch pieces and place, along with the butter, in the top of a double boiler over simmering water. Over low heat, slowly melt the chocolate and butter together. Remove from heat when the last chocolate chunks have disappeared. Cool.

While the chocolate is cooling, place the eggs in an electric mixer and whip, slowly adding the sugar until the mixture triples in volume, about 10 minutes. Then, reduce the mixer to its slowest speed and carefully pour

9 ounces bittersweet chocolate

5 tablespoons sweet butter (3½ ounces)

6 large eggs

7½ ounces granulated sugar (1 cup)

1¼ ounces all-purpose, presifted flour (¼ cup plus 2 tablespoons)

(continued)

Fresh Raspberry Sauce

1 cup firmly packed raspberries, plus about 30 extra left whole for garnish

3 tablespoons sweet wine (like Port)

~~~~~~~~~~~~~~~~~~~~~~~~~~~~~

Chocolate Cake with Fresh Raspberry Sauce

GOOD CHOICE

Nonvintage Cockburn's Special Reserve Port (a sweet, rich, not overly complex fortified red wine)

~~~~~~~~~~~~~~~~~~~~~~~~~~~~~

in the cooled chocolate mixture. Blend well. Gently fold in the flour, then pour into the prepared pan.

Place in the preheated oven, and bake for 10 minutes. Then reduce the oven to 350 degrees F, and bake for another 30 minutes. Remove, and let the cake cool to room temperature before serving.

Meanwhile, prepare the sauce: Place the ingredients in a food processor. Pulse about seven times, or until a chunky puree is reached.

For each serving, place about one tablespoon of the puree on a dessert plate. Place four thin slices of the cake on each plate, over the puree, and garnish each serving with 3–4 raspberries on top of the cake.

Serves 8

Our wine choice here was a lovely blended Port from the house of Cockburn, the nonvintage Special Reserve. The wine is sweet and rich to begin with—and, of course, fairly alcoholic (Ports have around 20 percent alcohol). The chocolate changed the wine by making it taste a little less rich and sweet. Superb! This actually enabled some of the subtler elements in the wine to come through—hints of raisins, nuts, vanilla. And these flavors were all highly complementary to the chocolate-raspberry flavors of the dish.

~~~~~~

Guidelines: Chocolate with Wine

❦ serve a sweet wine with chocolate desserts

❦ avoid very complex or aged sweet wines

❦ alcohol in the wine helps; a fortified wine like Port or Madeira is a good choice

❦ prepare a dessert that's not excessively sweet

❦ work something acidic into the chocolate preparation (such as fresh berries or other acidic fruit)

Once again, it is not a good idea to use a lovingly aged, top-flight Vintage Port in this situation. Such wines are already a bit dried out by time, and you wouldn't want to risk any further diminution of richness and sweetness. Those wines need no help to bring out subtlety. But a more obvious type of Port—like the Cockburn's Special Reserve—actually tastes more like a grand Vintage Port when drunk with this dish.

THE DUTIFUL DO'S

The Dreaded Don'ts have terrorized many a host—but steering clear of them only leads to sins of *omission*. True, you won't ruin a meal but you will miss some tasty things. However, the very proper cousins of the Dreadful Don'ts—the Dutiful Do's—regularly disappoint rule-following hosts by failing to live up to their inflated reputations. Blind adherence to the Dutiful Do's can cause some real sins of *commission* at table.

Many people mistakenly believe that some or all of the following Dutiful Do's are practically infallible:

Do drink Champagne with caviar!
Do drink Chianti with pasta and tomato sauce!
Do drink Cabernet with steak!
Do drink red wine with cheese!
To which we add: Do be careful!

You have no guarantees on any of these match-ups. Two of them—the pasta and the steak—will usually do well with their respective partners, as long as you follow some simple guidelines. But the traditional wine advice for the other two—Champagne for caviar and red wine for cheese—can charitably be labeled "science fiction."

CAVIAR AND CHAMPAGNE ARE NOT SOUL MATES

This is one of those classic matches that always seems to excite people. But it's an economic logic that brings these two items together, not a gustatory one. Raid your bank account, open a few bottles of bubbly with some fish eggs, keep an open mind, and see if you don't agree.

CAVIAR ON ICE

All you need to do is place about one ounce of caviar in a very small bowl. (The caviar should fill the bowl.) Place the bowl in a bed of shaved ice, and you're ready to go. For this experiment—and, to our taste, for caviar enjoyment in general—no accompaniments are needed. Eggs, onion, and sour cream all are useful to cover up the taste of second-rate caviar. But when the real thing is served—as it should be in this experiment—the only proper accompaniment is a small, exquisite spoon.

By the real thing, of course, we mean the eggs of sturgeons, exported either from Iran or Russia. Beluga caviar is the most expensive (larger eggs), but either sevruga or osetra caviar will perform admirably in this experiment—and at a much more reasonable price. Many connoisseurs and experts in fact prefer the smaller eggs. We carried out our taste test with osetra.

Serve as many people as you can, with one ounce of caviar per person (or two, if you're feeling really flush)

Almost every Champagne and sparkling wine in our tasting seemed coarser, sweeter, hotter after eating the caviar. It's the rare sparkling wine that stands up to eggs that, even at their best, retain some saltiness and fishiness. We found in general that frozen vodka, which washed over the eggs in a Siberian cloud of velvet, was the best accompaniment.

If you insist on Champagne, your best choice is an extremely dry, light, elegant Champagne which will suffer minimal interference from the caviar. This means French Champagne; lots of good sparkling wines are being made around the world, but none has the austere delicacy of the lighter French Champagnes. Our favorite was a Champagne made with no additional sugar (a very rare thing in the world of Champagne): Piper Heidsieck's Brut Sauvage. It served as a simple refreshment for the caviar, and did not turn fishy, hot, or coarse. But we emphasize once again: This was an anomaly. Once in a while, you will also hit a complex, aged Champagne that scores with caviar . . . particularly with Osetra.

USE CAUTION WITH CHIANTI AND TOMATO-SAUCED PASTA

There are so many styles of Chianti today—and so many new-fangled pasta dishes going around—that this once-simple choice has become increasingly complex. Prepare the following dish in late summer with about three cups of fresh tomatoes, skinned, seeded, and cut into strips. But for the rest of the year the canned variety provides a reasonable substitute.

LINGUINE WITH PANCETTA, CAPERS, AND TOMATO

Heat 2 tablespoons of the olive oil in a sauté pan over medium heat. Add the garlic, and sauté for 1 minute. Slice the pancetta rounds into ½-inch strips, and add to the oil. Sauté for 2 minutes, stirring. Add the capers. Drain and squeeze the liquid out of the canned tomatoes. Coarsley chop and add the tomato pulp—there should be about 3 cups—to the sauté pan. Stir well, bring to a simmer, and cook over medium-high heat for 3 minutes. Add a generous grind of black pepper.

Meanwhile, prepare the pasta. Cook the linguine in a large pot of salted water until just al dente. Drain in a colander, tossing up and down to remove the excess water. Add the remaining 2 tablespoons of olive oil, along with the cheese. Toss well.

Divide the pasta among six plates, and top with the sauce.

Serves 6

¼ cup olive oil

2 tablespoons finely chopped garlic, about 4 large cloves

4 ounces pancetta, cut in very thin rounds

4 teaspoons capers

4 28-ounce cans of peeled tomatoes

Freshly ground black pepper, to taste

1 pound linguine

Salt

½ cup freshly grated Parmigiano-Reggiano cheese

Tomato sauce poses problems for wine; it's extremely acidic, which makes wines with even a hint of sweetness and/or richness taste too

Linguine with Pancetta, Capers, and Tomato
BAD CHOICES

Two-year-old Ruffino Chianti Classico (a fruity, young Chianti)

Four-year-old Fattoria di Felsina Chianti Classico Riserva (a tannic, concentrated, rich Chianti)

sweet or too rich for such a simple dish. The best wine is a light, simple, fairly acidic red; the acid in the sauce and the acid in the wine cancel each other out, with happy results.

The traditional style of Chianti—not too fruity, light (from the addition of white grapes), fairly acidic—is a good bet with tomato-sauce pasta dishes. But there are many Chiantis on the market today that are either exuberantly fruity (because they have very little age and have retained their young fruit) or very serious (because they have been made with high-quality grapes, then aged for some time in small barrels, which gives them more richness and structure).

Both of these styles are departures from the Chianti tradition.

In our tasting, a traditional Chianti—a six-year-old Nozzole Chianti Classico Riserva—performed beautifully with the dish, merging seamlessly with the acid of the tomatoes. But a two-year-old Ruffino Chianti Classico—with lots of yummy, young fruit—seemed a little sweet when drunk with the sauce. And a spectacular Chianti built to age—a four-year-old Fattoria di Felsina Chianti Classico Riserva—was wasted on this dish; the simple acidity of the tomato sauce ate away the deep concentration of fruit and new wood.

We gave the new style Chiantis every advantage we could—by supplying the salty cheese and pancetta, by supplying the additional flavor interest of capers. But the old-fashioned stuff—reminiscent of what you'd find in straw-covered flasks—won the day. Save the wonderful new Chiantis for dishes other than tomato-sauce pasta.

Guidelines: The New World of Chianti and Tomato Sauce

❦ avoid fruity young Chiantis

❦ avoid serious, built-to-last Chiantis

❦ serve old-fashioned Chiantis that have been aged for 4–8 years (enough to lose their young fruit)

❦ include cheese and other salty-meaty elements in the dish to help smooth out the match

HOW TO RUIN STEAK WITH CABERNET

There's no doubt about it: A simply grilled steak with a bottle of Napa Valley Cabernet Sauvignon is a real high-odds proposition. Other Cabernets from around the world—even some from Bordeaux, the homeland of Cabernet—can sometimes be too light for the heft of a grilled steak. And if you deviate from the basic preparation, there are no guarantees whatsoever. Substitute other cuts of steak for the skirt steak in this recipe if you must—but don't leave out the pepper, the coriander, or the lettuce. They make the point well that "the preparation is all" when it comes to this classic match.

PEPPERED SKIRT STEAK BUNDLES WITH CORIANDER SEEDS

Place a heavy cast-iron skillet over high heat for about 10 minutes. Meanwhile, coat the skirt steak on both sides with the pepper, pressing it well into the meat. When the pan is hot, add the steak. After 10 seconds, shift its position slightly with a spatula to prevent sticking. Cook for about 2 minutes on the first side. Flip over, adjust position again after 10 seconds, then cook for another 1½ to 2 minutes for rare meat. Remove from pan and set aside.

Cut scallions into eighteen 2-inch lengths. Use mostly the white parts, leaving just a touch of green at one end. Place in the hot pan, cover, and cook, shaking the pan often, for about 2 minutes (until charred and tender). Remove.

Lay out the lettuce leaves with the stem end to the left. Thinly slice the steak along the grain into about thirty-six slices. On each lettuce leaf, place six steak slices, evenly spaced along one half of the leaf. Salt to taste. Lay three scallions across the meat on each leaf, and top with ¼ teaspoon of coriander seeds. Roll up and serve.

The flavor improves if you make the bundles about 1 hour in advance and keep them at room temperature.

Serves 6 as a pass-around appetizer

1 8-ounce piece of skirt steak, about ½-inch thick

1 rounded ½-teaspoon of coarse-ground black pepper

18 scallions

6 large, soft lettuce leaves, such as hydroponically cultivated Boston or butter lettuce

Salt

1½ teaspoons coriander seeds, lightly crushed

Peppered Skirt Steak Bundles with Coriander Seeds

BAD CHOICE

Eight-year-old Château Pichon Longueville Baron (an elegant, subtle red Bordeaux near its peak)

While preparing this dish, we were sampling the intended victim: an eight-year-old Château Pichon Longueville Baron, from a very fine vintage, just approaching its peak of drinkability. This was a lovely red Bordeaux, with a pretty bouquet that mingled cassis, herbal qualities, and a touch of tar. On the palate, the wine had medium texture, good balance, and just a moderate degree of tannin. Our anticipation was rising.

Unfortunately, the wine was obliterated by the dish. The char on the steak thinned the wine out immediately. The pepper killed the wine's subtlety. The lettuce diluted the wine's flavors, bringing out an unattractive mineral-like quality. The coriander had too much flavor for the wine; in the finish, all you tasted was coriander. It's a delicious dish and a delicious wine, but this marriage took a quick detour to Reno.

Forceful flavors in conjunction with steak—and this can mean something as seemingly innocent as the flavors of outdoor grilling—can wreak havoc with Cabernet-based wines of elegance. So unless you're having a simple pan-broiled steak with minimal flavor enhancement, it's probably best to think rich California or Australian Cabernet when it comes to steak.

Guidelines: Steak with Cabernet

❦ for simple preparations, most Cabernets—including elegant Bordeaux—will be fine

❦ for preparations that involve additional strong flavors, richer Cabernets—there are many from California and Australia—are preferable

RED WINE AND CHEESE DOESN'T

ALWAYS PLEASE

According to an old Bordeaux wine-merchant's maxim, the secret to a successful business is simple. When you buy wine, taste apples with it—for the wine will be at its worst, and you can judge it severely. When you sell wine, have the buyers taste it with cheese—because every wine tastes better with cheese.

No wonder there aren't many old Bordeaux wine merchants left.

If only wine always did taste better with cheese, this world would be a finer place. But there are many variables. Cheese can be crafted from the milk of cows, goats, sheep, donkeys, yaks, and reindeer; can be dry, soft, oozy, spreadable, or capable of inflicting damage when fired from fifty paces; can be inconsequential from an olfactory perspective . . . or can smell like hell.

We gave cheese a rough time in our test, but we think it makes the point that when you say cheese—whether you're smiling or not—you'd better be specific.

A SERVICE OF ÉPOISSES

Go to your local cheese shop and ask for a soft-ripened, washed-rind cow's milk cheese. Two ounces per person of almost any will do the job: Époisses, Livarot, Munster (not the anemic sliced wax from Wisconsin, but the real smelly stuff from Alsace). Just make sure it's not over the hill. If there's any doubt in your mind, ask the cheesemonger behind the deli counter (he's the one with the nose clips and rebreather).

Get it home quickly, avoiding other human beings at all cost, and let it come to room temperature—approximately 16 hours is a good rule of thumb for cheese. Serve it with bread (No butter, please!), crackers (No herbs and flavorings, please!), or with knife and fork.

For our tasting, we bought a small wheel of Époisses—a venerable Burgundian fromage with a history as long as its scented plume—and proceeded to our underground test site, reds at the ready.

A Service of Époisses

BAD CHOICES

A five-year-old Domaine Dujac Gevrey-Chambertin, Côte de Nuits (a medium-bodied, spicy and earthy Burgundy)

A two-year-old Coturri Zinfandel from Sonoma (a young, robust, alcoholic red Zinfandel)

A 12-ounce wheel of Époisses serves 6 as part of a cheese course

To the Burgundians, this wonderfully flawed discus—oozing mortal perfume from every crack and fistula—is best with wines from their native soil. Red Burgundy and Epoisses is one of the time-honored biggies.

So out came the red Burgundy—a five-year-old Gevrey-Chambertin from the Domaine Dujac. It was a fine bottle of Pinot Noir, all earth, sweet fruit, and exotic spice—until we had a bit of the cheese. In a single stroke of a malevolent dairy product, the wine's lovely, somewhat fragile alliance of flavors was sent scurrying for cover. The cheese was just too brutish; our poor wine never stood a chance.

Never willing to run from a fight, we popped a robust, alcoholic Zinfandel from California—a brash, young two-year-old from Coturri's Cooke Vineyards in Sonoma—and pushed our southpaw into the ring. It wasn't a taste rout as in the Burgundy versus Burgundy main event, but the wine's assertiveness seemed humbled by the staying power of the Époisses. What's more, a mean streak of fulsome tobacco flavor emerged. In the end, it was still all cheese and no wine.

Just for fun—by this time we were a bit punchy—we tried a rich, six-year-old Vendange Tardive Gewürztraminer from the Alsatian house of Willm. The white wine paired more easily with the Époisses than any of the reds! The Gewürz, by sheer dint of density, protected our tongues from too much bullying by the cheese. Even more impressively, the wine's inherent spiciness danced around the Époisse's sharp jabs, softening each blow that came its way. A regular Gewürztraminer might not have had the moves, but this late-harvest beauty was a knockout.

Try this test for yourself, to experience an extreme example of the potential incompatibility of red wine and cheese. But you don't have to stack the deck as we did, serving a subtle red with an extremely

Guidelines: Red Wine with Cheese

❦ firm, dry cheeses (including chevre) stand the best chance with red wine

❦ cheeses that are soft, fatty, or creamy make red wine taste dull

❦ smelly cheeses overwhelm red wine

❦ salty cheeses, particularly blue-veined types, overwhelm red wine

❦ if you must pair red wine with cheeses, look for dry, mild cheeses and for rich, fruity young reds

powerful cheese. Most creamy, fatty cheeses will knock the stuffing out of most red wines. Tannin is neutralized by the fat in the cheese, and reds often taste flat, spineless, and bland when served with runny cheeses. Try a Camembert with a good red Bordeaux. It should work, according to the books . . . but see if you don't agree that the wine is much better on its own.

Other kinds of cheese pose different problems. Blue cheeses—from Roquefort to Maytag Blue—are just too much for most red wine. Better to serve a sweet white, like a Sauternes, than to sacrifice one more red to the Dutiful Do's.

In our tasting experience, only chevre consistently marries well with red wine. If the cheese is not too aged, and the wine is not too powerful, you can expect good results. Medium-bodied, graceful Bordeaux in particular—of a certain age (5–8 years)—blend extremely well with aged chevre.

THE SACRED ORDER OF THINGS

So much for the Do's, the Don'ts, and the Great Commandments. We hope that for sensible menu-planners everywhere, their tyranny is a thing of the past. But the rule-masters of the world have one other set of prescriptions for us, one last challenge to the emergence of good sense at table, and that is the order of wine service.

These rules go something like this:

DRINK YOUNG WINE BEFORE OLD! Attend a fancy, seven-course wine and food dinner and the evening's oldest wine will almost invariably be served only slightly earlier than David Letterman delivers his monologue.

DRINK WHITE WINE BEFORE RED! Peek at any book or article that discusses the stately progression of wine in a menu and, with the exception of dessert wines, whites never get sent down the aisle after reds.

DRINK DRY WINE BEFORE SWEET! Dine out and order a glass of Sauternes along with your first course and, except in cities where they can pronounce Pouilly-Fuissé, you're apt to be escorted to the door (if not the county line).

We were never very comfortable with these rules to begin with, but after what we hope is a definitive tasting on the subject we're downright scornful of them. Follow our lead—set up the same tasting—and you too, perhaps, can be the first enlightened heretic on your block.

YOUNG BEFORE OLD

The logic of pouring young wines prior to more mature wines is grounded in the belief that older wines are, by definition, more complex and, therefore, more deserving of attention. Simply stated, the idea is that you build up to the big guns. We concede that dramatic tension and the thrill of crescendo are important components of any theatrical experience. Dining certainly has its drama, and it is often said that younger wines set the stage for their elder statesmen, playing the role of supporting actors to the meal's more worthy stars. To serve old wine before new is to invite the disappointment of anticlimax; if Marlon Brando gets killed in the first act, the other two acts can be distinct let-downs.

To test this, we selected three red wines to taste, separated in age by a span of ten years, from the right-bank regions of Bordeaux.

The youngest wine, a two-year-old St.-Émilion—Château Haut Sarpe, Grand Cru Classé—was all berry-fruit: soft, delicious, despite its youthfully exuberant tannin.

The middle-aged wine, a five-year-old Pomerol from a rich vintage—Château Beauregard—was less fruity, but nonetheless quite smooth and supple, with soft tannin and elements of ginger and spicy wood.

The oldest wine, a twelve-year-old St.-Émilion from a long-lived vintage—Château Gaillard de la Gorce, Grand Cru Classé—was showing its age without doddering off into the abyss. It's a fairly fragile wine reminiscent of wet leaves, allspice, licorice, and dried fruit.

The first part of our tasting followed The Sacred Order of Things. We moved from the young Château Haut Sarpe, to the middle-aged Château Beauregard, to the elderly Château Gaillard de la Gorce. The youngest wine was fine—until we started sipping the second wine. Our perception of the second wine—the Château Beauregard—was

---

Tasting Bordeaux of all Ages
GOOD DIRECTION
Tasting the oldest first (a twelve-year-old Château Gaillard de la Gorce), the middle-ager second (a five-year-old Château Beauregard), and the youngest last (a two-year-old Château Haut Sarpe)
BAD DIRECTION
Tasting the youngest first (a two-year-old Château Haut Sarpe), the middle-ager second (a five-year-old Château Beauregard), and the oldest last (a twelve-year-old Château Gaillard de la Gorce)

---

radically altered by the lingering tastes of that first, youthful wine. The tannins of the second wine were exaggerated, and the fruit was depressed; the Château Beauregard seemed more solemn, and harsher in the finish. This unpleasantness continued as we tasted the twelve-year-old Château Gaillard de la Gorce, which seemed to unravel at the seams when placed anywhere near its younger confrères.

An even greater surprise awaited us, for we then tasted the wines in reverse order: oldest to youngest. The old Château Gaillard de la Gorce had no problem with its new role as starter. In fact, its complexity seemed more evident, its flavors more integrated, when it wasn't forced to follow a junior. The wine in the middle also seemed more focused by the shift in order. And when we finally found our way back to the fruity youth, all was just fine—as if nothing had been amiss in the first place.

Thus we came to the conclusion that placing younger wines before older ones—while certainly useful for dramatic effect—isn't always the best strategy.

We found that a far better way to show off an older, more subtle wine is to get it into the taste race as soon as possible, preferably before the withering abuse of a younger wine's fruit and tannin can have a chance to upset the grape cart.

This is not to say that moving along a time-line from new to old never works. But you must exercise good sense, not a blind adherence to The Sacred Order of Things. Consider flavor intensity and texture, not just age. If a progression of wines from new to old leads to increasingly fragile specimens, then your best bet is to stand conventional wisdom on its head. But if your selection of wines takes you up the ladder from light to heavy as you pour more and more mature bottles (e.g., Beaujolais Nouveau, to five-year-old middling Bordeaux, to ten-year-old Hermitage from a great vintage), then by all means climb away!

Guidelines: Should Young Wines Be Poured Before Old Wines?

❦ tasting an old wine first diminishes drama, but increases the chances for appreciation

❦ old wines of subtlety and complexity may be difficult to appreciate after tasting younger wines filled with fruit and/or tannin

❦ if the old wine in question is rich and intense, younger wines that are lighter and simpler can precede it

---

WHITE BEFORE RED

The second part of The Sacred Order of Things is actually a spin-off of The Great Wine Commandment—white with fish, red with meat—since fish inevitably precedes meat in a menu of classic form. So, if you're doing everything by the book, you must have white wine with your turbot before you proceed to red wine with your beef.

Today, of course, we eat much more fish and far less red meat. It's pretty common for restaurants to offer as many seafood as meat entrees—if not more. And lighter meat dishes often precede fish entrees; we see nothing wrong with a carpaccio of veal with a light red followed by a grilled slab of tuna with a rich white. But wine-menu traditions are always slow to follow changes in diet and lifestyle.

We thought it simple enough to test these premises, and we procured the following wines:

A two-year-old Hunter Ashby Chardonnay from the Napa Valley in California. It was a quintessential California white, oozing with rich, ripe tropical fruit, fat on the palate, juicy right through to the finish.

A one-year-old Château d'Acqueria Tavel Rosé from the south of France. It was everything a Tavel rosé should be: light and fresh, with hints of pear and cherry-blossoms, balanced and clean.

A two-year-old red Burgundy, a Pommard from Antonin Rodet. The Pommard was chock full of good, clean Pinot Noir fruit: cherry-berry, whiffs of spice—light in style but quite well made.

We moved, at first, along the color line: white, to rosé, to red. We quickly discovered that the big, alcoholic white washed out the rosé's more delicate flavors. When we went from rosé to red, there was no problem: The richness of the red spread out after the Tavel.

Working backward from red-rosé-white, we ran into a familiar problem when we arrived at the rosé: It didn't have the strength to stand up to the more assertive flavors coming from the red, just as it failed to impress when tasted after the white. When we finally returned to the Chardonnay, it had no problem handling the switch from rosé. It is clear that a light rosé should precede both red and white wines of some substance.

Now came the big question: What would happen when we tasted the white just before the red, and the red just before the white? White to red—the transition that we've all made, thousands of times—was just fine, as expected. But, in this particular case, it wasn't perfect; the size of that California Chardonnay seemed to scale down the red

Burgundy a bit. But with buffers of food—and the weight of The Sacred Order of Things on your side—you'd probably never notice it at a dinner party.

Tasting the Color Continuum

GOOD DIRECTION

A heavy white (a two-year-old Hunter Ashby Chardonnay, Napa Valley) and an elegant red (a two-year-old Pommard, Antonin Rodet, from Burgundy) were content to play leap-frog; serve either one first.

BAD DIRECTION:

A lovely but light rosé (a one-year-old Château d'Acqueria from Tavel in the south of France) was clobbered when served after either the white or the red.

The big news was the performance of the white wine *after* the red wine. Superb! The red had more tannin, of course, but the white had more body—and, due to this, it was not altered one iota in our perception when we tasted it second.

The notion that one must proceed from white to red, then, didn't hold up very well in our tasting. While following the conventional route down the river didn't give us fits, it certainly didn't prevent us from enjoying the trip back up. And the informing logic, once again—as with our young-to-old experiment—is not the arbitrary logic embodied in The Sacred Order of Things; it is the simple logic of flavor intensity and texture.

Guidelines: Should White Wines Be Poured Before Red Wines?

❣ the issue of white before red or red before white has little to do with color

❣ if the white is light and the red is heavy, the red will probably show better if served second

❣ if the white is heavy and the red is light, the white will probably show better if served second

❣ rosés, which are usually extremely light, will probably do best before any white or red of substance

Dry Before Sweet

The last order in the Sacred Order of Things concerns the issue of relative sweetness. Once again, we find this suggestion to be rooted in the past, shadowing the traditional sequence of savory dishes before sweet dishes in a "proper" meal. There is something to be said for this logic. After all, beginning dinner with a hot fudge sundae loses much of its appeal past the eighth birthday.

But not all sweet dishes speak with the same tongue, and there are literally thousands of rousing dishes—from starters on up through main courses—that contain sweet elements of one kind or another. From carrot soup to glazed ham, from barbecue to duck à l'orange, sweetness is often a critical element in otherwise savory dishes, and enhances their flavors. So, too, can sweet wines be judiciously used throughout a meal, from palate-whetting aperitifs to the ultimate in sticky-gooey treats.

Our taste experiment included three extremely different wines:

A two-year-old Alsatian Riesling from Hugel. It was a textbook Alsatian Riesling: completely dry, hinting at quince, allspice, and that much-discussed and to us attractive scent of petrol.

A two-year-old German Riesling from the Mosel, a Serriger Würtzberg Kabinett. This off-dry wine was lively and balanced, with notes of green apple, lemon, and chalk.

A four-year-old Sauternes from Château Rieussec. The Sauternes was wrapped up in a glorious bouquet of vanilla, oak, lemon, honeysuckle, pineapple, and spice. Fat and sassy, it was succulent, rich, and sweet.

Following the Sacred Order of Things was a natural. Each wine seemed to set up the next, and none had difficulty standing in the sugary shadow of its predecessor. Amazingly, however, the Sauternes didn't have a negative effect on the drier wines on our way down the step-ladder of sweetness, as long as we took time to pause on each rung during our descent. With the off-dry Kabinett as a buffer, the sweet Sauternes couldn't threaten the integrity of the bone-dry Alsatian Riesling.

Thus we discovered that we could indeed have it both ways, if we took care to move in sweet increments up and down the sugar line. While this is not exactly radical, the implications are liberating for those of us still tethered to the old rule. Sweet wines, like sweet dishes, can take many different places in the gastronomic scheme of things; they needn't be avoided before the dessert course, just because they're a bit sticky.

Tasting from Dry to Sweet

GOOD DIRECTION

A two-year-old Alsatian Riesling from Hugel (dry), then a two-year-old Mosel Kabinett Riesling from Serriger Würtzberg (semi-dry), then a four-year-old Château Rieussec Sauternes (very sweet). Tasting them backward was also reasonable.

BAD DIRECTION

A four-year-old Château Rieussec Sauternes (very sweet), then a two-year-old Alsatian Riesling from Hugel (dry)

In fact, there were those in the nineteenth century who dared to reverse The Sacred Order of Things when it came to this issue. There is an old tradition—coming back into fashion now—of serving Sauternes along with a first course of foie gras terrine. We've tried it in meal sequences, and have had no problem getting back to dry wines as long as the very next wine is not excessively dry, thin, and tart.

If they broke The Sacred Order of Things at fancy gatherings in the nineteenth century—why on earth are we so timid now?

We'll now let the spirits of the nineteenth century rest in peace. Since the twentieth century didn't make significant improvements, in the next chapter we'll tackle the food and wine principles that we hope will inform the diners of the twenty-first century.

Guidelines: Should Dry Wines Be Poured Before Sweet Wines?

❦ the classical order, dry to sweet, makes a lot of sense

❦ if you're going to serve a dry wine after a sweet wine, make sure it's not extremely dry, tart, and thin

CHAPTER 3

A NEW DAY

DAWNS

ave you exorcised the hidebound rules of yester-year? Can you say "red wine with fish" without experiencing lifethreatening attacks of social conscience? If so, you're ready for our formulation.

It's all very simple. We propose that food and wine go well together because:

1. They're strikingly similar in some way, or . . .
2. They're strikingly different in some way.

And we propose that food and wine can be similar or different in three ways:

1. They can have similar COMPONENTS, such as sugar, acid, salt, or bitterness. Or they can have contrasting COMPONENTS.
2. They can have similar FLAVORS, such as herbal, fruity, peachy, earthy, or minty. Or they can have contrasting FLAVORS.
3. They can have similar TEXTURES, such as thin, velvety, medium-bodied, or viscous. Or they can have contrasting TEXTURES.

That's it. Now you're nearly an expert on matching wine with food. Once you can see the limitless menu of the world and the infinite wine list of the universe in this fashion, you'll never be stumped again by a food-wine choice. And you'll be able to predict things that the food-and-wine books never told you. After absorbing this chapter, you'll be able to predict that an acidic red will go well with your salad, a rich, toasty white with your grilled chicken, an herbal, young Cabernet with your rosemary-scented roast lamb, and a Sauvignon Blanc from France, New Zealand, or Australia with your goat cheese.

Of course, it's going to take a little practice. You must train yourself to see the possible contrasts or similarities in foods and wines. Even more importantly, you must develop an instinct for the key element in a dish, or in a wine—whether it's a component, a flavor, or a texture—so that you can guess what wines and foods are going to go well together. The identification of key elements is probably the most important thing that a menu-planner can do when choosing wines for a meal. To take a dish like sage-scented roast pork with apricot sauce, for example, and anticipate that the sweetness in the sauce will be the key element for matching wine—and not the sage, or even the pork itself—is of prime importance. Similarly, to recognize that the acid of a Muscadet, for example, is a key element in a match is also supremely important.

Fear not. To do this well, you won't have to approach every meal for the rest of your life actively charting the possibilities of your food and wine, boring everyone—including yourself—in the process. But by devoting a little thought to it, every once in a while, you'll develop a strong set of reflexes that will make you a matching miracle without a lot of applied effort at mealtime. The best way to start negotiating those key elements is to gain a clear understanding of what we mean by components, flavors, and textures.

COMPONENTS

We use this word to designate the very basic elements in wine and food that correspond to the basic sense perceptions on the tongue. The tip of the tongue perceives sweetness. The sides of the tongue perceive sourness. The middle of the tongue perceives saltiness. And the back of the tongue perceives bitterness. Food and wine have basic components that provide sensations for these areas on the tongue.

SWEETNESS. In food, sweetness comes from natural sugar, or from the addition of sugar. In wine, sweetness comes from the natural sugar in grapes (if fermentation has stopped before all the sugar has been converted into alcohol).

SALTINESS. In food, saltiness comes from natural salt (as in briny oysters), or from the addition of salt. Wine does not frequently offer salty flavors, though some wines—like Manzanilla sherry—are sometimes described as having a salty tang.

SOURNESS. In food, sourness comes from high levels of acidity, whether natural (as in lemons) or added (as in salad dressings). In wine, sourness also comes from naturally occurring high levels of acidity (often in northerly growing regions). Sometimes, in warmer regions, acid is added to make a wine more sour.

BITTERNESS. In food, natural bitterness is occasionally found, but it's rarely a pleasant perception. In wine as well, bitterness is usually a turn-off, often the accompaniment of too much tannin or too much wood. But, in food and wine both, a trace of bitterness can supply an interesting undercurrent to other tastes.

> Components are food and wine elements perceived on the tongue such as sweetness, saltiness, sourness, and bitterness.

All of these components, then, are perceived on the tongue, before the more complex flavors of food and wine have had a chance to work their way up to the olfactory nerve. The components supply the initial impression for any taste. And, as the brain begins to register other tastes (which we'll discuss below as flavors), the initial impression of the components remains, forming a kind of bass line for the melody of flavors.

In our tasting experience, it is this bass line that is the most important factor in determining the success of a food-wine match. Flavors and textures are always important—and can sometimes be the most important factors—but more often than not a match is made or broken on the components. They are always leading contenders for key elements. Consider the following recipe:

NUTMEG-SCENTED SORREL SALAD WITH ROASTED SHALLOTS AND MONKFISH

20 medium-sized shallots

1¼ teaspoons freshly grated nutmeg

2 teaspoons plus ¾ cup olive oil

6 tablespoons coarse salt

Preheat oven to 400 degrees F. Peel the shallots, keeping the root ends intact. Place them in a bowl, and mix well with ¼ teaspoon of nutmeg and 2 teaspoons of olive oil. Make a bed of coarse salt in a roasting pan, and spread the shallots out in a single layer over the salt. Roast in the oven for about 20 minutes, basting with additional olive oil to prevent the outer layer of the shallots from toughening. The shallots are done when they're browned outside and just soft inside. Keep warm.

Rinse the sorrel and the greens. Dry well, and keep cool.

Prepare the vinaigrette: Place the mustard in a bowl. Whisk in the fruit vinegar. Add ½ cup of the olive oil slowly, in a thin stream. Add ½ teaspoon nutmeg, and season with salt and pepper to taste.

Lay out the monkfish fillets. Cut ¼-inch notches all around the perimeter of each fillet. (This prevents the fillets from curling up in the pan.) Dredge the fillets well in flour, seasoned with salt and pepper. Place the remaining ¼ cup of olive oil in a sauté pan over medium-high heat. When the oil is very hot, sauté the monkfish quickly, about 1 minute per side, until golden-brown and just cooked. Remove from pan, and brush each fillet very lightly with a bit of the vinaigrette.

Assemble the salad: Place the dried greens in a large bowl. Cut the warm shallots in half, lengthwise, and toss with the salad. Add the vinaigrette, and mix well. Divide the salad among four plates, and nestle two monkfish fillets into the salad on each plate. Grate about ⅛ teaspoon of nutmeg over each salad.

Serves 4

2 cups sorrel leaves, thick ribs removed

6 cups assorted greens, such as mâche, Italian chicory, Bibb lettuce

1 tablespoon Dijon mustard

8 teaspoons mild fruit vinegar (like raspberry)

Salt and freshly ground black pepper, to taste

10 ounces monkfish, cut into 8 thin fillets

Flour for dredging

A Good Match Based on Similar Components: Sourness and Sourness

Nutmeg-Scented Sorrel Salad with Roasted Shallots and Monkfish

Two-year-old Sancerre Rouge, Côtes de Champtin, Pascal Jolivet

	COMPONENTS	FLAVORS	TEXTURES
SIMILARITY	■		
CONTRAST			

There are lots of interesting textures and flavors in this dish, but the trained menu-planner will recognize that the sour flavor of the sorrel leaves and the sour flavor of the vinaigrette are the key elements to consider in choosing a wine. Nutmeg, roasted shallots, even monkfish will go nicely with a wide range of wines; however, the prominent component of this dish—sourness—needs special attention.

For this reason, we chose a two-year-old Sancerre Rouge, Côtes de Champtin, made by Pascal Jolivet. Sancerre Rouge is made from the Pinot Noir grape, in the Loire Valley, a very northerly region for red wine. Cool growing regions, like Sancerre, give wine a fairly acidic character. Employing the principle of similarity of components, we were fairly certain that the acid of the wine would meet the acid of the salad and become fast friends. It worked perfectly. The acid in both the dish and the wine were cancelled, letting other flavors—such as the spicy Pinot Noir fruit of the wine—emerge more strongly. And the wine taste richer because of that impression of lower acid.

Imagine what might happen with another kind of wine. A red or a white with medium body—but low acid—would probably taste thinned out by the acidity in the salad. A complex wine would probably have its delicate balance altered by the sourness in this dish. But a simple, high-acid red fits like a glove.

Had you paid attention to the old rules, you would have been completely lost in this dish. True-blue rule-mongers would not have served wine at all. (No wine with salad!) Ambivalent rule-keepers would probably have broken that rule, but would have replaced it with an equally meaningless rule. (White with fish!) So, by paying careful attention to the rules, you wouldn't have gotten further than Perrier or Pouilly-Fuissé. You can see now that all of these rules are irrelevant; in this case, it's the similarity of components that counts.

Or consider this match-up:

ROAST PORK WITH OYSTER SAUCE GLAZE AND DEEP-FRIED CELERY ROOT

1 3½-pound pork loin, rib portion with about 4 ribs, bone in

5 tablespoons Chinese oyster sauce

Preheat oven to 325 degrees F. With a heavy cleaver, make four evenly spaced notches in the chine bone of the pork loin. Also, at corresponding points on the meaty side of the roast, cut ½-inch slits in the meat. This will facilitate cutting into portions when the roast is ready, and improve browning. Or ask the butcher to prepare the roast in this fashion.

Brush 3 tablespoons of the oyster sauce all over the roast. Place the roast in a heavy roasting pan, just a bit larger than the roast itself. Stand the roast in the pan on its broad end; the ribs will stand vertically, and the whole roast will be higher than it is wide. Place in the oven, and roast for one hour.

Remove, and brush with the remaining 2 tablespoons of oyster sauce. Pour 3 tablespoons of Manzanilla into the pan. Return to oven, and check every 20 minutes or so; add small amounts of Manzanilla to the pan as necessary to prevent the drippings from burning. When the pork roast is finished, there should be about ¼ cup of liquid in the pan.

Roast for another hour or so, or until the pork reaches an internal temperature of 150 degrees F. Total cooking time should be a little less than two hours.

Prepare the celery root: Remove the outer skins of the roots with a vegetable peeler. Continue to peel off as many very thin bands of celery root as you can manage. (Each band should be about 2 inches long, and 1 inch wide.) This will yield about 2 cups of very thin slices. Place in a bowl of cold water until ready to use.

When the roast is ready, let it stand for 20 minutes. Meanwhile, skim the fat from the pan drippings, and add ¼ cup water. Place over medium-high heat, scraping up the dark spots stuck to the pan. Simmer for about 1 minute.

Deep-fry the celery root: Heat the oil in a deep-bottomed pan over very high heat. When the oil reaches 375 degrees F, remove the celery root from the water, shake off excess water, and drain in a colander for a few minutes. Immerse in the oil. (It will spatter just a little.) Stir. The slices will

About ½ cup Manzanilla or dry sherry

DEEP-FRIED CELERY ROOT

2 ½-pound knobs of celery root

4 cups vegetable oil

Salt

A Good Match Based on Contrasting Components: Saltiness and Sweetness

Roast Pork with Oyster Sauce Glaze and Deep-Fried Celery Root

Four-year-old Hattenheimer Wisselbrunnen Riesling Spätlese, Hans Lang

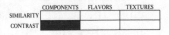

	COMPONENTS	FLAVORS	TEXTURES
SIMILARITY			
CONTRAST	■■■		

become golden-brown within 3–4 minutes. Remove, and place them on paper towels to dry and crispen, about 30 seconds. Sprinkle liberally with salt.

Cut the pork roast into four thick ribs, and serve with the pan-drippings sauce and the deep-fried celery root. Steamed mustard greens go well with this ensemble.

Serves 4

Pork pairs nicely with many wines, but—once again—in trying to select a wine for this dish, we searched for the key element that would make or break the match. And, with the combination of salty oyster sauce, salty Manzanilla, and salted, deep-fried celery root, there is no escaping the ugly truth: This is not a dish for people with high blood pressure. We're talking sodium chloride.

Component similarity? Somehow, the thought of more salt on top of the dish's salt did not seem appealing. After all, there was our own health to consider. And it was not so easy to find a wine with a prominent salty component. So we thought about contrast . . . and this led to the notion of serving a slightly sweet wine with the pork. We came up with a four-year-old Riesling from the Rheingau in Germany, a Hattenheimer Wisselbrunnen Spätlese, made by Hans Lang. The wine and food were delightful together. And—will the cardiologists ever forgive us?—the more salt we put on the celery root chips the better the match became. The wine was a perfect refreshment after the salt of the dish, and the dish tasted meatier, more substantial, more satisfying next to the sweetness of the wine.

The principle of similar or contrasting components stands behind some of the great all-time matches. Oysters and Muscadet is a classic; it's based on the contrast of salty and sour. Roquefort cheese and Sauternes is another classic; it's based on the contrast of salty and sweet. Fruit tarts and demi-sec Champagne, based on the similarity of sweetness and sweetness, is also traditional.

So, when considering a food-and-wine match, the first area to explore is the components. If a dish has prominent acidity, saltiness, sweetness, or bitterness, those factors are likely to be the leading factors in wine selection. If a wine has prominent acidity, sweetness, or bitterness, those factors are likely to be the leading factors in food selection.

Good Matches Based on Components

		COMPONENTS	FLAVORS	TEXTURES
CONTRAST	Raw oysters — Muscadet salty acidic			

		COMPONENTS	FLAVORS	TEXTURES
CONTRAST	Roquefort — Sauternes salty sweet			

		COMPONENTS	FLAVORS	TEXTURES
SIMILARITY	Fruit tart — Demi-sec Champagne sweet sweet			

Here are a few basic things to keep in mind when considering the contrast or similarity of components:

- acidic foods and acidic wines often go well together; the similarity of sourness renders both less sour (salad and Beaujolais)
- acidic wines go nicely with salty foods (Muscadet and oysters)
- acidic foods can wash out low-acid wines (salad and white Hermitage)
- salty food and high-alcohol wine taste bitter together (potato chips and Alsatian Gewürztraminer)
- salty food and sweet wine go nicely together (Roquefort and Sauternes)
- sweet wine and sweet food go nicely together (usually it's best if the wine is sweeter than the food, like demi-sec Champagne and a light fruit tart)
- bitter food and bitter wine don't cancel each other out; they simply taste bitter together (the meat and skins of walnuts with over-oaked Chardonnay)

It all sounds intimidating, but it's not. The important thing is to start considering food and wine with the notion of components in mind; before long, you will develop your own instincts about which components to match or contrast.

FLAVORS

We use this word to designate the range of complex tastes that give distinction to all foods and wines.

After your tongue has perceived the basic components in food or wine, the olfactory nerve takes over. What is usually described as flavor is actually something that people smell. The tongue can't pick up fruity flavors, or tarry flavors, or minty flavors. It's the interaction of nose and palate that enables us to find those specific flavors.

In both food and wine, components are often measurable. Wine labels sometimes tell you how much sugar or acid is in a wine. Strawberry jam could be analyzed for the components sugar or acid in the same way. But the complex array of chemical traces that give steak a steak flavor, or peaches a peach flavor, or Beaujolais a Beaujolais flavor, is much more mysterious. And that's why our excitement over the taste of food or wine usually revolves around these more complex perceptions, the flavors.

Ironically, though they're less intellectually stimulating, it's the simpler components—sugar, acid, etc.—that usually matter most in food and wine matching. But flavors can also exercise a powerful influence. When a certain flavor in a wine lines up sympathetically with a certain flavor in a food, the result can be magnificent. Fino sherry is often described as "nutty," and that same description, of course, could be applied to roasted almonds. And when you drink the sherry with the almonds, you experience a kind of nut fugue: The nutlike flavors of each component reverberate, back and forth, trading, comparing, illuminating—exploring areas of nuttiness that even Jerry Lewis never thought of. This is a grand match of similar flavors, and when the flavors. line up, they can be delicious indeed.

> Flavors are food and wine elements perceived by the olfactory nerve such as fruity, minty, herbal, nutty, cheesy, raisiny, smoky, flowery, earthy, oaky, . . . and hundreds of others.

Unfortunately, a wonderful match like the almonds and Fino sherry can also foster misconceptions. The precise nuttiness of sherry is rather a different taste from the precise nuttiness of almonds. In this case, the flavors were close enough to be complementary; but just because the flavors of wine and the flavors of food carry similar adjectives, it doesn't necessarily mean that they have much to do with each other when you taste them.

Many people have the mistaken notion that food-and-wine matching is principally an exercise in matching flavor adjectives. For example, Alsatian Gewürztraminer is usually described by wine-tasters as "spicy." Those who think of Gewürztraminer in this way, therefore, often suggest it as the proper wine to go with "spicy" food. This places Gewürztraminer in the frequent company of Chinese and Indian dishes.

To us, the fact that Gewürztraminer is described as "spicy" and the fact that Indian food is described as "spicy" is a quirk of language, not a prescription for wine-and-food matching. The components of wine and the components of food are often identical; it's sugar that makes them both sweet, it's acid that makes them both sour. But the flavors of wine and the flavors of food usually come from different sources. When we describe a wine as "spicy," or "fruity," or "herbal," it's usually a metaphoric use of those terms; those qualities in the wine don't come from spice, or fruit, or herbs. The "spice" of Gewürztraminer has no literal relationship to the "spice" of Indian food.

Don't take the adjectival descriptions of flavors to be necessary indications of good food and wine matches. Unlike the cooks who use them, spices are not created equal. Nor, for that matter, are fruits, herbs, or any other complex flavors. If you want to find a good wine and food match, you have to be as specific as possible: Which spice? Which fruit? Which herb?

Consider the specific flavor similarities at work in this dish:

TRUFFLES 'N' GRITS

Preheat oven to 250 degrees F. Butter a 9-inch baking dish. Prepare the grits: Bring 3½ cups water to a boil in a saucepan. Slowly stir grits and salt into boiling water. Return to boil, then reduce heat. Cover and cook slowly for 15 minutes, stirring occasionally. Remove from heat and pour into the baking dish, spreading out the grits to a uniform depth of ½ inch. Let cool to room temperature, and, using a cookie cutter, cut out four equal pieces.

Melt the butter in a nonstick pan, and sauté the cutouts until brown on both sides. Keep warm in the oven until the truffle sauce is completed.

Prepare the truffle sauce: Melt 3 tablespoons of the butter in a heavy saucepan.

GRITS

1 tablespoon sweet butter, plus additional for greasing dish

¾ cup enriched white hominy grits

¼ teaspoon salt

TRUFFLE SAUCE

4 tablespoons sweet butter (½ stick)

2 tablespoons finely minced shallots

(continued)

⅔ cup chicken stock
(or canned chicken
broth, low salt is
best)

2 ounces dry red wine

1 ounce shaved, fresh
black truffle

Salt and freshly
ground black
pepper

Add the shallots, and sauté over moderate heat for 3 minutes. Add the chicken stock, the red wine, and all but four shavings of truffle. Continue cooking until the mixture has reached one third of its original volume. Remove from heat, swirl in the remaining tablespoon of butter, and season with salt and pepper to taste. Serve immediately over the fried grit cutouts, garnishing each portion with a single truffle shaving in the center.

Serves 4 as a first course

A Good Match Based on Similar Flavors: Earthy and Earthy

		COMPONENTS	FLAVORS	TEXTURES
Truffles 'n' Grits	SIMILARITY		■	
	CONTRAST			

1967 Château Lafite-Rothschild

There are numerous factors at play in this dish (which, by the way, though it sounds extravagant, will only cost you about $6 a serving). But we knew from the start that the powerful, pungent flavor of black truffles—that sublime earthiness—would have to be the key element in wine selection.

With only a modicum of guilt, we splurged on an old bottle of red wine that we suspected would provide a wonderful match for the black truffles. Red wines that are capable of aging—the best Bordeaux, Burgundy, Hermitage, Barolo, Rioja—all develop a measure of earthiness as they mature. Usually, if the wine is holding up well, lots of other flavors are also present. But we purposely chose a wine from a fading vintage—a 1967 Château Lafite-Rothschild—to downplay the other flavors and emphasize the earthiness.

The wine was just right: kind of feeble, but reeking of mushrooms, dank cellars, holes in the ground, and—yes—truffles. And with the Truffles 'n' Grits, an amazing interaction developed before our very palates: A mushroom cloud of deep, dense flavors exploded over the test site. This was atomic fusion of the highest order, and with no fallout—unless you count two ecstatic wine tasters falling out of their chairs. Lots of other, younger, less expensive wines would have done well here also—but a perfect application of the flavor similarity principle gave those Truffles 'n' Grits their ideal mate.

You can also use the flavor contrast principle to your advantage, as in the following recipe:

INDIAN GRILLED CHICKEN

Bone the chicken thighs.

Prepare the marinade: Place the yoghurt and the next ten ingredients in the bowl of a food processor. Process for about 1 minute, or until you have a smooth puree. Place the chicken thighs in a large bowl, cover with the marinade, and marinate, refrigerated, for 24 hours. When ready to cook, remove the chicken from the marinade and pat completely dry with towels.

Prepare the sauce: Place the onions, the green pepper, the cinnamon sticks, and the cloves in a heavy saucepan. Add the chicken stock and the saffron, bring to a boil, and cook rapidly for about 30 minutes or until the mixture is reduced to 1 cup.

While the stock is reducing, begin grilling the chicken. Place the pieces over a medium-high charcoal fire, and cook for about 5 minutes per side. They are done when they're just past a rosy tinge at the center. Keep warm.

Melt the butter in a clean saucepan, and add the flour. Stir for 2 minutes over medium heat. Strain the reduced chicken stock into the flour-butter mixture, and whisk rapidly to blend. Simmer for 1 minute.

Place two chicken thighs on each of four dinner plates. Pour the sauce around the chicken, and place a few fresh coriander leaves on the chicken.

8 medium-sized chicken thighs

1 cup plain yoghurt

5 medium garlic cloves, peeled

1/4 cup coarsely chopped fresh ginger root

1 teaspoon ground coriander

1 teaspoon garam masala

1/2 teaspoon ground cumin

1/4 teaspoon ground allspice

1/4 teaspoon ground cinnamon

1/4 teaspoon Indian chili powder

1/4 teaspoon ground cardamom

1/4 teaspoon ground fenugreek
(continued)

Serves 4

2 small onions, quartered

½ green pepper, cut in chunks

2 cinnamon sticks

2 whole cloves

3 cups chicken stock (or canned chicken broth, low salt is best)

½ teaspoon saffron threads

1 tablespoon sweet butter

4 teaspoons flour

GARNISH

Fresh coriander leaves

Examples of Flavor Matches

SIMILARITY

Grilled leg of lamb with rosemary — Cabernet Sauvignon

herbal herbal

	COMPONENTS	FLAVORS	TEXTURES
SIMILARITY		■	
CONTRAST			

CONTRAST

Parmigiano-Reggiano cheese — young Italian red

cheesy cherrylike

	COMPONENTS	FLAVORS	TEXTURES
SIMILARITY			
CONTRAST		■	

CONTRAST

smoked ham — dry German Riesling

smoky flowery

	COMPONENTS	FLAVORS	TEXTURES
SIMILARITY			
CONTRAST		■	

We could have just said, "the food is spicy, so let's drink a spicy wine—like Gewürztraminer!" But we resisted the temptation. Instead, we determined what kind of spices were in this dish. Though it's a typically Indian blend of many spices, it's the sweetly fragrant Indian spices (such as cinnamon, clove, and saffron) that inform the dish and create its flavor.

Since Indian food often blends sweet spices with herbal flavors, we tried to create the same kind of blend in our wine selection. So, to create a flavor contrast, we chose a Sauvignon Blanc from New Zealand (Corbans, from the Marlborough region), blazing with the

A Good Match Based on Contrasting Flavors: Sweetly Fragrant and Herbal

Indian Grilled Chicken

	COMPONENTS	FLAVORS	TEXTURES
SIMILARITY			
CONTRAST		■	

One-year-old Corbans Sauvignon Blanc, Marlborough, New Zealand bright, grassy, herbal quality that is craved by lovers of Sauvignon Blanc. The gambit paid off. The herbal flavors of the wine were strikingly different from the cinnamon-clove-saffron flavors of the dish, but the two sets of flavors formed a fascinating attraction of opposites.

There are many great matches based on the principle of flavor similarity or contrast. An all-time favorite is a grilled leg of lamb, scented with rosemary, served with a wine made from Cabernet Sauvignon. This red grape often exhibits herbal nuances, so Cabernet Sauvignon wine can be a perfect flavor similarity with the rosemary. Or, imagine a strong young Italian red with aged Parmigiano-Reggiano: The cherrylike flavors of the wine form a flavor contrast with the cheesy flavors of the Parmesan. Another good contrast example is a slice of smoked ham with a dry German Riesling. Smoky and flowery flavors are fascinating together.

We suggest that any potential food-wine match should first be considered for its components. But a consideration of flavor similarities or contrasts will add depth to any match-up. Here are a few guidelines to keep in mind when considering flavor matches:

• use caution when it comes to flavor similarity, and avoid generalities whenever possible; the textbook description of a wine (like "spicy" for Gewürztraminer) may have nothing to do with the food
• if you find a food and a wine that really do have similar flavors (like almonds and Fino sherry, nutty and nutty), they will usually go together well
• for flavor contrasts, you must use your judgment. Will fruity and flowery go together? Will nutty and cheesy go together? Will herbal and fishy go together?
• keep in mind that some foods can *only* take contrasts, never similarities (you can't find a fishy wine, a lamb-y wine, a garlicky wine), but the addition of herbs, fruit, nuts, etc., to fish, lamb, garlic, will help to create flavors similar to wine if that's what you're after
• some of our favorite contrasts: fishy and herbal (shad with Pouilly-Fumé); smoky and flowery (ham with Riesling); cheesy and cherrylike (Parmigiano-Reggiano with Valpolicella); meaty and earthy (prime ribs with aged red Burgundy); fruity and honeyed (strawberries with Sauternes)

Once again, these are not restrictive rules. These suggestions are offered only to make you sensitive to the nuances involved in matching flavors. Once you're in the habit of thinking about similar and contrasting flavor matches, you'll be able to write your own infinitely more pleasing list of suggestions.

TEXTURES

We use this word to designate those qualities in food and wine that correspond to sensations of touch and temperature. Though most people are not accustomed to thinking of food and wine (especially wine) in tactile terms, textures often play an important role in setting up great matches. And keep in mind that the entire oral cavity is involved in sensing texture; while components involve only the tongue, and flavors involve mostly the nose, in textures the playing field is every corner of your mouth.

Textures are those qualities in food and wine that we feel in the mouth, such as softness, smoothness, roundness, richness, thickness, thinness, creaminess, chewiness, oiliness, harshness, silkiness, coarseness, . . . and hundreds of others.

Compared to the other key elements—components and flavors—textures can be rather easy to understand and identify. After all, it doesn't take much in the way of sensory training to recognize distinctions between rough and smooth, hot and cold, or thick and thin. Of course, these are only the most obvious textures; they can also be far more subtle, as anyone who has ever tasted a suave beurre blanc, a velvety Pomerol, a mucilaginous okra pod, or a hollow Pinot Noir will attest.

Once again, to make the most of texture you must bring the concepts of similarity and contrast into play. Some food-wine matches work because the food and wine reinforce each other texturally (like rich filet mignon with rich Merlot); some work because of a striking difference in textures (like soft, slippery oysters with thin Muscadet). Beware the double whammy; some matches can be ruined by too much of a good thing (like a gooey dessert with a highly viscous dessert wine). And, in some matches based on contrast, things get out of hand if the food is way too rich for the wine, or vice versa (like a chunky lamb stew wiping out a light red Burgundy, or a dense young Barolo overwhelming a lightly sautéed veal scallop).

Let's begin with a food-wine match based upon similarities of texture. Here's a dish that begs for a winter dining-room scene lifted from Currier & Ives:

BLACK-EYED PEAS WITH BRAISED DUCK AND OKRA

Cut the duckling into breast, leg, and thigh pieces. Bone them, keeping the skin intact. You will have two breast fillets, two thigh fillets, and two boneless legs. Reserve all scraps and bone.

From the scraps, remove all pieces of skin and fat and place in a large, heavy pan over medium heat for 10 minutes. You should render about ½ cup duck fat in the pan. Remove browned skin and fat from the pan, and discard along with any extra fat. Dredge the pieces of filleted duck in flour, then brown in the hot duck fat, skin-side down, until golden brown, about 10 minutes. Turn over, and sauté an additional 5 minutes. Remove the duck from the pan, and pour off the fat in the pan.

Add the wine and the stock to the pan, scraping up the brown bits that cling to the pan. Bring to a boil. Place all remaining cleaned duck bones and scraps, the leeks, and 6 sage leaves in the pan. Then position the browned duck fillets among the bones and vegetable so that the fillets are half in, half out of the braising liquid. Cover, leaving just a small opening, and simmer for about 2 hours. The duck is done when it's very tender. Cut the duck into eighteen pieces, salt and pepper it well, let come to room temperature and keep covered overnight in the refrigerator.

Strain the braising liquid into a clean container. Cool covered to room temperature and refrigerate overnight. The next day, remove the white fat and reserve. There will also be a good deal of dirty stock; remove and

1 5-pound duckling

Flour for dredging

2½ cups dry white wine

5 cups light brown stock (or chicken stock)

2 large leeks, cleaned, trimmed, and coarsely chopped

18 sage leaves

Salt and freshly ground black pepper, to taste

1 cup dried black-eyed peas, soaked in water for 8 hours

2 large garlic cloves, minced

1 medium green pepper, minced

½ pound fresh okra, cut in thirds

2 large canned Italian plum tomatoes, crushed, with 3 tablespoons puree from can

(continued)

*¼ pound garlic sau-
sage, such as kiel-
basa or cotechino,
sliced extremely
thin*

*8 tablespoons sweet
butter (1 stick),
cold*

*2 tablespoons very
finely chopped fresh
parsley*

**A Good Match
Based on Simi-
lar Textures:
Rich and Rich**

	COMPONENTS	FLAVORS	TEXTURES
SIMILARITY			■
CONTRAST			

**Black-Eyed Peas with
Braised Duck and
Okra**

**Six-year-old Conn
Creek Zinfandel, Napa
Valley**

discard. You should have about 2½ cups of clean duck stock.

When ready to serve, drain the peas, and place in a clean saucepan with 6 sage leaves, finely chopped. Add 2 cups of the clean duck stock. Simmer for about 25 minutes, or until the peas are just tender.

While the peas are simmering, place 1 tablespoon of the reserved duck fat in a sauté pan. Add the garlic and the green pepper, and sauté over medium heat for 5 minutes. Add the okra and the tomatoes. Stir well, and simmer until the okra just turns tender, about 15 minutes. Season well with salt and pepper.

Add the reserved duck pieces to the okra, along with the thin slices of garlic sausage. Add the peas, along with a bit of the remaining stock from the peas—just enough to moisten the okra-duck-sausage-pea mixture. Warm gently, and taste for seasoning.

Meanwhile, prepare the sauce: Place the remaining ½ cup of duck stock and the remaining 6 sage leaves, finely minced, in a saucepan. Bring to a boil, then, moving the pan off and on the heat as necessary, whip in the butter, 1 tablespoon at a time. When the butter is incorporated, divide the warm duck mixture among six warmed dinner plates, and divide the sauce among them. Sprinkle with the parsley, and serve.

Serves 6

Cooking with duck is always an exercise in fleshy abandon, because our web-footed friends come so well-insulated. From the moment we began rendering the cut-up bird, we knew we were in for a big, hearty treat. The addition of simmered black-eyed peas and thick, gooey okra only served to underline the dish's rustic density. Finding the key element here doesn't pose much of a problem: When braising a quacker, richness rules the roost. (Or should we say roast?)

As the pan slowly bubbled, we tasted the world's rich reds on our minds' palates, sizing them up against the glutinous source of those wonderful aromas in the kitchen. We considered country reds from Italy, France, Spain, and elsewhere. But in a fit of gastronomic patriotism—the duck was from New York, the peas from Virginia, the okra from Louisiana—we finally settled on a six-year-old Conn Creek Zinfandel, from the good old Napa Valley.

The wine was a perfect specimen of an older Zin: a bit diminished in its alcohol and fruity zeal, but rich and round, with soft, furry tannins dominating the finish. The duck's inherent richness—amplified by the reduction sauce made from pan drippings—combined seamlessly with the big-boned Zinfandel. And the furriness of the wine caught the okra in mid-ooze, adding another dimension of body to the match. All in all, a delightful pairing that perfectly captured the excitement of texture similarity.

Textures in wine and food can also be devastatingly effective when they form a contrast.

FLOURLESS PEAR SOUFFLÉ

Peel, core, and dice the pears. Combine with 4 teaspoons of the sugar, the pear juice, liqueur, and the *eau-de-vie*. Cover, refrigerate, and marinate for 12 hours.

When ready to serve the soufflé, preheat oven to 400 degrees F. Prepare two 2-cup soufflé molds. Butter them well, and prepare two collars of aluminum foil to fit around the molds. The collars should fit around the base and stand about 3 inches higher than the molds. Butter the inside of the collars well, wrap them around the molds, and hold in place with straight pins. Reserve.

Whip the egg whites until foamy. Add the cream of tartar and the salt, and continue whipping. Gradually add the remaining 2½ tablespoons of sugar. Whip until the egg whites hold stiff peaks.

Puree the marinated pears and liquid in a food processor. Place the puree in a large bowl, and mix a quarter of the whipped egg whites into the puree. Gently fold in the remaining egg whites; combine completely but do not deflate the egg whites.

⅔ pound fresh pears

4 teaspoons plus 2½ tablespoons sugar

3 tablespoons pear juice, fresh or bottled

1 tablespoon pear liqueur

2 teaspoons **poire eau-de-vie**

3 large egg whites, at room temperature

⅛ teaspoon cream of tartar

Pinch of salt

A Good Match Based on Contrasting Textures: Light and Heavy

	COMPONENTS	FLAVORS	TEXTURES
SIMILARITY			
CONTRAST			■■■■■

Flourless Pear Soufflé

Two-year-old Muscat de Beaumes de Venise, Paul Jaboulet Aîné

Pour the mixture into the soufflé molds. Smooth the tops, leaving a small peak at the center of each. Quickly place in a roasting pan, and pour boiling water around the soufflés—the water should come half-way up the sides of the molds. Place in the oven, and bake for about 15 minutes, or until the soufflé is puffed, and browned on top. Remove from the oven and remove the foil collars and discard the pins. Immediately bring the soufflés to the table, and divide them among four dessert plates.

Serves 4

NOTE: For the purposes of this wine experiment, serve the soufflés just as they are. If the food-wine match is not the main focus of this dessert, you may want to serve it with vanilla sabayon.

We engineered this soufflé so that its key element would be unmistakable; soufflés are always light, but without any egg yolks or flour this one was so light it threatened to float out the window. When you taste it, you'll respond to the moderate sweetness, to the lovely fresh pear flavor—but most of all you'll respond to that wispy, wonderful texture.

The game plan is simple. Find a rich dessert wine to provide a texture contrast. And we came up with a beauty: a two-year-old Muscat de Beaumes de Venise from the steady house of Paul Jaboulet Aîné. It is a beautifully honeyed melange of pear, peach, apricot—sweet and heavy, but with sufficient acidity to prevent it from cloying.

On the palate, the wine seemed to cut through the soufflé like a candied buzz saw, condensing and ultimately collapsing the delicate cloud into a short, sweet Bartlett gumdrop. In the end, we were left dizzy from the descent.

Just for fun, we popped a bottle of demi-sec bubbly to see if "light-on-light" would shine as brightly as "heavy-on-light." Texturally, nothing was wrong with the match; it was a decent example of similar texture. But the emphasis seemed to shift away from texture and toward components, with the match-up of sugar dominating our interest. It certainly wasn't as dramatic or satisfying as the Muscat-soufflé connection.

The principle of similar or contrasting textures—though less dominant in most match-ups than the principles of components or flavors—supports a number of intriguing combinations. Long-cooked lamb shanks and Gigondas, for example, unite similar rich textures. Creamed salt cod and bone-dry Fino sherry bring together the heavy and the light. A grilled paillard of veal and a simple Cabernet Franc from Friuli connect across a bridge of lightness and simplicity.

Once again, we suggest that you think first of components when pondering a wine-food match. Then, let flavor considerations come into play. Finally, imagine the feel of the food and wine in your mouth, and arrive at your conclusions concerning similar or contrasting textures. Here are a few guidelines to keep in mind when considering texture matches:

- there are many possible textures in food and wine, but the two most important to think about are rich and light
- light food with light wine is always reliable
- rich food with rich wine can be wonderful, but make sure the match isn't *too* rich
- rich food with light wine, or light food with rich wine—the two contrast possibilities—can be winning, as long as the rich partner doesn't overwhelm the light
- be on the look-out for other textural qualities: grainy, loose, dry (in food), oily, rough, etc., which can form the basis for strong textural associations
- temperature is also a tactile factor; warm food and cold wine can be a stunning contrast

Examples of Texture Matches

SIMILARITY	CONTRAST	SIMILARITY
Braised lamb shanks—Gigondas	**Creamed salt cod—Fino sherry**	**Paillard of veal—Friulian Cabernet Franc**
rich rich	**rich light**	**light light**

	COMPONENTS	FLAVORS	TEXTURES
SIMILARITY			■
CONTRAST			

	COMPONENTS	FLAVORS	TEXTURES
SIMILARITY			
CONTRAST			■

	COMPONENTS	FLAVORS	TEXTURES
SIMILARITY			■
CONTRAST			

THE WILD CARDS

It would be neat if every single facet of food and wine fit into one of the three divisions: components, flavors, or textures. But there are two elements—both found principally in wine—that cut across these divisions. They are alcohol and tannin. Depending on the context, they can be considered as components, flavors, or textures. Alcohol and tannin are the wild cards of wine-and-food matching.

Let's first look at alcohol, one of the main by-products of fermentation. When you notice alcohol in a wine, nine times out of ten you notice it as a texture. It usually announces its presence on the palate by making your mouth feel "hot"—a mild burning sensation that's pleasurable at low levels. Alcohol is a relatively heavy substance, so it registers texturally on the palate in another way as well: High-alcohol wines are rich wines.

You could also argue that alcohol works as a component in wine-food matches. High-alcohol wines carry an impression of sweetness, which acts as any sugar would in tandem with food. That's why dishes with a little sweetness in them often go particularly well with high-alcohol wines, such as Chardonnay from California. Also, alcohol can interact in significant ways with other components—such as the bitter effect that's produced when a high-alcohol wine pairs up with a salty food.

Alcohol can also operate as a flavor. If you taste a young Port, in which the added alcohol has not yet had time to marry with the wine, you can unmistakably taste a kind of brandied fruitiness that is the flavor of alcohol.

Tannin also has multiple dimensions. Most important is texture; a tannic wine feels astringent on the palate, drying out the mouth. If you've brewed a cup of tea that's too strong—or eaten the papery portion of a walnut—you know the way that tannin feels in the mouth. In tasting a wine, you usually feel the tannin in the finish, just as the wine is moving on to your throat. Tannin can be an important texture factor in a match, since it has the effect on the palate of cutting fattiness. For this reason, the highly tannic red wine called Madiran is the wine of choice, in southwest France, as a partner for the extremely fatty preserved duck of the region (confit de canard).

Tannin also can be considered as a component, since it is a measurable component of wine—just like sugar or acid. And though tannin is mostly a tactile sensation, certain forms of tannin can also taste bitter—again qualifying it as a component. Keep in mind that a bitter food and a tannic wine is clearly something to be avoided; here's a similarity of components that's most disagreeable.

The flavor of tannin is a very minor consideration. Some experts claim to detect a dusty cellar smell in young wines with a great deal of tannin, but this is so subtle it has no effect on wine-and-food matching.

In summary, alcohol and tannin—though hard to isolate in single categories—exercise powerful influence on food-and-wine matching. When looking for the key element of a wine, consider its components, its flavors, and its textures—but always remember that alcohol and tannin, working in various ways, are often leading candidates for the key element.

Consider a California Chardonnay, grown in a hot region during a hot summer. It may have close to 14 percent alcohol. If so, alcohol will probably be the key element in matching the Chardonnay with food. Avoid matching it with salty food (alcohol and saltiness-bitterness), and avoid matching it with very light food (many light foods—like airy omelets, for example—will be washed out by the richness of the wine).

Or, consider a young red Bordeaux from a top vineyard in a top vintage. The wine will undoubtedly have a great deal of tannin, and—should you decide to drink it young—this will be the key element in matching the wine with food. Do not drink a wine like this with sautéed broccoli rabe (a bitter Italian broccoli); it will create an unpleasant flavor. Do find something rich and fatty—leftover prime ribs, perhaps, on a sandwich—which will be cut beautifully by the wine's tannin.

THINKING ABOUT WINE AND FOOD
IN CATEGORIES

You will sometimes be looking for a salty food (component), or an herbal food (flavor), or a rich food (texture) to match with a certain wine. This is not difficult to conjure up; we're all familiar with the qualities of many foods, and it's not hard to imagine what their key elements might be. Here's a short list of some foods that fit into the main categories:

COMPONENTS

SALTY	ACIDIC	SWEET	BITTER
anchovies	lemon juice	barbecue sauce	broccoli rabe
bacon	tamarind	raisins	endive

FLAVORS

FRUITY	NUTTY	SMOKY	HERBAL
peach	almonds	ham	coriander
jam	praline	barbecued ribs	pesto

SPICY	CHEESY	EARTHY	MEATY
clove	Parmigiano	truffles	filet mignon
lamb curry	pizza	organ meats	prime ribs

TEXTURES

LIGHT	RICH	COARSE	FATTY
soufflé	crème fraîche	cracked wheat cake	confit de canard
salmon mousse	lamb chops	blood sausage	rillettes

For many people, doing the same thing with wine—determining which wines will feature sweetness, acidity, fruitiness, richness, etc.—is a great deal harder, since it obviously requires a working knowledge of the world's wines.

So—if you're not a hard-core wine buff—we've made the process as easy as possible for you. Some of our main categories—like the component of acidity—always suggest the same handful of wines to wine-lovers. We've listed these obvious choices in all the important categories for you, so the following guide will help you to quickly find an acidic wine, or a fruity wine, or a rich wine when you're thinking about food matches. For more detailed information on all of these wines—a complete breakdown of components, flavors, and textures—you should consult The Big List, see page 228.

COMPONENTS

SALTY
(rare in wine)

ACIDIC
whites: village-level Chablis (France)
Muscadet (France)
Mosel Rieslings (Germany)
Vinho Verde (Portugal)
New York State Chardonnay
reds: Beaujolais Nouveau (France)
light Burgundy (France)
Sancerre (France)
Valpolicella (Italy)
Bardolino (Italy)

SWEET
whites: Sauternes (France)
Coteaux du Layon (France)
Picolit (Italy)
Beerenauslese (Germany)
late-harvest Riesling (U.S., Australia)
reds: Vintage Port (Portugal)
Recioto della Valpolicella (Italy)

BITTER
whites: over-oaked Chardonnay (California, Australia)
over-oaked Burgundy (France)
old-fashioned woody Riojas (Spain)
dry vermouth
reds: tannic young Cabernets (California, Australia)
tannic young Bordeaux (France)
tannic young Rhônes (France)
Amarone (Italy)

FLAVORS

FRUITY
whites: young Riesling
young Chardonnay (especially California, Australia, New Zealand)
young Pinot Grigio (Italy)
reds: Beaujolais (France)
young Pinot Noir (especially California, Oregon)
young Dolcetto (Italy)
young Merlot (especially California, Italy)

NUTTY
whites: Fino, Amontillado sherry (Spain)
Greco di Tufo (Italy)
Meursault (France)

SMOKY

whites: aged white Burgundy (France)
reds: some aged Bordeaux (France)
         some aged Rioja (Spain)
         some aged Barolo (Italy)
         some aged Taurasi (Italy)

HERBAL

whites: Pouilly-Fumé, Sancerre (France)
         Sauvignon Blanc, Fumé Blanc (California, Australia, New Zealand)
reds: Chinon, Bourgeuil (France)
         some young Bordeaux (France)
         some young Cabernet (especially Monterey County, California)
         Cabernet Franc (Italy, California)

SPICY

whites: Mosel Riesling (Germany; especially Ürziger Würzgarten)
         barrel-fermented Chardonnay (California)
reds: Gigondas, Côte-Rôtie, Hermitage (France)
         Shiraz (Australia)
         Petite Sirah (California)
         Zinfandel (California)

CHEESY

whites: aged Greco di Tufo (Italy)
reds: some Chianti, Brunello, Valpolicella (Italy)

EARTHY

whites: some aged Burgundy (France)
         some aged Chardonnay (California)
reds: aged Burgundy (France)
         very old Bordeaux (France)
         aged Hermitage or Côte-Rôtie (France)

MEATY

reds: young Pomerol (France)
      young Merlot (California)

TEXTURES

LIGHT

whites: Vinho Verde (Portugal)
         Muscadet (France)
         Soave (Italy)
         Riesling QbA (Germany)
reds: Sancerre (France)
         many lesser Burgundies from lesser vintages (France)
         Valpolicella and Bardolino (Italy)
         lesser Riojas (Spain)

RICH

whites: California Chardonnay
Premier Cru and Grand Cru Burgundy
Hermitage Blanc (France)
Alsace Tokay from a rich vintage (France)
first-rate Bordeaux (France)

reds: Cabernet, Merlot, Zinfandel (California)
first-rate Pomerol (France)
great Bordeaux in rich vintages
Côte-Rôtie (France)
Amarone (Italy)
Pesquera (Spain)
Grange Hermitage (Australia)

THE WILD CARDS

ALCOHOL (high)

whites: Chardonnay from rich vintages (California, Australia)
Burgundy from very rich vintages (France)
Alsatian Gewürztraminer from rich vintages (France)
Rhône wines (France)
Sauternes from rich vintages (France)
sherry (Spain)

reds: Cabernet from rich vintages (California, Australia)
Zinfandel (California)
Petite Sirah (California)
Rhône wines (France)
Amarone (Italy)

TANNIN (high)

whites: over-oaked Chardonnay (California, Australia)
reds: young Bordeaux
young Cabernet Sauvignon (California, Australia)
young Rhônes (France)
young Brunello di Montalcino (Italy)
young Barolo, Barbaresco (Italy)
young Taurasi (Italy)
young Ribera del Duero (Spain)
young Port (Portugal)

We know there's a lot of information here, but the very last thing you should do is panic. In matching food and wine, there are no absolutes; if you don't use a wine from one of our categories with the indicated food in the indicated way, the chances are things will still turn out okay. You should not memorize the above list, by any means; it's largely subjective, anyway, and most wine experts would likely argue long into the night about which wines belong in which categories. But by being aware of the issues involved—components-flavors-textures, similarity-contrast—and by developing a rudimentary feel for the wines of the world, your ability to predict outstanding food-and-wine matches will improve dramatically.

If all of these terms begin to look confusing on paper, try thinking about them the next time you find yourself puttering about the kitchen or bumping around a wine tasting. You could then begin your approach to learning our gustatory principles by informally analyzing the food you're cooking or the wine you're sipping. The more often you play this game, the easier it will be to make brilliant spur-of-the-moment wine-and-food choices without undue mental effort.

We like to think of all this low-level thought as infield practice . . . to use a baseball metaphor. A third baseman will stand in the hot sun for hours on end, fielding practice ground balls. Some will be hit low, to his left, for example, so he can practice ground balls hit low to his left. He may field fifty of them in a row, just to develop his reflexes for that kind of ground ball. When he gets in a game, and a ground ball is hit low to his left, he will not say to himself, as the ball is approaching him, "Let's see. I remember that if I move this way, right foot over left, shoulders low, charging the ball, I can pick it up at 40 degrees. . . ." Far from it. He will, practically without thought, make the correct play on the ball. All of the thought that he devoted to the play in practice is now left behind.

Whether you're a baseball fan or not, this is exactly the way to approach the skill of choosing wine for your meal. If you think about these principles beforehand—and give them some attention every once in a while, when the fancy hits—you'll be able to order a Pouilly-Fumé with your grilled chicken and fresh coriander sauce as if you were Brooks Robinson picking up a sizzling shot to his left in the World Series. It just becomes habit after a while, not a cumbersome scheme that you must dredge up and explore at the approach of every sommelier.

Remember, the only thing you need to take from this chapter—far more important than any of the details we've presented—is a basic understanding of the categories and how they work. If you can see the differences between components, flavors, and textures—and if you can imagine the differences on the palate between similarity and contrast—you're well on your way to terrific matching.

INFIELD PRACTICE: A FEW SHORT DRILLS

We've put together some quizzes that will help you sharpen your understanding of the principles in this chapter. These quizzes have no immutable, writ-in-stone answers. There may be red and white in wine, but there's certainly no black and white; the answers are the answers *we'd* give to the questions, but they may not be the answers *you'll* give. Fine. The importance of these quizzes lies not in the answers themselves, but in the mental gymnastics you'll be doing as you try to arrive at the answers. Remember that we're not supplying any rules about food and wine in this chapter; we're merely trying to supply you with an effective framework for thought.

Keep in mind that, for most people, food-oriented answers will be easier to determine than wine-oriented answers. We all know the taste of chocolate, but not everyone knows the taste of Chenin Blanc. If you don't know enough about wine to take the wine quizzes, you can either just read them along with the answers for edification, or you can try to piece the answers together by consulting The Big List, see page 228.

QUIZ # 1: FILL-INS FOR FOOD

For each food item mentioned, fill in the category and the specific quality that add up to the key element. (For example: The key element in salted popcorn is the component of saltiness.)

The key element in a vinaigrette is the _____(category)_____ of _____(specific)_____ .

The key element in oysters is the _____(category)_____ of _____(specific)_____ .

The key element in macadamia nuts is the _____(category)_____ of _____(specific)_____ .

The key element in ripe melons is the _____(category)_____ of _____(specific)_____ .

The key element in pesto is the _____(category)_____ of _____(specific)_____ .

The key element in blue cheese is the _____(category)_____ of _____(specific)_____ .

The key element in smoked turkey is the _____(category)_____ of _____(specific)_____ .

ANSWERS:

SMOKED TURKEY: flavor of smokiness
BLUE CHEESE: component of saltiness
PESTO: flavor of herbs
RIPE MELONS: component of sweetness
MACADAMIA NUTS: texture of richness
OYSTERS: component of saltiness
VINAIGRETTE: component of acidity

Quiz #2: Fill-ins for Wine

For each wine mentioned, fill in the category and the specific quality that comprise the key element. (For example, the key element in Sauternes is the component of sweetness.)

The key element in a young Beaujolais is the _____(category)_____ of _____(specific)_____ .

The key element in a very young first-growth red Bordeaux is the _____(category)_____ of _____(specific)_____ .

The key element in an old red Burgundy is the _____(category)_____ of _____(specific)_____ .

The key element in a young Soave is the _____(category)_____ of _____(specific)_____ .

The key element in a German late-harvest wine (like Beerenauslese) is the _____(category)_____ of _____(specific)_____ .

The key element in a young Petite Sirah from California is the _____(category)_____ of _____(specific)_____ .

The key element in an off-vintage village Chablis is the _____(category)_____ of _____(specific)_____ .

ANSWERS:

OFF-VINTAGE VILLAGE CHABLIS: component of acidity
YOUNG PETITE SIRAH: texture of tannin
GERMAN LATE-HARVEST: component of sweetness
YOUNG SOAVE: texture of thinness
OLD RED BURGUNDY: flavor of earthiness
VERY YOUNG FIRST-GROWTH RED BORDEAUX: texture of tannin
YOUNG BEAUJOLAIS: flavor of fruit (cherries, strawberries, banana)

QUIZ #3: FILL-IN FOR FOOD AND WINE

Identify the key elements that make the following food-wine matches work. (For example: filet mignon and merlot/similarity of textures—rich and rich.)

ROASTED NUTS AND FINO SHERRY

	COMPONENTS	FLAVORS	TEXTURES
SIMILARITY			
CONTRAST			

ANSWER:
Similarity of flavors—nutty and nutty

OYSTERS AND CHABLIS

	COMPONENTS	FLAVORS	TEXTURES
SIMILARITY			
CONTRAST			

ANSWER:
Contrast of components—salty and acidic

FETTUCINE CARBONARA AND AMARONE

	COMPONENTS	FLAVORS	TEXTURES
SIMILARITY			
CONTRAST			

ANSWER:
Similarity of textures—rich and rich

GRILLED DUCK BREAST WITH BEAUJOLAIS

	COMPONENTS	FLAVORS	TEXTURES
SIMILARITY			
CONTRAST			

ANSWER:
Contrast of flavors—meaty and fruity

ROQUEFORT AND SAUTERNES

	COMPONENTS	FLAVORS	TEXTURES
SIMILARITY			
CONTRAST			

ANSWER:
Contrast of components—salty and sweet

QUIZ #4: MATCHING FOOD AND WINE

For each food item on the left, choose the wine on the right that is most likely to match well:

DILLED GOAT CHEESE
TARTLETS   Kabinett Riesling

SMOKY TEXAS-STYLE
BARBECUED RIBS   Sercial Madeira

OXTAIL SOUP WITH
BACON AND KALE   Sauternes

SMOKED SALMON   California Zinfandel

VANILLA PUDDING
WITH HAZELNUTS   Pouilly-Fumé

ANSWERS:

Dilled Goat Cheese Tartlets *Pouilly-Fumé*
Smoky Texas-style Barbecued Ribs *California Zinfandel*
Oxtail Soup with Bacon and Kale *Sercial Madeira*
Smoked Salmon *Kabinett Riesling*
Vanilla Pudding with Hazelnuts *Sauternes*

QUIZ #5: THE RESTAURANT TEST

PART ONE: THE FRENCH RESTAURANT

You are at a first-rate French restaurant, and have selected the cassolette of langoustines with wild mushrooms and chervil (a small dish of crayfishlike tails in a light cream sauce). The very creative sommelier has suggested the following wines to go with this dish:

• two-year-old Chateau St. Jean Chardonnay, Robert Young Vineyard
  (white, fruity, rich, fairly high alcohol)

- six-year-old Meursault, Charmes (Premier Cru) Michelot-Buisson
  (white, balanced, nutty-earthy, good acid)
- three-year-old Yamhill Valley Vineyards Pinot Noir (Oregon)
  (red, young berry-fruit, medium body)
- four-year-old Taltarni Shiraz (Australia)
  (red, peppery, medium body)

Which would you choose—and why?

ANSWER:
We would pick the Meursault, a white Burgundy, for this dish, hoping that its richness would go nicely against the richness of the shellfish, that its acid would cut the cream, that its developed earthiness would play well with the mushrooms. The young, fruity California Chardonnay might leave an impression of sweetness that would cloy on top of the cream. Red wine and cream is tricky—and red wine with shellfish is tricky—so both reds here are low-odds choices.

PART TWO: THE ITALIAN RESTAURANT

At an Italian restaurant specializing in bizarre twists on regional dishes, you've ordered the ricotta-stuffed agnolotti with sardine, raisin, and pine-nut sauce (little cheese-stuffed pasta pillows with a traditional Sicilian sauce). All of the following wines are in an agreeable price range:

- two-year-old Livio Felluga Tocai Friuliano
  (white, ripe fruit, almond, possibly a touch bitter, low acid)

- three-year-old Ruffino La Cabreo Chardonnay
  (white, medium body, slightly earthy)

- five-year-old Le Haut-Lieu Vouvray, Gaston Huet, demi-sec
  (honey and flower nose, slight sweetness, light body, great acid)

- two-year-old Gigondas, Domaine St.-Gayan, Roger Meffre
  (red, big, tannic, muscular, peppery)

Which would you choose—and why?

ANSWER:
The Vouvray is our choice, in the hope that it will balance everything perfectly—the great acid will probably cut through the ricotta as well as the sardines. This dish needs something to cut the fishiness, but

stand up to the sweetness of the raisins. For this reason, we would pass over the two Italian whites, two dry wines that would do nothing for the raisins and might make the sardines taste fishy. The big red Rhône is almost certain to taste coarse and clumsy with this dish.

PART THREE: THE CHINESE RESTAURANT

Your order at an upscale Chinese restaurant is Hunan chicken with scallions and fresh coriander leaves (stir-fried chicken, hot and spicy, in a salty brown sauce). Beer is a strong possibility, but you've noticed four very interesting wine possibilities:

- three-year-old Arbor Crest Merlot, Columbia Valley Washington, Bacchus Vineyard
  (red, medium body, good acid, light tannin, fruity-herbal)

- two-year-old Côtes-du-Rhône Blanc, Etienne Guigal
  (white, big, alcoholic, tropical fruit)

- eight-year-old Château Talbot
  (red, medium body, earthy-herbaceous, gentle)

- two-year-old Fieldstone Gewürztraminer, Alexander Valley
  (white, grapefruit-litchi nut, a little sweet, hot)

Which would you choose—and why?

ANSWER:
The Washington state Merlot is our choice. Its bright fruit should be a good foil to the brown saltiness of the dish, and its herbal dimension should pick up the coriander nicely. The acid should cut through, and, because there's low tannin and low alcohol, there'll be no interference with the heat of this dish. The hot Rhône white will probably taste even hotter and coarser against this dish. The delicate, aged Bordeaux will be washed out. And the old standby for Chinese food—Gewürztraminer—seems likely to fail here; sweetness doesn't seem appropriate, the alcohol might be too hot, and these particular flavors don't suggest a perfect marriage with the flavors of this dish.

PART FOUR: THE STEAKHOUSE

Sawdust on the floor, no nonsense from the staff, and a broiled sirloin steak with hash-brown potatoes on the way. There's no sommelier, but there is a range of interesting reds available:

- four-year-old Mercurey, Clos des Myglands, Faiveley
  (red, light, slight earthiness, good acid)

- three-year-old Marqués de Cáceres Rioja Crianza
  (red, light, fruity-woody)

- twelve-year-old Château Cantenac-Brown
  (red, gentle tastes of age, elegance)

- six-year-old Ridge Cabernet Sauvignon, York Creek
  (red, forceful, berry-tarry, rich feel)

Which would you choose—and why?

ANSWER:
The deck is stacked here—the rich steak will probably wash out all of
the light reds. A texture similarity is required here, and the Ridge
Cabernet is an ideal choice.

PART FIVE: THE NEW AMERICAN RESTAURANT

The restaurant specializes in fashionable regional American food, and
you're topping off your meal with a fairly sweet pecan and vanilla
terrine with maple-bourbon sauce. The wine steward has brought a
separate dessert wine list, and these are the possibilities:

- nonvintage Lanson Extra Dry Champagne (white, light, slightly
  sweet, fruity)

- four-year-old Erbacher Marcobrunn Riesling Spätlese (white, light,
  slightly sweet, high acidity, peach-apricot)

- five-year-old Château La Tour Blanche, Sauternes (white, medium
  body, medium sweetness, honey)

- Ferreira Duque di Bragança twenty-year-old tawny Port (brown,
  rich feel, nutty-buttery, quite sweet)

Which would you choose—and why?

ANSWER:
It would be interesting to try all of these, but we suspect that the first
three won't have the sweetness or the body to stand up to the terrine.
Sweet desserts usually require wines that are even sweeter, and the
tawny Port is the only wine here with a good chance. Moreover, its
flavors seem more appropriate with this dish than do the flavors of the
other wines.

QUIZ #6: THE FINAL EXAM

For the final exam, we would like you to prepare a dish, open a wine that we've recommended, and comment on the match. Food and wine matches often work on multiple levels at the same time. The following complex dish has a wide range of components, flavors, and textures all actively involved in the total palate impression:

HIDDEN QUAIL EGG WITH GINGER CREAM

¾ pound very fresh fluke or flounder fillet

1 heaping tablespoon chopped chives, plus 12 whole chives for garnish

¾ teaspoon wasabi paste

6½ teaspoons lemon juice

1 teaspoon Japanese ground red pepper (available at Japanese specialty stores, optional)

Salt, to taste

6 tablespoons coarsely cut fresh ginger root

6 large egg yolks

6 tablespoons peanut oil

6 tablespoons heavy cream

Prepare the fluke: Chop the fluke until it's a coarse paste. Add the chopped chives, the wasabi, 2 teaspoons of the lemon juice, and half of the red pepper. Mix well. Season to taste with salt, cover, and refrigerate.

Prepare the ginger cream sauce: Place the ginger in the bowl of a food processor. Add the large egg yolks and process for about 10 seconds. Add the remaining 4½ teaspoons of lemon juice. With the motor running, add the peanut oil, drop by drop at first, until completely incorporated. Slowly add the heavy cream, taste for seasoning, and refrigerate the sauce for at least 30 minutes.

Prepare the salad and garnishes: Tear the greens into small pieces, and rinse well. Wrap in paper towels and hold in the refrigerator. Preheat oven to 550 degrees F., then toast the sesame seeds for 3 minutes, or until they turn golden. Reserve. Toast the sheet of nori over an open flame, 8 inches away, for about 20 seconds per side or until it is crisp. Cut the nori into very thin strips; you will need 6 tablespoons. Reserve.

When ready to serve, arrange the fluke mixture into low, flat mounds, about four inches in diameter, with a small hole in the center on each of six dinner plates. Fill the holes with a quail's egg yolk. Top with a slice of smoked salmon, completely covering the yolk and the mound of fluke.

Moisten the reserved salad greens with a

little of the ginger sauce. To the salad, add ¼ teaspoon of the red pepper and the sesame oil, and stir well. Season to taste. Place ½ cup of the salad at 12 o'clock on each of the salmon plates, topping the salad with the toasted sesame seeds. Stir the ginger sauce well, and pass through a fine strainer. Pour the sauce around, but not on top of, the salmon on each of the plates.

Garnish the sauce on each plate with 1 tablespoon of the toasted nori shreds. Place two chives across the salmon on each plate. Dust the rim of each plate with the remaining ¼ teaspoon of red pepper.

Serves 6

3 cups very loosely packed chicory and other greens, such as red leaf lettuce and sprouts

¾ teaspoon sesame seeds

1 sheet nori (dried Japanese seaweed)

6 quail egg yolks, raw

9 drops Japanese sesame oil

½ pound top quality smoked salmon, cut in 6 broad, thin slices

With this dish, we recommend a four-year-old Coulée-de-Serrant from Mme. Joly. It's a dry Loire white, made from the Chenin Blanc grape. You can substitute dry Vouvray, Savennières, or Quarts de Chaume. American Chenin Blancs are a possible substitute, as long as they're bone-dry and with good acidity. Enjoy the wine with the dish . . . and then figure out why it worked so well (or why it failed to work for you).

ANSWER:
For us, this is a spectacular match . . . and one that demonstrates, in just one mouthful, all of the principles described in this chapter.

Let's start with components. The wine features high acidity, and this is a perfect contrast to the saltiness of the smoked salmon. Additionally, that acidity cuts right through the bitterness of the chicory, turning something potentially unpleasant into something delicious.

In this case, flavors are even more important. The wine features a gingersnaps kind of aroma, and this is exquisite with the ginger in the sauce. Furthermore, the honeyed fruit that the wine offers is a wonderful contrast with the overall seafood flavor of the dish.

Texture is also a key player in this match. Overall, it's a rich dish, what with the silkiness of the sauce, the velvetiness of the salmon, the unctuousness of the quail egg. A thin white would probably get wiped out. A super rich white might cloy. *This* white is on the rich side, but just to the proper degree; it is a lovely texture similarity that doesn't go too far. Furthermore, the wine forms a wonderful texture contrast with the dish's one light element, the tossed greens.

If you have the opportunity to make this dish and taste this wine, you'll see in a second what we're trying to express. One mouthful is worth a thousand words . . . and the more comfortable you become with our system, the fewer words you'll need to make it work for you, time and time again.

By paying attention to compo-
nents, flavors, and textures, you
now have all the tools you need to
set up thrilling wine-food
matches in any course of a meal.
And if a meal consisted of a
single course, our discussion of
the subject would now be com-
plete. 🐟 *But a course, of*
course, is not a meal; it's part of

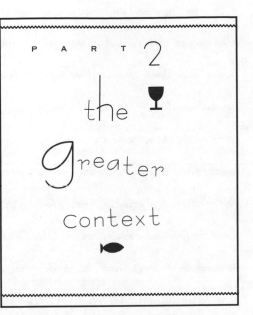

P A R T 2

the

greater

context

a meal, part of a greater structure, a building block in what will become the

cook's equivalent of a funky shack, a bourgeois split-level, or an alabaster

palace. You must know all about building blocks to begin raising the building—

but then you must learn how to put them together. And . . . you must learn to

raise the structure on the proper site; an alabaster palace might be perfect on the

plains of Andalusia, but it would probably seem out of place in America, even in

Beverly Hills. ♟ *The architecture of great meals is no accident, and in the*

next five chapters we'll show you how to build gastronomic structures of great

beauty, practicality, and appropriateness. We'll lead you through a widening

circle of concerns:

1. Plotting the course-to-course rhythm of your meal. 2. Finding the proper

balance between great wine and ordinary food, and great food and ordinary wine.

3. Deciding how to select wines when foods from other countries are being served.

4. *Creating food and wine menus with respect to the seasons.* 5. *Creating food and wine menus with respect to your guests and the occasion.* ➤ *Each of these issues boils down to a conflict between two principles, the gustatory and the psychological. In every case, the things your palate tells you are not precisely the same as the things your mind tells you. Foods and wines that might taste great together in a true blind tasting—when you're blindfolded, and have no idea what you're eating and drinking—may leave a different impression entirely when you know the food, have read the wine label (and seen what country it comes from or how much it cost), and are placed in a specific dining context (ethnic, socio-economic, seasonal, etc.)* ♛ *The following chapters attempt to sort out the gustatory from the psychological. Now that you've mastered the source of each course (based on gustatory principles), you must develop your feel for the meal (which usually involves the ultimate gastronomic zone, the mind).*

CHAPTER 4

THE

RHYTHM

ISSUE

N othing brings a menu to life like variety. The French, for example, have perfected a varied menu sequence that traditionally progresses from raw shellfish, to cooked fish, to roasted meats, to cheese, to sweets. The Italians are less formal about it, but salads, pastas, fish dishes, meat dishes, cheeses, and sweets are arranged in some order to keep the eye and palate in a state of constant excitement. The Chinese are masters at presenting a simultaneous variety of flavors, temperatures, and textures; the Japanese are perhaps the most subtle of all in this regard.

Variety is also a key concept for the selection of wine. You could serve only one wine with a meal, but it wouldn't match the gastronomic energy of a meal that ranges from tingling Champagnes to velvety fortified wines, from very crisp whites to very rich, buttery ones, from fading, delicate reds to robust red monsters in the prime of life.

In each case—varied food and varied wine—the excitement is based more on a psychological response than on a gustatory one. Your taste buds are fairly constant, and they will usually react similarly to taste stimuli. (There may be minor physical changes in receptivity.) But it's really your mind that's setting you up; after eating three purees in succession a crusty chunk of meat or bread is going to taste better than ever. After drinking a series of light white wines, an enormous Chardonnay is going to be welcome.

Variety is widely accepted as a desirable goal in the selection of food and in the selection of wine. But variety is equally important in setting up a series of wine-and-food matches. *How* the wine and food interact in the first course, in an ideal menu, should vary from *how* the wine and food interact in the second course, and so on. Matches based on similarity are most effective when set off by matches based on contrast. Just as jumping from a cold oyster to a warm soup, or from a tart Vinho Verde to a rich, red Zinfandel creates gastronomic thrills, so jumping from a rich smoked salmon with a light, acidic, rapierlike Riesling (a match based on contrast) to an herbed, lightly grilled chicken paillard with a fragrant light red Burgundy (a match based on similarity) will delight the mind and the palate. The alternation of principles in matching food and wine will create an ineffable harmony and excitement in your meals that your guests will probably be hard-pressed to explain. It's subtle, to be sure . . . but it's a detail that can elevate good meals to great meals, solid workmanlike efforts to brilliant, artistic designs. We call it the gastronomic rhythm method, and it works.

To illustrate, we've set up a menu for a dinner party for six, including wine recommendations for each course. We urge you to prepare this meal, and to serve the wines we've listed (or reasonable facsimiles):

BELON OYSTERS	**EIGHT-YEAR-OLD CHABLIS, GRAND CRU LES CLOS, WILLIAM FÈVRE**
SCALLOP AND LEEK SOUP WITH SAFFRON AND SHERRY	**MANZANILLA SHERRY EMILIO LUSTAU SOLERA RESERVA "PAPIRUSA"**
NOISETTES OF VENISON WITH CUMBERLAND SAUCE	**TWO-YEAR-OLD RIDGE ZINFANDEL, LYTTON SPRINGS**
GORGONZOLA CHEESE	**THREE-YEAR-OLD AMARONE GIUSEPPE QUINTARELLI**
BUTTERY APPLE TART WITH RUM AND CINNAMON	**TWO-YEAR-OLD AUSTRALIAN LATE-HARVEST RIESLING, PEWSEY VALE, BOTRYTIS-AFFECTED**

Here's a menu that ranges over the entire gastronomic map. For all its bristling variety it proceeds logically, offering diners a hearty mid-winter meal, both elegant and comforting. There's only one problem, as we see it. Every match of food and wine is based on the principle of texture similarity, with rich meeting rich enough times to thicken your blood by just reading the menu.

Belon oysters, now cultivated in Maine, are among the creamiest bivalves known to man. In this menu, they are set against their frequent partner, Chablis. But this is no ordinary Chablis; this is one with a difference. When you age a Grand Cru Chablis—especially if it comes from a great vintage, as ours did in this experiment—it becomes as rich, velvety, and complex as any Chardonnay-based wine from more southerly vineyards. So the texture similarity here is very much the point: cream meets velvet, and—isolated from the rest of the menu—the results are delicious.

For the next course, one would anticipate some relief from the richness of the first course. Not in this menu. The sweet scallops and the rich Lustau sherry also work together beautifully—more texture similarity, along with other similarities—but it may not be fully appreciated right after the oyster course.

On to the main course—and again, there's no relief in sight. Rich chunks of marinated venison are sautéed rare, and served with a sweet, traditional English game accompaniment, cumberland sauce. To match a dish like this, you *must* offer a wine with at least a touch of sweetness (component similarity) and the richness to survive the weight of the food (texture similarity). The Zinfandel and the venison is a lovely match, but lovely matches become increasingly difficult to notice.

For the cheese course, once again, there's no let-up in the onslaught. A powerful, creamy Gorgonzola is tough on wine . . . unless you unleash the power of a wine like Amarone on it. This massive Italian red—especially when it's young—has the stuffing to stand up to strong cheeses. It is another good texture similarity, but diners at our table found extremely creative excuses to pass up this course.

The aroma of the warm apple tart was so seductive that no one could pass up dessert—but a post-prandial glass check revealed that the amount of wine that guests consumed with this course could be measured in drops. The rich, honeyed, botrytised wine was a perfect texture similarity with the rich, buttery tart—with a good component similarity (sweetness) and a good flavor similarity—but it was certainly too much of a good thing, especially as the *coup de gras* in this overwhelming meal.

You might think that we never wanted to see this menu again. But one week later we served it a second time.

This time, however, we changed some of the wines. We deliberately set out to break the chain of matches based on texture similarity to see if we could resuscitate this meal—which, after all, included a number of truly delicious dishes and wines. Could the alternation of matching principles save the day? Could the elimination of a similarity here and the inclusion of a contrast there turn things around? Could variety in food-and-wine matching make the crucial difference? The answer was a resounding yes. By offering different wines in most cases—and by making one small but decisive change in the food—we had a meal that pleased us, delighted our guests, irrefutably demonstrated our principle, and yield no leftovers whatsoever!

The new menu:

BELON OYSTERS	**ONE-YEAR-OLD MUSCADET**
	CHÂTEAU DE LA CASSEMICHERE
SCALLOP AND LEEK SOUP	**MANZANILLA SHERRY EMILIO LUSTAU**
WITH SAFFRON AND	**SOLERA RESERVA "PAPIRUSA"**
SHERRY	
NOISETTES OF VENISON	**FIVE-YEAR-OLD CALIFORNIA PINOT**
WITH WILD MUSHROOMS	**NOIR, MOUNT EDEN**
GORGONZOLA CHEESE	**THREE-YEAR-OLD AMARONE**
	GIUSEPPE QUINTARELLI
	MUMM NONVINTAGE EXTRA DRY
	CHAMPAGNE
BUTTERY APPLE TART	
WITH RUM AND CINNAMON	

It's a great help to start the meal with a match based on contrast. The young, light Muscadet is a texture contrast (light and rich) to the rich Belons, a component contrast (acidic and salty) and a flavor contrast (fruity and briny). The Chablis match is more thrilling—in a gastronomic vacuum—but the Muscadet clearly launches *this* menu with more grace. Now the richness of the soup-sherry match can be fully appreciated. A light opener is always a great set-up for a rich second-course, and that strategy works perfectly here.

With the balance of the first two courses established, something rich and meaty for the third course is a natural follow up. But the sweetness and richness of that cumberland sauce—and of the requisite Zinfandel—threaten to throw the succeeding courses out of whack. So we permitted ourselves one fairly significant change in the menu: The venison is not marinated, and is served with a deglazed pan sauce made with red wine, brown stock, butter, and wild mushrooms. The Zinfandel, clearly, is now out; it's too broad and rich for this subtler dish. We needed a red wine that is rich enough to stand up to the venison's texture but light enough to provide some relief at this crucial point in the meal (with an Amarone lurking just around the corner). We found a lovely solution: A Pinot Noir from California that didn't shrink from the texture challenge of the venison, but supplied just enough lightness and acidity to keep the match delicate and graceful. The further affinity of the wild mushrooms for the earthy flavor of aged Pinot Noir—a great flavor similarity—strengthens the match-up.

We left the cheese course alone, because the palate was now ready to tie into the heft of Amarone and Gorgonzola—and what a difference this made! The match, in this menu, was not only acceptable—it is positively welcome! The venison course became a set-up for the cheese course, introducing the palate to stronger flavors, teasing with a lick of a moderate red, inducing one to fairly beg for the exquisite consummation of Amarone. The venison course and the cheese course formed a two-part crescendo, just as the oyster course and the soup course did in this revised menu.

We considered keeping the botrytised Riesling with the apple tart in this second menu, but decided that—though the palate could possibly handle rich on rich after the changes we made in the menu—it would be better to set up something light. Since it's difficult to serve a light dessert wine with a rich dessert—the wine usually gets overwhelmed—we chose to offer a slightly sweet Champagne to precede the tart as an "intermezzo". This is not a common practice, and we had no idea how it was going to work out. We need not have worried. It was the perfect wine for the moment. The bubbles washed the palate, clearing away the heaviness of the two previous courses. The wine's charming young fruit announced that a change in flavors was coming. And the touch of sweetness gave notice that we had subtly—but irrevocably—crossed the border into dessert territory.

When the tart itself arrived, it was as if the promise of the glass of Champagne had been fulfilled. No sticky-gooey wine was needed to wash down the buttery crumbs, and the meal ended on a satisfyingly light note. The differences in these two menus will undoubtedly deepen your understanding of wine and food matches. Here are the recipes:

BELON OYSTERS

2 dozen belon oysters

Cracked ice

Lemon wedges

Open the oysters as close to serving time as possible. Spread cracked ice and place four oysters on each of six dinner plates. Serve with lemon wedges.

To enjoy the wine match fully, refrain from serving any sauce with the oysters.

Serves 6

SCALLOP AND LEEK SOUP
WITH SAFFRON AND SHERRY

2 cups shellfish stock
(such as clam,
shrimp, or lobster;
substitute fish stock
or bottled clam
juice)

2 cups chicken stock

scant ½ teaspoon saf-
fron threads

3 tablespoons sweet
butter

3 tablespoons all-
purpose flour

2 medium leeks, white
parts only, rinsed
and cut in rounds

2 stalks celery

6 large sea scallops,
about ½ pound

1 medium tomato,
peeled, seeded, and
diced

1 tablespoon dry
sherry

Combine the stocks in a small saucepan along with the saffron threads, saving a few threads for garnish. Bring to a boil.

In a larger saucepan, melt the butter over medium heat. Add the flour, and stir with a wooden spoon for two minutes. Remove from the heat, and add the boiling liquid all at once, stirring vigorously with a wire whisk until smooth. Add the leeks to the soup. Reserve the leaves from the celery and add the stalks to the soup. You should have about ¼ cup of leaves. Simmer for 20 minutes.

While the soup is simmering, slice each scallop into 5–6 very thin slices.

When ready to serve, bring the soup to a boil, and add the sherry, maintaining the boil for 1 minute. Divide the scallop slices, the diced tomato and the celery leaves among six wide, shallow soup plates. Scatter a few reserved saffron threads on top. Bring the bowls to the table, and serve the hot soup from a tureen. Ladle about ½ cup of soup into each bowl.

Serves 6

NOTE: The sliced scallops are slightly cooked right in the soup bowl by the hot liquid. If you prefer to cook them more—or if your scallops are not fresh—add them to the hot soup for two minutes before serving.

Now you have your choice of two recipes for Venison Noisettes:

NOISETTES OF VENISON WITH CUMBERLAND SAUCE

In a bowl, combine the wine, onion, juniper berries, bay leaves, salt, and pepper. Add the venison, and marinate for 12 hours.

Prepare the sauce: Combine the jelly and the Port in a heavy saucepan. Cook over medium heat, until the jelly is melted, about 3 minutes. Add the stock, the orange rind and the lemon rind, and simmer for 3 minutes. Add the orange juice and the lemon juice, and simmer for an additional 2 minutes. Stir in the mustard. Serve the sauce, or save and reheat it.

When ready to serve, prepare the venison noisettes: Remove the venison from the marinade and dry carefully. Melt the butter in a sauté pan over medium-high heat until it foams and the foam begins to recede. Add the noisettes to the pan. Cook about 3 minutes per side for rare meat. Remove the noisettes when done and drain on paper towels for a moment. Divide among six dinner plates, and surround with the heated cumberland sauce. Chestnut puree and sautéed Brussels sprouts are good accompaniments to this dish.

Serves 6

1 cup dry red wine

1 medium onion, thinly sliced

1½ teaspoons crushed juniper berries

2 small bay leaves

⅜ teaspoons salt

¼ teaspoon freshly ground black pepper

1½ pounds boneless loin of venison, cut into 6 4-ounce fillets

½ cup red currant jelly

½ cup young ruby Port

¼ cup brown stock (or canned beef broth, low salt is best)

Rind of 1 orange, cut in strips

Rind of 1 lemon, cut in strips

Juice of 1 orange

Juice of 1 lemon

1 teaspoon Dijon mustard

3 tablespoons sweet butter

And the alternative:

Noisettes of Venison with Wild Mushrooms

6 tablespoons sweet
butter (¾ stick)

1½ pounds boneless
loin of venison, cut
into 6 4-ounce fil-
lets

2 small shallots,
finely minced

½ pound wild mush-
rooms cut into
halves or quarters
if very large (we
used chanterelles)

6 tablespoons dry red
wine (preferably the
same wine you'll
drink with the dish)

¾ cup brown stock (or
canned beef broth,
low salt is best)

2 tablespoons finely
chopped chives

Melt 3 tablespoons of the butter in a sauté pan over medium-high heat until it foams and the foam begins to recede. Add the venison to the pan. Cook about 3 minutes per side for rare meat. Remove the noisettes when done, and keep warm.

Discard all but 1 tablespoon of the butter from the pan. Add the shallots and sauté, stirring, over medium-high heat, for 1 minute. Add the mushrooms, and sauté, stirring, for 1 minute. Add the wine, and boil for 30 seconds. Add the brown stock, and reduce rapidly for about 3 minutes. Whisk in the remaining 3 tablespoons of butter.

Divide the noisettes among six plates, top with the mushrooms and sauce, and sprinkle the chopped chives over all. A thin potato galette is a good accompaniment.

Serves 6

Gorgonzola Cheese

Place 2 ounces of Gorgonzola on each of six small plates. The cheese is best with the wine if spread on crusty bread.

Serves 6

BUTTERY APPLE TART WITH RUM AND CINNAMON

Combine 1⅓ cups flour, 4 teaspoons of the white sugar, and the salt in a large bowl. Lightly beat one egg, and add to the flour mixture. Work the dough with your hands until the egg is well blended. The dough will be crumbly. Cut 8 tablespoons of the butter into sixteen pieces, and add to the flour mixture. With your hands, quickly work the butter into the flour, adding more flour if necessary. The pastry should just hold together, with pieces of butter evident; don't overwork the dough or the pastry will be tough. Form into a disc, cover with wax paper, and chill for 2 hours.

Roll the chilled dough out into a ⅛-inch-thick, 10-inch diameter circle on a floured board, turning the dough constantly to prevent it from sticking. Work quickly. Place a buttered 7–8-inch tart pan with a removable bottom on the counter. Roll the dough onto the rolling pin, place it over the tart pan, and gently unroll it into the pan. Tuck the dough into the pan. There will be a few inches of dough overlapping the top of the pan. Run the rolling pin across the top, and the extra dough will fall away. Save for another use. Cover the tart with a sheet of buttered wax paper and refrigerate.

Meanwhile, prepare the apples: peel, core, and quarter the apples, and cut each piece into 4 or 5 slices. Place the remaining 2 tablespoons of butter in a heavy sauté pan over medium-high heat. When it starts to foam, add the apple slices and cook, stirring, for 2 minutes. Add 2 tablespoons of the brown sugar, ½ teaspoon of the cinnamon, and the lemon juice. Cook, stirring well to distribute the ingredients, for 4 minutes. Add 2 tablespoons of the rum, and ignite

1⅓–1½ cups sifted all-purpose flour

6 teaspoons granulated sugar

½ teaspoon salt

2 large eggs

10 tablespoons sweet butter, chilled

1 pound Golden Delicious apples, about 2 large

2 tablespoons plus ¼ teaspoon brown sugar

⅝ teaspoon ground cinnamon

1 teaspoon lemon juice

2½ tablespoons dark rum

3 tablespoons heavy cream

with a match. Cook for one minute, while the flames die down. Remove the apples from the heat.

When ready to cook, prick the bottom of the chilled tart shell all over with a fork, place in a 350-degree F oven, and bake for 12 minutes or until golden. Add the apple filling, distributing it evenly. Continue baking for 15 minutes.

Meanwhile, prepare the custard filling: Beat the remaining egg in a small bowl, and add the remaining 2 teaspoons of granulated sugar, the remaining 1½ teaspoons of rum, and the cream. After baking the apple filling for 15 minutes, pour the custard mixture into the tart pan, distributing it as evenly as possible throughout the apple mixture. All the liquid may not fit into the tart pan. Discard this, or save for another use. Sprinkle the top evenly with the remaining ¼ teaspoon of brown sugar, and the remaining ⅛ teaspoon of cinnamon. Return to the oven, and bake 15 minutes more, until the custard is just set, and the top of the tart is puffed up. Remove from the oven, slip off the rim of the tart pan, and place the tart on a wide plate. Let it rest for about 5 minutes, then cut into six slices. The tart is best when eaten warm.

Serves 6

CHAPTER 5

THE

QUALITY

ISSUE

For all of the issues in Part Two—variety, quality, ethnicity, seasonality, occasionality—there are two forces simultaneously at play. One is purely gustatory: Apart from considerations of context, how do the food and the wine taste together? The second principle is psychological: What is the context, and how does it affect our enjoyment of food and wine?

The subject of this chapter, the quality issue—must grand food be served with grand wine? must humble food be served with humble wine?—is usually settled in the psychological sphere. Most people just feel comfortable serving humble food with humble wine. And we don't object to this sort of solution, as you'll see presently. However, we must all keep in mind that enforcing a gastronomic caste system at the dining table is not necessarily grounded in good gustatory logic.

To begin with, there's a pretty firm wine-and-food "rule" that we'd like to challenge, defeat, cut up into little neutrinos, and erase from the collective unconscious. The rule concerns the type of food one is supposed to serve to accompany a grand bottle of wine. Wine snobs will tell you that only simple, but elegant food—rack of lamb, prime ribs of beef, grilled quail—is appropriate for showing off a complex wine. In the popular mythology, humble, homey foods and dishes that feature as much complexity as the wine itself, are equally out-of-bounds when the big ones are uncorked. We disagree, and we're prepared to back up our position. But we hasten to point out that this particular dispute is just a small part of an even more important wine-and-food issue that, in the worst tradition of wine intimidation, tends to make people crazy.

When it comes to wine and food at the economic edges of gastronomic experience—very expensive wines, very cheap wines, very expensive foods, or very cheap foods—hosts, diners, and even sommeliers start to sweat. If you make a mistake with a $10 bottle of Bordeaux, these perspirers seem to feel, no one will notice. Similarly, choosing a wine for pot roast doesn't cause sleepless nights. But drag an oenological gem up from the cellar, and watch the anxiety levels soar. Truck in the truffles and foie gras, and observe the quickening heartbeats. At the funky end of the gastro-socio-economic continuum, the same phenomenon takes place: An innocent little hamburger can, it seems to some, be an express lane to social disgrace if you serve an inappropriate wine with it (which usually means any wine at all).

We'd like to defuse all of this potentially explosive nonsense. Bringing together the high and the low, in whatever form, will always make some people nervous. But, to us, the gastronomic yoking of high-bred wines and white-bread foods, or simple wines and simply exquisite food, presents no difficulties whatsoever . . . beyond the usual difficulties. We reiterate: The most important thing in matching wine with food, from a purely gustatory point of view, is getting the components, flavors, and textures to line up correctly. This applies equally to $5 Bordeaux with roast chicken, and to a Château Latour with chateaubriand. The heightening or lowering of the social stakes that attends the selection of wine and food has no effect on the pure taste of those items.

Herewith, then, are a pair of gustatory principles for culinary princes and paupers. These principles reflect the stark, objective palate-reality of the situation, outside of the psychological factors:

GUSTATORY PRINCIPLE #1: *Top-quality wine can be served with all sorts of food, as long as the components, flavors, and textures match up.* The only problem is that you have to be careful. Why are top-quality wines top-quality? Usually because they offer great complexity, or great subtlety, or great harmony—sometimes all three. The wrong foods can clash with complexity, overwhelm subtlety, or rearrange harmony into discord. This is why many people take the safe route, serving only simply roasted fillet of beef with a great red wine. If you're not sure of yourself, it is a wise course; but keep in mind that nothing can equal the thrill of a full-throttle bottle of great complexity next to a complicated dish that matches the wine flavor for flavor. It takes some thought to achieve, but it's worth the effort.

GUSTATORY PRINCIPLE #2: *Simple wines can be served with top-quality, expensive food, as long as the components, flavors, and textures match up.* A monochromatic, $6 Muscat next to a slice of foie gras may well be a glimpse of heaven, so never reject a simple wine for expensive food just because it's simple. But do keep one potential pitfall in mind: If the food is not only hoity-toity, but also *complex*—don't expect the match to be a marriage in the truest sense. A simple, inexpensive Chablis next to a bank-breaking, baroque combination based on beluga caviar, Dover sole, crayfish, and lobster sauce may be just fine if the profiles match up. In fact, it's the safe way out; you can expect the simplicity of the wine *not* to clash with the riot of rich flavors in the dish. However, at best, the wine will serve only as a simple refreshment; taking the opposite route—rolling the dice on a very complicated, grand Corton-Charlemagne, though the odds are stacked against you—could lead to a more memorable match.

In many situations—particularly if the crowd is relaxed, if the evening is not dedicated to the analysis of food and wine, and if the atmosphere is not heightened with extraordinary social or culinary expectations—the two gustatory principles above can be relied upon.

BEYOND THE GUSTATORY:
THE POWER OF THE MIND

However, there are psychological forces potentially at play that could turn everything topsy-turvy. Some people might be almost offended by a glass of low-brow Muscadet with beluga caviar, or at best find it odd. Some people—culinary Dadaists, or perhaps those who like to *épater le bourgeois*—might find the match exhilarating in its rejection of convention. Whichever crowd you entertain, be aware that when the issue of food and wine gets blended with the issue of dollars and cents attitudes and preconceptions can have a powerful effect on how things taste. Expectations can escalate dramatically.

Ask yourself this question: Would you enjoy an ounce or two of beluga caviar served on a paper plate, with a plastic spoon? How about a foie gras sandwich on white bread, eaten out of your hands? Or Château Margaux out of a paper cup? Again, there are people who might be thrilled by these reversals. But most would find the context inappropriate and would probably enjoy the food less. To some, the food and wine actually wouldn't taste as good!

THE TEST

To test this further, we set up an elaborate tasting of "high" and "low" foods, along with "high" and "low" wines . . . and, of course, we urge you to do the same.

We decided to use one basic food as a base for a range of dishes, so that we might reduce the variables. We chose beef, and we prepared it in a variety of ways up and down the gastro-economic continuum.

Furthermore, we selected two wines—one grand, one humble—to taste with the beef in all its permutations. Our guiding principle throughout was to create matches that would work on gustatory grounds alone; the two wines, technically, go well with every dish we prepared. The key question: Would they also be psychologically satisfying?

The wines:

1. A one-year-old Beaujolais Regnié. (Regnié is a town in the region that produces particularly good Beaujolais.) Textbook Beaujolais. Light, frivolous ruby color. Strawberries and bananas on the nose. Full of fruit and fun on the palate, light but grapy, good acid, slight impression of sweetness. A wine to guzzle merrily; certainly not a wine to discuss long into the night.

2. A ten-year-old Romanée-Conti from the Domaine de la Romanée-Conti. The greatest vineyard in Burgundy . . . and the wine is as impressive as the label. Rich ruby-garnet in color, with a developing bouquet of enormous complexity: spice, licorice, clove, soy, and the sexy decadence that makes great Burgundy one of the world's most desirable and expensive wines. Silky on the palate—though not heavy—with all of the bouquet's components reincarnated as taste sensations. A monumental wine . . . for talking about late into the night and for many years after.

The foods:

1. At the high end of the scale, we served a *Filet Mignon in Puff Pastry with Seared Foie Gras, Truffles, and Sauce Perigourdine.* A selection of purees—pea, carrot, cauliflower—molded into small ovals surrounded this elaborate creation, which looked like something out

of the eighteenth century, or out of a horribly pretentious cooking school. We based the sauce on a deep reduction of veal and beef stock, enriched with pureed foie gras, and flavored with a week's salary worth of minced, fresh black truffle.

2. *Roast Prime Ribs of Beef.* One rung down the ladder in our test. We coated the beef liberally with salt and pepper, placed it fat-side up in a roasting pan in a 325-degree F oven, and cooked it for 18 minutes per pound, or until the meat reached about 115 degrees F on a meat thermometer. (This is for very rare, practically quivering roast beef.)

3. *Carpaccio.* Simplicity is best here. Have your butcher machine-slice high-quality top round into the thinnest slices possible. (Some butchers call this cut London Broil.) Have this done as close to serving time as possible. One pound will serve six people nicely. Sprinkle with a little salt and pepper, drizzle with fruity extra-virgin olive oil, and grate some Parmigiano-Reggiano over all.

4. *Beef Stew.* Here's the rustic recipe we used:

PROVENÇAL BEEF STEW
WITH ZUCCHINI AND TOMATO

Mix the beef cubes with 1 tablespoon of the olive oil, 2 cloves of garlic, chopped, ½ teaspoon of salt, and a few grinds of black pepper. Marinate in the refrigerator for 6 hours.

Meanwhile, preheat oven to 550 degrees F. Place the beef bones in a large roasting pan, and add 2 garlic cloves, smashed, the shallots, and the carrots. Roast for 20 minutes, or until the bones are browned. Pour off the fat from the roasting pan, and place the bones and vegetables in a pot. Pour the red wine into the roasting pan, and cook over high heat for one minute, scraping up any brown bits that cling to the pan. Pour the wine into the pot, and add the beef stock, the water, and the bay leaf. Bring to a boil, then lower the heat and simmer for 1½ hours, removing any scum that accumulates on the surface.

2 pounds beef chuck, cut in 1-inch cubes

7 tablespoons olive oil

5 large cloves garlic

1½ teaspoons salt

Freshly ground black pepper

3 pounds beef bones

4 shallots, peeled and smashed

2 carrots, peeled and sliced coarsely

½ bottle dry red wine

(continued)

1¼ cup beef stock

1¼ cup water

1 bay leaf

1 cup flour for dredg-
ing

2 medium zucchini

16-ounce can toma-
toes

GARNISH

Parsley

Scrape the garlic off the marinated beef cubes. Place the flour in a shallow bowl and dredge the cubes. Place 2 tablespoons of olive oil in a Dutch oven over high heat. Add the floured beef cubes in one layer and sauté until browned on all sides, about 3–4 minutes. Repeat this process if the cubes don't fit in one layer. Pour the oil out, and strain the cooked beef stock into the Dutch oven. The liquid should just cover the beef cubes; add a little water if necessary. Simmer for about 2 hours, or until the beef is fork-tender.

Rinse the zucchini, and cut into 1-inch chunks. Place in a colander in the sink or over a bowl, sprinkle with the remaining teaspoon of salt, weight down, and let drain for 1 hour. Meanwhile, slice each canned tomato into four pieces. When ready to cook, remove the zucchini from the colander and dry well in a towel. Place the remaining 4 tablespoons of olive oil in a large saucepan over medium-high heat. Add the zucchini. Cook, stirring occasionally, until just softened, and light brown, about 4–5 minutes. Add the remaining clove of garlic, minced, and the sliced tomatoes. Set this mixture aside until the stew is ready.

When ready to serve the stew, add the zucchini-tomato mixture, stir well, and simmer for 5 minutes. Taste for seasoning. Sprinkle minced parsley on top, and serve.

Serves 4

5. *Steak Frites*. Every Frenchman's fast-food lunch. We pan-fried a 1-inch shell steak—crusty outside, rare inside—and cooked up some golden, crispy French fries.
6. *Cheeseburger*. The American equivalent of steak frites. Grilled, served on a hamburger bun, with just a touch of ketchup. (We figured that lots of sweet ketchup would not be kind to the Romanée-Conti.)
7. *Roast Beef Sandwich*. We tried it two ways: with mayonnaise and lettuce, and with a mixture of mustard and horseradish. Both times on crusty Italian bread.

From a gustatory perspective, everything worked out perfectly: Both wines went at least reasonably well with all of the foods. The real action, of course, was on the psychological front, where—even in our soulless, laboratory environment—some matches that were perfectly palatable on gustatory grounds just didn't seem right because of high cost–low cost juxtaposition.

The chart on the following pages contains our comments on every match:

DISH	Filet Mignon in Puff Pastry with Seared Foie Gras, Truffles, and Sauce Perigourdine	Prime Ribs of Beef au Jus
WITH BEAUJOLAIS	Fine with the dish, and a lot of fun as usual. But who wants fun? You spent too much money on this dish for fun. Steven Spielberg's *1941* isn't funny because forty million dollars is not a laughing matter. The Beaujolais just goes down too easily. It's amusing, but somehow it's irrelevant.	To some, prime ribs conjures up visions of white-gloved penguins in formal English dining rooms, expertly carving trim portions of exquisitely rare beef on gleaming silver trolleys. If you think of your prime ribs in this way, use the Beaujolais to slake the thirst of those in the scullery.
WITH ROMANÉE-CONTI	After what you spent on this dish, you want to savor every morsel . . . and savoring every drop of wine at the same time seems most appropriate. The richness of the dish slows you down, and then—when you sip the wine—you get slowed down further as your palate strains to understand every nuance. If the food and wine didn't go together on gustatory grounds, we wouldn't recommend the match; but they do go together well, technically, and this marriage of luxury creates a delicious aura that goes beyond the stimuli your taste buds are recording.	Prime ribs, like the filet mignon, has a slow, contemplative rhythm; both dishes are expensive, and both invite casually paced savoring. For prime ribs, there are other reasons as well to slow down: you can't chew it too quickly, and if you do it begins to cloy. So the measured savoring of great Burgundy is just right with this dish. And it doesn't hurt one bit that this combination is perhaps the best in the entire experiment, with the beef unlocking the key to even deeper levels of spice, game, and fresh thyme in the wine.

Carpaccio	Beef Stew	Steak Frites
With the peasant wine, carpaccio, essentially a peasant dish that's gone upscale, seems elemental, rough, even brash . . . all in a most attractive way.	A tonal bull's-eye. Stew is a convivial food; it thaws, in more ways than one. Diners share from the communal pot, and conversation flows—usually on any subject but the food. This Beaujolais is as buoyant as the stew and, since we were feeling the chill of the day, the food and warming wine disappeared rapidly.	The wine finds another soul-mate in this dish. This is the dish of a hundred thousand bistros . . . and bistro means quick. If you slow down on those French fries, they'll lose their crispness. The wine assumes its rightful place here as a quick gulp, and will make you feel that no other wine solution is appropriate, or even possible.
With the expensive Burgundy, everything changes. Again, the match is delicious . . . but this time it is also refined. The beef now seems suave, sophisticated. We ate it more slowly. We imagined we were in the Cipriani Hotel in Venice, rather than some boisterous trattoria in the countryside. It's amazing what fermented grape juice does to the imagination.	If you were served this wine blind, by no means would you object to it with the food. It seems to be pulled south by the stew, showing some lovely pepper flavors that no other dish in the experiment brings out. But the wine is not remarkable in this context—just a good, solid stew-mate. If you then discovered you'd drunk your $300 bottle of Romanée-Conti without having had the chance to appreciate it at its best and most subtle, you'd probably give up blind tastings forever. We loved the wine with stew, but this jewel from Vosne-Romanée deserves better.	Certainly not a Grand Cru Burgundy. This dish, unlike the stew, does not flatten the wine; you know what you're tasting here, whether it's blind or not. And, because of this, it just seems awkward, out of place, far too serious for the gastronomic moment.

<u>DISH</u>	**Cheeseburger**	**Roast Beef Sandwich**
<u>WITH</u> <u>BEAUJOLAIS</u>	Because there's ketchup on the burger, a little sweetness in the wine helps . . . and the Beaujolais scores another triumph. Slightly chilled, it seems as familiar as Coca-Cola with the burger.	What do you think? Beaujolais and a sandwich is as natural as can be.
<u>WITH</u> <u>ROMANÉE-</u> <u>CONTI</u>	Like popcorn with Champagne, here's a great intellectual conceit: the world's most exalted wine with America's basest food. But the idea of slumming is to set up a contrast that makes you see something in a different way. That just doesn't happen here. The match is fine, but you long for more grown up food to take the measure of that very grown-up wine.	This comes close to working. Because Romanée-Conti is so damned good with roast beef, this match has an irrepressible appeal. We felt like the servants at some grand manse, late at night, stealing the dregs of a great wine in the pantry along with the grand dinner's leftover meat on a hunk of bread. This is a match for the imaginative; we still feel that for the highly organized, it won't be very satisfying.

We were amazed how often the higher-class foods did not take to the Beaujolais, and how consistently the lower-class foods seemed odd with the Romanée-Conti. Remember that these are not gustatory responses, but psychological ones. We proved to ourselves that the mind plays tricks when it comes to this issue, and these psychological factors should not be ignored when you're considering a marriage of gastronomic partners from different sides of the tracks.

We do note with a kind of subversive joy, however, that our peak Romanée-Conti moment (with the prime ribs) was no more pleasurable than our peak Beaujolais moment (with the steak frites). Had we tasted the Romanée-Conti next to the Beaujolais without any food on the table, we would have smiled gently at the Beaujolais—and no doubt rhapsodized for hours over the Romanée-Conti. But take the two wines with their respective ideal partners, and the pedigree diminishes in value. On a hedonic scale, both of these matches were near the outer limits of the stratosphere.

Wine snobs will never yield the point, but food—if you get it just right with the wine—is the great leveler.

CHAPTER 6

THE
ETHNIC
ISSUE

f you're serving the cuisine of a specific country, should you serve wines from the same country? Or will other wines work just as well? The answer, as you'll discover below, is—it depends. Once again, the psychological and the gustatory are waging war over your palate.

SECTION ONE: THE PSYCHOLOGICAL ARGUMENT FOR ETHNIC WINES WITH ETHNIC FOODS

The occasion was perfect for a spectacular match of ethnic food and wine. Sitting in the dining room of a large winery in the Veneto region of Italy, not far from Verona, a cadre of local women had been recruited to create for us one of the region's more uncommon specialties: *bigoli*. (Long, thick round pasta that is made with the unusual addition of corn flour, extruded at home through brass rings, and lightly dried.) Its chewy but elastic texture is another one of Italy's miracles, and the aromas of the bubbling veal ragu wafting through the room left no doubt that pasta and sauce would enjoy each other's company immensely. The dining experience was the kind of unfussy, nouvelle-be-damned one that every modern traveler dreams of.

The oenologic imagination fairly danced in anticipation. Would they treat us to a special version of one of the light local whites with this homespun dish? A wood-aged Soave, perhaps? A single-vineyard Gambellara? A barrel sample of Bianco di Custoza? What about one of the regional reds . . . an unusual Valpolicella or Bardolino that would give those tired names new respectability? All the way with an enormous Amarone, maybe? Or, best of all, some local treasure that we'd never heard of but was quite obviously *the* wine to drink with *bigoli*, *the* wine to round off a perfect ethnic circle?

"We've got something special for you to enjoy with the *bigoli*," said the proud winery owner . . . and our hearts skipped a few more beats. "You may not be aware of the fact," he continued, "that we have opened a new winery within the last few years. In your country. In Virginia. So we thought you'd especially enjoy a glass of American Chardonnay with the *bigoli*."

If you couldn't see beneath the skin, at that moment you would have observed broad smiles, happy eyes open wide. If you were not trained to distrust the mask, you might not have noticed that the smiles and eyes were frozen in position, that we were terrified to shift expressions, not knowing what looks of horror might rush in to fill the void.

Oh, there are worse things in the world, to be sure. On an absolute scale of suffering, the Virginia Chardonnay debacle nestles in somewhere between hangnails and belated birthday cards. However, at that moment, in that place, with that fabulous local pasta, the well-intentioned but gravely misguided wine selection ruined an otherwise terrific day. We were on the brink of ethnic perfection, one of the finest moments imaginable in the increasingly elusive pursuit of the authentic . . . and then the spectre of Thomas Jefferson snatched it away from us.

The Chardonnay was pretty lousy with the pasta—kind of alcoholic and coarse—but it probably would not have registered even if it had fit like a glove. The *bigoli*, in all its exquisite ethnic strangeness, had set us up for the local beverage. We had been led into a regional frame of mind, and not a single wine from any other of the world's wine regions could have satisfied the psychological craving. Lafite-Rothschild? Take that swill away, my good man! And bring us your finest Soave!

Had we lost our minds? Not really. Gastronomy is the most intimate tourism, and no dedicated tourist can resist a glimpse of the preserved, the pristine, the way things really are. This spirit often affects the decision-making when it comes time to choosing a wine for ethnic foods.

We spend a good deal of energy in the U.S. seeking authentic ethnic dining experiences. "Continental" restaurants—with their pastiche of veal cordon bleu, veal Parmigiania, and wiener schnitzel—are distinctly unfashionable. The adventurous eater is looking for the restaurant that offers a consistent lineup of one country's foods. Sometimes, the most discriminating diners even look for those restaurants that offer the foods of a particular *region:* Hunan food, Tuscan food, Provençal food, Catalan food. . . . Can a restaurant dedicated to the food of the west shore of Lake Garda be far off?

There's a certain thrill, to be sure, in remaining ethnically consistent: It helps you to pretend that you're paying a visit to another country. For your dining dollar, you get food, drink, ambience . . . and a journey fueled by the imagination. It may taste just as good to slip in a coquilles Saint-Jacques Parisienne between your Provençal ratatouille and your Provençal daube de bouef, but it makes it a lot harder to spend an imaginary night in Nice.

This powerful psychological principle is the most compelling reason to serve ethnic wine with ethnic food. As you leap from authentic course to authentic course, the pleasure of the game is multiplied geometrically by treating the wines in the same fashion. The Burgundian dining adventure begins with a light Aligoté. The moderately-aged white Chassagne-Montrachet that follows gleams against the backdrop of its lesser regional cousin. It's a short leap to a nearby red, as the Premier Cru Beaune thrills us with the achievements of red-wine grapes from the same soil that created the Chassagne-Montrachet. And then a powerful Chambertin Clos de Bèze lifts the party to the sky, deposits it safely in a corner of Burgundy . . . and no one returns until the next morning.

Ethnic Wines with Ethnic Foods?

Pro There's a psychological thrill in matching the foods and wines of one country. It makes you feel as if you're there.

Con It's only the similarity or contrast of key elements in wine and food that really determines the success or failure of matches.

But make no mistake about it. This sort of Burgundian excursion is only for those willing to follow the scenario, only for those willing to play the game.

From a pure tasting perspective, a California Zinfandel will do just as well as a Gigondas with a Provençal daube de boeuf. Similarly, you can serve with confidence a rich, young Rioja alongside a Tuscan-style beefsteak with white beans, in place of the more traditional Chianti. In fact, if you served these wines blind—out of a decanter, with no label showing it—it would be the rare guest or fellow diner who would know the difference. Wines and foods match up because their elements are similar or contrasting . . . and, but for the psychological dimensions of the match, it doesn't matter where the wines or foods come from.

Our feeling, then, is this: The psychological dimension is a powerful one, and should not be ignored. In the right context—when you have interested guests and diners, perhaps about to take a trip to the country in question—the wines of one country with the foods of that country are a multi-level delight. But if the context is not right—when you have a crowd, perhaps, not willing to pay attention to every label and to the regional history behind every dish—wines from other countries can do just as well as wines from the country represented by the food.

In the next section we set up a tasting exercise, free from the psychological fervor of an ethnic excursion at your dining table, to demonstrate that in most cases nonethnic wines are entirely acceptable with ethnic foods.

SECTION TWO: THE GUSTATORY ARGUMENT AGAINST ETHNIC WINES WITH ETHNIC FOODS

Put aside the re-creation of that summer in Tuscany, that honeymoon in Burgundy, that romp through the Costa del Sol. You can always show slides after dinner. What we'd like you to do now is step into our laboratory—a place far removed from the magic of travel memories.

The following three dishes are general representatives of their respective countries. Not one is a classic dish from a specific region. Each could have been created in the capital city, in a smaller city, in the country, or in a kitchen or restaurant in America. But each dish captures a true ethnic taste, and is a good test sample in this ethnic wine experiment.

With each dish, we have selected three wines. One is a logical ethnic accompaniment to the dish; the other two are equivalent wines from other countries. You will get the most from this exercise if you prepare the dish, and serve *all three* wines with it so you can compare. You might want to serve them out of decanters, so that neither you nor your guests know which is which.

We begin with a dish that is brimming with the flavors and the gastronomic spirit of France: a terrine of duck, flavored with Calvados. If you don't have the time to prepare this recipe, try the experiment with a slice of pâté that you've purchased. It should be a coarse, meaty, country pâté, with only hints of liver and garlic flavors.

r

Duck Terrine Flavored with Calvados

Bone the duck. Reserve the skin, bones, and giblets for the optional parts of this recipe, if desired (see page 131). Reserve one duck breast fillet. Separate the remaining meat into two piles. Add the duck liver to one pile, and, with a sharp cleaver, chop to a fairly smooth paste. Coarsely dice the other pile. Combine the two piles in a large bowl. Chop the 12 ounces of pork fat into tiny dice, and combine with the chopped meat. Add the Calvados, thyme, paprika, nutmeg, cloves, salt, pepper, garlic, and potassium nitrate. Mix very well with a wooden spoon. Fry a small amount of the mixture, and taste and adjust seasoning. (Remember that when it's cold, it tastes less salty than when it's hot.)

Salt and pepper the reserved breast fillet, and bury it inside the pâté mixture. Cover the bowl, and refrigerate overnight.

When ready to prepare the pâté, preheat the oven to 325 degrees F. Line a 3–4 cup terrine with the slices of fatback. They should completely cover the bottom and sides of the terrine, and there should be enough fatback overhanging the terrine to enable you to completely enclose the terrine on top.

Remove the breast fillet from the pâté mixture, wipe off, and cut into five long strips. Add one-third of the pâté mixture to the fatback-lined terrine, smoothing the top so that it's in an even layer. Add three strips of duck to the terrine, spaced evenly (one at a far edge, one in the center, the third at the other edge). Cover with half the remaining pâté mixture. Place the remaining two strips of duck so that they sit immediately to the left and right of center. (This will create an attractive pattern of the five strips when you slice the pâté.) Cover with the remaining pâté.

1 5-pound duckling

12 ounces smooth pork fat, plus 3–4 thin sheets of fatback

¼ cup Calvados or other brandy

¼ teaspoon dried thyme

⅛ teaspoon paprika

Large pinch of freshly ground nutmeg

Pinch of ground cloves

1 teaspoon salt

½ teaspoon freshly ground black pepper

½ teaspoon fresh garlic, chopped to a paste

¼ teaspoon potassium nitrate (also called saltpeter) for color, optional

1 bay leaf

½ cup all-purpose flour

Garnish

Parsley sprigs

Three Wines with French Duck Terrine Flavored with Calvados

AN ETHNIC MATCH

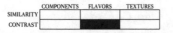

	COMPONENTS	FLAVORS	TEXTURES
SIMILARITY			
CONTRAST		■	

One year-old Musca-det, Château du Cléray, Sauvion & Fils (France)

TWO NONETHNIC MATCHES

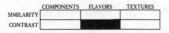

	COMPONENTS	FLAVORS	TEXTURES
SIMILARITY			
CONTRAST		■	

Three-year-old Pies-porter Michelsberg Qualitätswein, Julius Kayser (Germany)

	COMPONENTS	FLAVORS	TEXTURES
SIMILARITY			
CONTRAST		■	

One-year-old Yarden Galil Sauvignon Blanc (Israel)

Smooth the top, and fold the overhanging fatback over the pâté mixture. Tuck into the terrine where necessary, so that the pâté mixture is completely covered. Place the bay leaf on the top of the fatback.

Seal the top of the terrine with a flour-water mixture: Mix the flour with enough warm water to make a sticky dough. Spread this dough around the edges of the terrine, so that there are no crevices visible between the fatback-enclosed pâté mixture and the walls of the terrine. Spread out the dough so that it clings to the top edges of the terrine. Then cover the dough with a fitted cover or aluminum foil. The point is to force the fat—which will melt in the oven—to remain inside the terrine during cooking.

Place the sealed terrine in a roasting pan, and pour boiling water into the pan until it comes half-way up the sides of the terrine. Place in the preheated oven, and bake for 1 hour, 40 minutes.

When cool enough to handle, remove and discard the sealing dough. Place a 5-pound weight on the terrine, and let rest in the refrigerator for at least 24 hours. Remove the weight after one day. The terrine could be served at this point, but it will taste better if it "ripens" for 5–7 days in the refrigerator.

When ready to serve, slip the terrine out of its mold. Scrape away any excess fat or jellied stock, but keep the surrounding fatback in place. Save the jellied stock, if desired, for garnish. Remove the bay leaf. Let the terrine come almost to room temperature, then cut it into twelve slices. Place each slice on a plate, topped with a little jellied stock if desired. Garnish with parsley sprigs, and serve with crusty bread.

Serves 12

OPTIONAL: DUCK STOCK FOR TERRINE For additional flavor, place the duck bones in a large, heavy saucepan. Add 1 medium onion, 1 carrot, and 3–4 sprigs of thyme. Barely cover with water. Bring to a boil, remove the scum, lower heat, and simmer for 5–6 hours, or until the stock has reduced to about 3 tablespoons. Cool, and blend into the pâté mixture just before stuffing the terrine.

OPTIONAL: RENDERED DUCK FAT FOR TERRINE For additional flavor, chop all of the duck fat and skin into ½-inch pieces. Place in a heavy saucepan with 2 tablespoons of water, and simmer over low heat for about 1 hour. Strain the fat from the pan, let cool, and blend ¼ cup of this rendered duck fat into the pâté mixture just before stuffing the terrine. Reserve the rest for other uses such as sautéing potatoes and other earthy vegetables.

There's little argument in France over the best type of wine for terrines such as this one: dry white. On a visit to the Loire Valley a few years ago, we asked a local wine official to name his favorite wines with charcuterie. Every single wine he named was a dry white from the Loire. When we asked him to name other wines, non-Loire wines, he began mentioning dry whites from other parts of France. When we asked him why he drinks only white wine with pâté, he paused, thunderstruck—he had never thought about this before. Finally, he spoke, "Because it's *a priori*." This philosophical term refers to something you can know before experiencing it. We'd heard it applied to moral absolutes, pure beauty, and the existence of God, but never to meatloaf made from pork.

That Loire official will never experience the joy of a fruity, light, chilled red with pâté—but that's okay. Whites *do* usually score best with charcuterie. And in our tasting, we discovered that a white with good acid (to cut through the richness of the pâté), medium body (to stand up to the fattiness), and some pronounced flavor (to match the strong pâté flavor) works best of all. From France, this could mean a range of wines. Many of the Alsatian types work nicely, particularly when they have the acid of so-called "off-vintages." Village Chablis is another strong prospect, along with a clutch of lesser southern Burgundies made from Chardonnay grapes.

We kept that Loire official in mind, and came up with a delicious young Muscadet: a one-year-old Château du Cléray, the flagship wine of the great house of Sauvion & Fils. Its applelike flavors were a great flavor contrast with the meaty terrine flavors, and its acidity lightened the terrine considerably. Most important, drinking the Muscadet with the terrine supplied the unmistakable sense-memory of hundreds of bistro meals in France; taste and smell are powerful memory-enhancers, and this very ethnic match-up brought back a flood of warm recollections. Of course, had we never experienced French wine with rich pâté in France, we could not have recalled the sensation of being there.

For those who don't have this experience in their memory banks—or for those more interested in the best match than in nostalgia—we tasted other wines, from other countries, that probably would work with the pâté. And, sure enough, we found a pair that—psychological factors aside—worked as well as, or better than, the Muscadet.

The second wine was from Germany: a three-year-old Piesporter Michelsberg Qualitätswein from the Mosel, produced by Julius Kayser. Its floral flavors were also a great flavor contrast with the duck, its higher acid cut through even better, and helped to create a long, tingling finish. The wine featured a touch of sweetness, which was acceptable—but more sweetness would not have been appropriate. If you must substitute a wine for this one, limit yourself to Qualitätswein or Kabinett wine from less-than-rich vintages. On the other hand, the so-called "dry" German wines—called "Trocken" or "Halbtrocken"—may feature too much alcohol for this match.

We continued the experiment with a tingling Sauvignon Blanc: green and grassy, with lots of lemon acidity. Many of the Australian and New Zealand Sauvignon Blancs fit this description, but we found gastronomic bliss in a wine from Israel: a one-year-old Yarden Galil Sauvignon Blanc. The good acid was instrumental once again, but the real key here was in the flavor. The grassiness supplied the initial flavor contrast, but this yielded to a long finish in which a series of spicy-clovey flavors supplied a more profound flavor contrast. Things happened all over the palate in this highly successful third match. It didn't bring back any memories of bistros near the kibbutz, but it sure tasted good.

The next experiment took us to Italy, and we created a pasta dish that is unmistakably Italian in every way:

PAPPARDELLE WITH PORCINI AND SAUSAGE

Place the flour, the semolina, the olive oil, and the salt in the bowl of a food processor. Break the eggs into the bowl. Process for about 5 seconds, until the mixture is crumbly. With the motor running, slowly add the water through the feed tube. The dough should form a ball along the sides of the bowl. Depending on the weather, you may need a little more flour (which you should distribute evenly around the ball) or a little more water, so that the ball is smooth—neither sticky nor dry. Remove the dough from the bowl, wrap in wax paper, and let it rest for ½ hour at room temperature.

When ready to roll out, divide the ball into quarters. Cover three quarters with wax paper. Knead a quarter by running it through a pasta machine set on #1. When it comes through the machine, fold the dough neatly and run it through again—folding the dough in such a way as to create an even rectangle as the dough comes through the machine. Repeat one more time. Now roll the sheet of dough through the machine on progressively thinner settings. (Roll it through on #2, then #3, then #4, then #5.) At this point, cut the long sheet of pasta in half, crosswise. Roll each half through the machine on the thinnest setting, #6. Hand-cut each half into pappardelle, 1½ inches wide, 3 inches long. Spread out sheets of wax paper, sprinkle lightly with corn meal, then place the pappardelle on the wax paper. Repeat the process with the remaining dough pieces.

Cover the dried porcini with boiling water. Let soak for ½ hour. Drain. Set the mushrooms aside and reserve the liquid.

Preheat the oven to 450 degrees F. Place

PASTA

1¼ cups all-purpose flour

½ cup semolina

1 teaspoon olive oil

½ teaspoon salt

2 large eggs

2 tablespoons water, more or less

ASSEMBLY

1½ ounces dried porcini mushrooms

3 sweet Italian sausages, about ¾ pound

2 teaspoons fruity olive oil

4 large eggs, well-beaten

½ cup freshly grated Parmigiano-Reggiano cheese

Pinch of freshly grated nutmeg

Salt and freshly ground black pepper, to taste

GARNISH

Italian parsley

the sausages in a small baking pan, and cook for about 15 minutes, or until brown outside and cooked inside. Time the cooking so that the sausages are ready just as the pappardelle are cooked.

Boil the pappardelle in a large pot of salted water. When done—about 1 minute—pour the pappardelle into a colander. Toss in the colander, over the sink, to let excess water drain off. Toss with the accumulated fat from the sausages. If the pappardelle are sticking together, add a little extra olive oil. Quickly sear the porcini in a small sauté pan in the 2 teaspoons of olive oil. Add to the pappardelle. Add the eggs to the pappardelle, combining well to make a light sauce. Crumble the sausage and toss with the pasta and eggs. Add the Parmigiano-Reggiano, mixing well. Add the nutmeg, and season to taste with salt and pepper.

Divide among four plates, topping each one with a broad leaf of Italian parsley.

Serves 4

Three Wines with Italian Pappardelle with Porcini and Sausage

AN ETHNIC MATCH

Two-year-old Pagliarese Chianti Classico (Italy)

	COMPONENTS	FLAVORS	TEXTURES
SIMILARITY			
CONTRAST	■		

TWO NONETHNIC MATCHES

Seven-year-old Vina Monty Gran Reserva Rioja from Bodegas Montecillo (Spain)

	COMPONENTS	FLAVORS	TEXTURES
SIMILARITY			
CONTRAST		■	

Seven-year-old Trapiche, Cabernet Sauvignon from Mendoza (Argentina)

	COMPONENTS	FLAVORS	TEXTURES
SIMILARITY			
CONTRAST		■	

Pasta with any kind of rich sauce—made from eggs, or cream, or cheese—poses problems for wine. If a wine has too much young fruit, it can taste inappropriately sweet with rich pasta dishes. If it's a little high in alcohol, it can taste "hot" with these dishes. If you serve a very thin, light, refreshing wine with rich pasta, the wine can disappear next to the dish.

Our favorite solution to the problem is a light red wine, with just enough character to stand up, but not enough fruit and/or alcohol to cloy. There's a wide variety of wines from Italy that fits in here—all of which offer that unmistakable cherry-cheesy Italianate character, so attractive with pasta dishes. Bardolino and Valpolicella, both made near Verona, are usually perfect in this context. The light Nebbiolo-based wines of Lombardy—such as Inferno and Grumello—also work well. And light Cabernet Francs from Friuli and Trentino-Alto Adige are always good prospects.

For our experiment, we chose a light-style Chianti Classico, a two-year-old Pagliarese. There are many rich, important, highly structured Chiantis that would be wrong here. But a light wine like this cuts through the dish, adds its slightly cheesy flavor to the Parmigiano, and prevents any threat of an unpleasant cloying sensation. Once again—if you've been there and consumed something similar—the match is as good as a ticket on Alitalia.

But other wines are also good. We opened a seven-year-old Spanish wine, a Rioja—the Vina Monty Gran Reserva from Bodegas Montecillo—and it was extraordinary with the pasta. Its fruit was subdued from bottle age, so it didn't cloy with the rich sauce. Its modest flavors of age were a perfect flavor contrast to the egg-and-cheese flavors of the dish, and, simultaneously, a flavor similarity with the earthy porcini mushrooms. Modest alcohol, light body, and decent acidity all helped in the effort.

We reached all the way to Argentina for our third wine, and a seven-year-old Trapiche Cabernet Sauvignon from the Mendoza region worked in much the same way as the Rioja. Its flavors of age—not too complex or subtle—were lovely with the dish, and its overall light profile prevented any rough edges on the match.

We concluded the experiment with the dish that is practically emblematic of Spanish cooking: paella. If non-Spanish wines can work with something so definitively Spanish as a dish of paella, then there's hope for ethnic cross-fertilization everywhere.

PARSLEY PAELLA WITH PEPPERED SHRIMP, STRING BEANS, AND SNAILS

1/3 pound medium-sized shrimp, about 12

Salt

1/2 teaspoon freshly ground coarse black pepper

1 tablespoon fruity olive oil

2 large chicken thighs, boned, cut in quarters

2 ounces chorizo, sliced fairly thin

2 large shallots, chopped

3 medium cloves garlic, chopped

2 ounces string beans, cut in 1/2-inch lengths

1 cup short-grained rice, such as Italian arborio

1/2 cup very finely chopped fresh parsley leaves

2 cups chicken stock

1/2 teaspoon saffron threads

12 large canned snails

2 pimientos, cut in strips

Butterfly each shrimp by cutting along the back, through the shell, to remove the black vein. Rinse, then spread it wide open, leaving the shell on. Sprinkle with salt and the freshly ground black pepper. Set aside for at least 1/2 hour.

In a large, heavy pan, with a tight-fitting lid, heat the olive oil over medium-high heat. Season the chicken thighs well with salt and pepper, then add to the hot oil, skin-side down. Cook for about 2 minutes, or until the skin just begins to brown. Add the chorizo slices, and toss with the chicken. Cook for 1 minute. Add the shallots, the garlic, and the string beans. Mix well. Add the rice and half of the parsley, stirring to incorporate well and to coat the rice thoroughly with oil. Add the chicken stock and the saffron threads. Stir well. Bring the mixture to a boil, reduce the heat, cover, and simmer for 15 minutes. Embed the shrimp in the top part of the rice, then scatter the snails and the pimiento strips around the shrimp, all in a decorative pattern. Cover, and cook for 10 minutes more, or until the liquid has been absorbed and the rice is just cooked. Serve at the table out of the pan, sprinkling the portions with the remaining 1/4 cup of parsley.

Serves 4

We weren't sure about the best type of wine for this dish, so we experimented with several. But we had reached a firm opinion: Rich, juicy reds—plump with young fruit, but not stiff with tannin—proved to be the paella wine *nonpareil*. A Spanish beauty that fit the bill was a three-year-old Coronas, made by Miguel Torres in the northeastern region of Penedés. The wine's exuberant fruit, and its rich, round body, perfectly covered the rich, intensely flavored paella. Since the paella contains no eggs or cream (unlike the Pappardelle with Porcini and Sausage), you don't have to worry about a rich wine cloying alongside the dish. Here's a case where texture similarity—rich on rich—works beautifully.

But you don't need Spanish wine to pull off the trick. Every bit as good was a one-year-old Montepulciano d'Abruzzo, made by Cantina Zaccagnini in central Italy. Its seductive fruit, and rich body—all without a great deal of complexity—were perfect next to the paella.

The best wine of all, however, came from our own shores—the north shore of Long Island, in fact. A two-year-old blend of Cabernet and Merlot from Bedell Cellars in Cutchogue, New York, was absolutely exquisite with the dish. Its rich and soft texture was lovely against the fat grains of rice, the creamy shrimp, the moist chicken, and the velvety snails. Its fruity flavors worked as the fruity flavors of the other two wines worked; but this wine added an herbal dimension that picked up the parsley flavor running through the dish, adding an extra frisson to an already superb match.

Clearly, in a laboratory situation, the national heritage of a wine is not a key factor in the success of its marriage to food. But don't take our word for it, please—try these experiments yourself.

Three Wines with Spanish Parsley Paella with Peppered Shrimp, String Beans, and Snails

AN ETHNIC MATCH

Three-year-old Coronas, by Miguel Torres (Spain)

TWO NONETHNIC MATCHES

One-year-old Montepulciano d'Abruzzo by Cantina Zaccagnini (Italy)

Two-year-old Long Island Cabernet/ Merlot by Bedell Cellars (United States)

SECTION THREE: THE GUSTATORY ARGUMENT FOR ETHNIC WINES WITH ETHNIC FOODS

The experiments above cover most of the situations in which you might be tempted to serve ethnic wine with ethnic food; remember that matching them can work for psychological reasons, but nonethnic wines, if properly chosen, can taste just as good as ethnic wines can with ethnic foods.

That said, we hasten to add that there are three special situations in which it's a good idea to reach for a bottle of ethnic wine with an ethnic dish! Here they are:

1) **WHEN YOU'RE HAVING A REGIONAL DISH WITH A STRONG TRADI-TION OF BEING SERVED WITH A PARTICULAR REGIONAL WINE.** The three recipes presented above are ethnic, but not regionally traditional. That is, not a single one of them is identified with one region in particular. (They could be found in many parts of their countries of origin.) And not a single one of them suggests a regionally "mandatory" wine. But there is a range of dishes throughout the wine-drinking world inextricably tied to certain regional wines. We believe that substitutes are possible, but it's hard to improve these time-honored matches. And since they're such high-odds propositions, why bother to stray? Here are some of the world's leading regional matches:

CHOUCROUTE GARNIE	**(ALSACE)**	*ALSACE RIESLING*
RAW BELON OYSTERS	**(LOIRE)**	*MUSCADET*
CROTTINS DE CHAVIGNOL (SMALL MOUNDS OF GOAT CHEESE)	**(LOIRE)**	*SANCERRE*
LYONNAIS GARLIC SAUSAGE	**(LYON)**	*BEAUJOLAIS*

RISOTTO WITH SQUID	**(VENETO)**	*SOAVE*
LASAGNE VERDI AL FORNO (BAKED GREEN LASAGNA)	**(EMILIA-ROMAGNA)**	*LAMBRUSCO* (NOT THE POP WINE VERSION—THE REAL STUFF AS SERVED IN EMILIA-ROMAGNA)
CROSTINI DI FEGATO (LIVER SPREAD ON BREAD)	**(TUSCANY)**	*CHIANTI*
CASSATA (SPONGE CAKE WITH CANDIED FRUIT)	**(SICILY)**	*MOSCATO DI PANTELLERIA*
MARINATED GREEN OLIVES	**(ANDALUSIA)**	*AMONTILLADO SHERRY*
CALDO VERDE (PORTUGUESE SOUP WITH KALE, GARLIC AND SAUSAGE)	**(THE MINHO)**	*VINHO VERDE*

2) WHEN YOU'RE HAVING AN ETHNIC DISH THAT REQUIRES A SPECIFIC ETHNIC WINE IN THE COOKING. These dishes usually taste best when served with the same wine at table. The affinity is especially strong if the wine in the dish has been subjected to little or no cooking. (After long cooking, the wine loses its character.) The dish can be traditional or the creation of some regionally oriented modern chef. Here are some of the leading examples:

OEUFS A LA MEURETTE (EGGS POACHED IN BEAUJOLAIS)	**(FRANCE)**	*BEAUJOLAIS*
STRAWBERRY TART WITH SAUTERNES SABAYON	**(FRANCE)**	*SAUTERNES*

ZABAGLIONE WITH MARSALA	**(ITALY)**	*MARSALA*
COQ AU RIESLING	**(FRANCE)**	*ALSACE RIESLING*
BLACK BEAN SOUP	**(SPAIN)**	*OLOROSO SHERRY*
GRANITE DE MARC DE CHAMPAGNE	**(FRANCE)**	*ICED MARC DE CHAMPAGNE*
PEARS POACHED IN MUSCAT DE BEAUMES DE VENISE	**(FRANCE)**	*MUSCAT DE BEAUMES DE VENISE*
LIVER TERRINE IN VOUVRAY ASPIC	**(FRANCE)**	*DRY VOUVRAY*

3)**WHEN YOU'RE TRAVELING.** We must confess that we are true believers in the agri-mystical theory of wine with food. Somehow—and we know not why—the food that is grown in a region *does* taste better with the wine of that region. For this reason, we always like to drink local wines with local foods when we're traveling, unless we find ourselves in an Amazon rain forest.

To eat Italian food with Italian wine in New York is not really to eat Italian food with Italian wine. With the exception of a few imported white truffles, perhaps, you're really eating *Italian-style* food with Italian wine—and Italian-style food can be good with many wines. But when you are actually eating Italian food—i.e., when you're in Italy—then the whole game changes. The style is Italian, the flour is Italian, the hands rolling the pasta are Italian, the air you're breathing is Italian . . . and you should try to make sure that the wine is Italian, not Virginian.

CHAPTER 7

THE

SEASONAL

ISSUE

f you've ever trudged in from the cold, and come face to face with
a steaming bowl of bean and cabbage soup, and lunged for the
nearest stout red wine . . .

If, after the first romp through a field in spring, you've ever set
a lacy tablecloth and covered it with platters of asparagus and cool
glasses of Muscat . . .

If you've picnicked on the beach, with lobster sandwiches, salads
galore, and cold jugs of simple wine . . .

If, in autumn, you've sat down to a concatenation of fresh game and
fresh white truffles—accompanied by the first glass of tannic red
you've had in many months . . .

Then, you know that the seasons have a mighty effect on the
appreciation of food, wine, and food and wine together.

HOW THE SEASONS AFFECT FOOD

Everyone is aware of the seasonal influence on what we eat. Like the
other food-wine issues in Part Two, the seasons affect us on a
gustatory and a psychological level.

The gustatory level is simple to explain: Some foods are associated
with specific seasons because that's when they're produced; to eat
them in other seasons is to consume food that's been frozen, stored, or
produced in less than ideal circumstances.

Beyond the physical considerations of availability and freshness,
however, lie a range of psychological considerations. Our salad

Some Foods that Actually Taste Better in Season

tomatoes in September	navel oranges in winter
melons in September	morels in spring
apples in fall	soft-shelled crabs in
chanterelles in fall	late spring
white truffles in November	peaches in the summer
oysters in winter	corn in August

Some Foods with Psychologically Determined Seasons

bright green vegetables such as asparagus or peas in spring	bosky flavors in fall
salads in summer	stews in winter
cold soup in summer	hearty roasts in winter
sushi and sashimi in summer	hot soup in winter

consumption goes up in the summer—not just because salads taste better, and not because we're less hungry in summer than in winter. It just seems appropriate, in the summer, to ingest something lighter, crisper, more in tune with the world around you.

HOW THE SEASONS AFFECT WINE

In wine, the differences are more subtle. To begin with, there's only one wine available to the consumer that tastes different at a specific time of year: Beaujolais Nouveau. The grapes for this unique wine are harvested in September to October, vinified, and the finished wine is ready for sale in November! By contrast, most of the world's fine wines are not available for at least 4–5 months after the harvest, and some not for years.

Beaujolais itself (which is available later in the year, around April) is already a light-hearted, frivolous wine. But when it's made as Nouveau, it's lighter and more frivolous still; it's a virtual party in a bottle, with amazingly vivid, young, simple fruit (smelling something like bananas), and not enough concentration or complexity to waste any time talking about. By the spring, its buoyant fruit has faded, and, by next autumn, most examples of Beaujolais Nouveau are merely vinous spectres.

On the psychological front, the seasons of wine are very distinct. Generally, the heavier, richer, more complex the wine, the more it seems appropriate for a winter setting—when no one has anywhere to go beyond the hearth, when the warmth of such wines provides as much comfort to sensitive palates as the warmth of stews and soups. But racy, floral wines—served chilled, of course—are the wines of summer, and there can be little in all winedom to compare with the sipping of a lightly sweet Mosel in a

Wines that Actually Taste Better in Season

❧ Beaujolais Nouveau and other Nouveau pretenders from Italy, California, Australia

blooming June garden. Try a vintage Port in that same context, and you'll find yourself longing for winter's fireplace, or an ice cube, or a trip to the freezer.

Wines with Psychologically Determined Seasons

❧ light German Riesling in spring

❧ cool, simple wines, such as sangria, in summer

❧ rich whites, rich reds in winter

❧ medium-weight reds in fall (as your palate wends its way back to red after a summer of cool whites and rosés)

HOW THE SEASONS AFFECT
FOOD-AND-WINE MATCHING

When you bring food and wine together, you have the opportunity to powerfully reinforce the seasonal appropriateness of a food you're serving, or of a wine you're offering. The most seasonally correct dish can suddenly seem distinctly unseasonal if you offer a wine that's six months ahead of its time; and this works in reverse as well. For example, if you serve a summertime salad entree—a mess of greens, let's say, with slivers of grilled chicken and a light olive oil dressing—

you'll need to clinch the season by serving a light rosé, or a fairly simple Chardonnay, or a Chenin Blanc. Serving a hearty red from the south of France with this salad may be amusing in some contexts, but your summertime guests might wilt on the patio more quickly than the lettuce. Or, you're in front of that roaring hearth in January and the decanter of Port is being passed around. This is winter bliss . . . so don't spoil it by offering a selection of Chilean peaches, plums, and nectarines. Oh, they should go well with the wine, technically—but why deny your guests the full, wintry consummation of Stilton and walnuts?

To test the point further, we conducted a year-long study that yielded four delicious seasonal recipes along with four seasonally appropriate wine choices. Try each of these recipes in its given season, and open the recommended wine. We have also included, with each recipe, a wine that goes perfectly well with the food—but seems hopelessly out of sync with the season. Try that wine as well with the dish, to gain a better understanding of the calendar's uncanny culinary power.

A MATCH FOR SUMMER

Summer is synonymous with patios and grills, outdoor parties and jugs of wine. So we brought together several of America's favorite summer ingredients—lobster and corn—and designed the package for outdoor merriment:

SOUTHWESTERN LOBSTER ROLLS

4 live 1½-pound lob-sters

2¼ cups cornmeal

12 large eggs, plus 2 large egg yolks

1½ cups water

½ teaspoon salt

6 tablespoons melted sweet butter

For the lobster: Bring a large pot of salted water to a boil. Add the lobsters, cover, and bring the water back to a boil. As soon as it's boiling, remove the cover, and simmer the lobsters for 15 minutes. Remove lobsters and cool. When cool enough to handle, remove the lobster meat, coarsely chop, and reserve. Discard shells, reserve tomalley.

For the cornmeal crêpes: Place the cornmeal in a food processor. (You may have to do this in two stages.) Add the twelve eggs, the water, the salt, and the butter. Process for about 30 seconds, or until the mixture is well blended. Let rest in the refrigerator, covered, for ½ hour.

When ready to prepare the crêpes, grease a 6- to 7-inch frying pan, or a crêpe pan, with vegetable oil. Use a brush or a paper towel. Place over medium-high heat, until the oil just begins to smoke. Remove the pan from the heat, and pour a scant ¼ cup of batter into the pan, all at once. Immediately begin swirling the batter around the pan so that the entire bottom surface of the pan is covered. You will have a round, thin crêpe. Place the pan back on the heat for about 30 seconds, or until the batter has congealed and the bottom side is lightly browned. Flip over, and cook for another 30 seconds. Place on a plate, cover with a linen towel, and continue until sixteen crêpes are made. Stack and reserve, unrefrigerated, for up to 3 hours.

For the mayonnaise: Place the 2 egg yolks in a food processor. Add the mustard and 1 tablespoon lime juice. Process for 3 seconds. Combine the olive oil and the vegetable oil. With the food processor running, begin adding the oils, drop by drop. After you've added a few teaspoons of oil you can start adding the oil in a steady, thin stream until you have a stiff mayonnaise. Immerse the ½ cup of coriander leaves in boiling water for 3 seconds. Remove, run under cold water, and squeeze dry. Place in the food processor with the mayonnaise, and process until the green flecks are evenly distributed. Let the mayonnaise rest in the refrigerator for at least ½ hour.

For the final assembly: When ready to serve, peel and stone the avocados. Cut into sixteen broad slices, and sprinkle the slices with salt, pepper, and remaining lime juice. Set aside.

Place the lobster meat in a large bowl. Add the red and green pepper, and the corn

½ teaspoon dry mustard

3 tablespoon lime juice

¼ cup fruity olive oil

¼ cup vegetable oil

½ cup plus ⅛ cup tightly packed fresh coriander leaves

2 avocados

Salt and freshly ground black pepper, to taste

1 red pepper, finely minced

1 green pepper, finely minced

2 ears corn, boiled, kernels removed

A Match for
Summer

The Food Southwestern
Lobster Rolls

The Seasonal Wine Rosé
Sangria

The Out-of-Season Wine
two-year-old
Chassagne-Montrachet,
Les Morgeots, (Premier
Cru) Chartron &
Trebuchet

kernels. Add the remaining ⅛ cup of corian-der leaves. Mix in the mayonnaise, and blend well. Taste for seasoning; add salt and pepper if necessary.

Use the reserved cornmeal crêpes just as they are, at room temperature. Or, for addi-tional flavor, grill the prepared crêpes over a very hot charcoal fire for about 30 seconds per side. In either case, place a few table-spoons of the lobster mixture inside the crêpe, cover with a slice of avocado, and fold the crêpe in half. No silverware is necessary—eat this roll out of your hands.

Makes 16 rolls

With the lobster, we served the following wine in summer:

ROSÉ SANGRIA

1 bottle California rosé (choose white Zinfandel, rosé of Cabernet Sauvi-gnon, rosé of Pinot Noir or others . . . just make sure that it's not too sweet)

1 orange

1 lime

½ lemon

3 tablespoons Grand Marnier

1–2 tablespoons gran-ulated sugar, de-pending on your taste and the sweet-ness of the base wine

Ice cubes

6 ounces soda water

Pour the rosé into a large pitcher. Wash the orange, lime, and lemon, cut them into thin slices, and add to the pitcher. Add the Grand Marnier and the sugar. Marinate for at least a few hours. (The sangria will taste better if you leave it overnight.) When ready to serve, fill up the pitcher with ice cubes, pour the soda water over all, and stir well. Serve with a wooden spoon in the pitcher.

Serves 3–6

Perfect! Not only a good match, but in the perfect seasonal key. We also tried a serious white Burgundy—a two-year-old Chassagne-Montrachet, Les Morgeots (Premier Cru) from Chartron & Trebuchet. It's a fabulous wine, with lots of rich fruit, spicy flavors, and delicious acidity. It fit the lobster well, as white Burgundy sometimes does—but it is just too serious for a boisterous crowd on a hot summer night. We felt as if we wasted it; we would have enjoyed it far more in the fall or winter at a formal sit-down dinner.

A MATCH FOR AUTUMN

Autumn brings a wealth of ingredients—such as game, and squash, and woodsy mushrooms. It's a season when, with leaves burning and the alluring smells of nature's decadence in the air, we seek an analog on our plates and in our glasses. Here's a match-up that wouldn't be as good at any other time of year:

SAUTÉED QUAIL WITH ACORN SQUASH AND KASHA

Preheat oven to 400 degrees F. Cut the squash in half, and remove the seeds and fibers with a spoon. Trim the squash bottoms so they rest squarely on a baking sheet. Place the halves, cut-side up, on a baking sheet and place a tablespoon of the butter in the middle of each piece. Salt and pepper the sections and cover with foil. Bake for 35 minutes, uncover and continue baking until tender and lightly browned.

For the kasha: Combine the stock, salt, pepper, and butter in a small saucepan and bring to a boil. In a separate bowl, combine the beaten egg with the kasha and mix well, making sure that all the kernels are coated. Place into a 1-quart heavy skillet with a tightly fitting cover.

Over high heat, constantly stir, flatten, and chop the egg-coated kasha with a fork or wooden spoon for 2–4 minutes or until the

ACORN SQUASH

2 acorn squash, medium sized, rinsed clean of dirt

4 tablespoons sweet butter, (½ stick)

Salt and freshly ground black pepper, to taste

KASHA

2 cups chicken stock

1 teaspoon salt

1 teaspoon freshly ground black pepper

(continued)

*2 tablespoons sweet
butter*

*1 large egg, slightly
beaten*

*1 cup kasha (coarsely
granulated buck-
wheat kernels)*

QUAIL

4 quail, cleaned

*Salt and freshly
ground black pep-
per, to taste*

4 slices bacon

*4 tablespoons chopped
scallions*

*3 cups chicken or veal
stock*

*1 tablespoon chopped
fresh tarragon*

*2 tablespoons grappa
or brandy*

¼ cup tawny Port

GARNISH

Fresh tarragon leaves

egg has dried on the kasha and the kernels are very hot and mostly separate. Momentarily remove the skillet from the burner, and quickly add the boiling liquid. Cover the skillet, and return to the burner. Reduce the heat to low and cook gently for 10 minutes. Remove the cover, stir, and check to see if the kernels are tender and the liquid is fully absorbed. If not, cover and continue steaming for 3–5 minutes. When done, remove the cover and fluff with a fork.

Remove the squash from the oven and reduce the heat to 200 degrees F. Season the quail inside and out with salt and black pepper. Fry the bacon in a nonreactive 12-inch skillet over medium heat until crisp. Remove bacon to a paper towel. When dry, chop and reserve. Reheat the bacon fat over medium heat, and add the quail and scallions. Slowly cook the quail until the birds are nicely browned, about 15 minutes. Then, transfer the birds to the warm oven and drain off the excess fat from the skillet. Add the stock, chopped tarragon, grappa, and port to the pan, and bring the mixture to a boil. Reduce the mixture by two-thirds, then remove it from the heat. Salt and pepper to taste.

To assemble: Place a section of the cooked squash on each of four large dinner plates. Surround the squash with kasha. Take a quail and position it, breast-side up, opposite the squash. Pour some sauce over the kasha, then pour the remaining sauce on both sides of the bird. Sprinkle the dishes with the reserved chopped bacon and decorate with fresh tarragon leaves.

Serves 4

To us, there is a quintessential autumn wine: red Burgundy, especially aged red Burgundy. It's a wine that occasionally smells like burning leaves in autumn, and its delicious decadence is the vinous equivalent of earthy mushrooms, falling leaves, and encroaching darkness. A seven-year-old Mazis-Chambertin from G. Vachet-Rousseau (a Grand Cru wine from a small proprietaire in Gevrey-Chambertin) was autumn itself with the quail. Since it came from a vintage known for thin, acidic wines—like many Burgundy vintages— it was not too powerful for the delicate birds. But it was from the right side of the barnyard, filled with all of those funky nuances that makes aged Burgundy so sexy. A Pinot Gris from Alsace—a three-year-old Martin Schaetzel—was also good with the dish, but its overtly fresh fruit failed to confirm that summer was really finished.

A Match for Autumn

The Food Sautéed Quail with Acorn Squash and Kasha

The Seasonal Wine seven-year-old Mazis-Chambertin, G. Vachet-Rousseau

The Out-of-Season Wine three-year-old Martin Schaetzel Pinot Gris, also known as Tokay d'Alsace

A MATCH FOR WINTER

It's easy to predict what will play in February; make it hot, make it rich, make it plentiful. We followed those precepts, and came up with a rustic dish guaranteed to chase away the wintertime blues. You may have cabin fever, but you won't want to leave the cabin that's heady with these fragrances:

TRIPE WITH LENTILS, SAGE, AND PROSCIUTTO

Rinse the tripe well, then place in a large pot filled with salted water. Bring to a boil, lower heat, and simmer for ½ hour. Remove from water and, when cool enough to handle, cut into slices approximately ½ inch wide and 3 inches long. Toss with ½ teaspoon of the sage, and with lots of freshly ground pepper. Set aside.

While the tripe is simmering, chop the carrot, the celery, two of the onions, and the

3 pounds fresh honey-comb tripe or frozen tripe, defrosted

1 teaspoon powdered sage

Freshly ground black pepper, to taste

(continued)

1 carrot

1 stalk celery

3 medium onions

4 cloves garlic

5 tablespoons fruity olive oil

⅛ pound or 3 thin strips bacon, cut into matchstick-sized strips

1 cup dry white wine

2 cups beef stock

¼ pound prosciutto, cut in tiny dice

½ cup dried lentils

¼ cup freshly grated Parmigiano-Reggiano cheese

GARNISH

6 tablespoons chopped fresh parsley

garlic into extremely fine dice, practically a paste. Place 3 tablespoons of the olive oil in a large pot, and add the bacon. Cook over medium heat for 3 minutes. Add the chopped vegetables, stir well, and cook very slowly for 30 minutes, covered, stirring often so as not to brown the onion and garlic.

Add the tripe to the vegetables and stir well. Add the white wine, along with 1½ cups of the beef stock. Bring to a boil, and cook for 2 minutes. Lower heat, and simmer for 3 hours, partially covered, stirring occasionally, until the tripe is fairly tender. If the liquid evaporates during the cooking, add more white wine and beef stock (in a 2:3 ratio) to keep the stew moist. After 3 hours of cooking, add the diced prosciutto, stir well, and cook for an additional hour.

Add the remaining 2 tablespoons of olive oil to a medium saucepan. Finely chop the remaining onion, and add to the pan over medium heat. Sauté for 2 minutes. Rinse the lentils well, and add to the onion. Sprinkle with the remaining ½ teaspoon of sage and stir well. Add the remaining ½ cup of beef stock (just enough to cover the lentils) and simmer until just tender. Most packaged lentils available today cook within 45 minutes, but check package instructions to make sure. If the lentils are still firm and the liquid has evaporated, add more liquid.

When the tripe has cooked for 4 hours, add the cooked lentils and the Parmesan cheese. Stir well. There should be a moderate amount of sauce in the pot—the dish should be stewlike; add additional beef stock if too dry. Cook over low heat for 20 minutes. Serve in broad, shallow soup plates, sprinkled with chopped parsley.

Serves 6

The dish had a clear Italian accent, but we knew that a rich red from anywhere would firmly fix this dish in its proper season. So we grabbed a bottle of a legendary Portuguese wine—a ten-year-old Barca Velha, made by the Port house of Ferreira, from the same types of Douro Valley grapes that usually go into Port. At ten years of age, it was still purple with youth, moderately tannic, and could easily go another 10–15 years. But this bottle's time—wintertime—had come and it was the perfect snowbound mate for the bubbling tripe. White wine is often drunk with tripe, and a South Australian Sauvignon Blanc—a two-year-old from Wolf Blass—has just the right acidity to cut through, just the right fruit to stand up. But it did not make a seasonal point, and, while we fought over the dregs of the Barca Velha, most of the Sauvignon Blanc passed a comfortable night in the refrigerator.

A Match for Winter

The Food Tripe with Lentils, Sage, and Prosciutto

The Seasonal Wine ten-year-old Barca Velha

The Out-of-Season Wine two-year-old Wolf Blass
South Australian Sauvignon Blanc

A MATCH FOR SPRING

Blend one part spring ingredients, one part froth, and one part brightness—and you've got a perfect spring recipe. Try this after a light, delicious meal with the windows wide open:

COLD STRAWBERRY SOUP

Select eight large strawberries, about ½ pint. Cut into thin slices, place in a bowl, and combine with 1 teaspoon of sugar, ¼ teaspoon of the lemon juice, and the Grand Marnier. Mix well, and marinate for at least 1 hour, at room temperature.

Place ½ pint of strawberries in a food processor. Add 1 tablespoon of sugar, and

2 pints fresh strawberries, about 24 ounces

1 teaspoon plus 5 tablespoons granulated sugar

(continued)

*¾ teaspoon lemon
juice*

*¾ teaspoon Grand
Marnier*

1⅛ cups heavy cream

*1 teaspoon unflavored
gelatin*

*¼ cup mint leaves,
loosely packed*

**A Match for
Spring**

The Food Cold Strawberry Soup

The Seasonal Wine one-year-old Cascinetta Moscato d'Asti

The Out-of-Season Wine Sandeman's Founders Reserve Port

puree. Whip 1 cup of the heavy cream until it's stiff and forms soft peaks. Heat the ⅛ cup of cream until just simmering, then pour the cream over the gelatin in a small bowl. Stir until the gelatin is dissolved. Stir the dissolved gelatin into the strawberry puree, then gently fold in the whipped cream. Mix well, to reach an even pink color, but preserve the airiness of the whipped cream. Refrigerate for ½ hour.

Prepare the soup: Place the remaining pint of strawberries in a food processor. Add 3 tablespoons of sugar, and the remaining ½ teaspoon of lemon juice. Puree. Ladle the strawberry puree into four soup bowls. Remove the whipped cream-strawberry mixture from the refrigerator, and shape into twelve ovals, by lifting a heaping tablespoon of the mixture from the bowl with an oval-shaped soup spoon. Using a second spoon, shape and smooth the oval right in the bowl of the spoon. As you work, dip the second spoon in hot water to achieve a smoother oval. Place three ovals on the strawberry puree in each bowl, at 12 o'clock, 4 o'clock and 8 o'clock.

Garnish the bowls with the marinated strawberry slices, resting them against the ovals in a decorative pattern. Distribute the mint leaves over the soup, and serve.

Serves 4

There are many dessert wines that could handle this luscious bowl of fruit. But we opened a sparkling wine from the Piedmont—a one-year-old Moscato d'Asti, called Cascinetta—that seemed the very soul of spring. Moscato d'Asti is a little lighter, a little less sweet than its more famous regional cousin, Asti Spumante—and for these reasons, it was superb with the berries. We tried a ruby Port as well—the top-value Sandeman's Founders Reserve. It was a very fine match, technically . . . but it knocked us back a few months, and could not compare to the springlike optimism carried by those Moscato bubbles.

CHAPTER 8

THE

OCCASIONALITY

ISSUE

S pecial occasions demand special foods and special wines. This is a simple fact of culinary life. It all started with that gooey cake—bearing a single candle—that they pushed under your nose when you were one year old. You don't remember it now, of course, but by the time those cakes started bearing two, three, and four candles you knew that something special was going on here: When everybody made a big fuss about "your" day, you got this great round thing to eat with frosting all over it. And you learned your first lesson in gastronomic occasionality.

Today you play the culinary reflex game with great ease on all the notable occasions. We say Thanksgiving . . . you say turkey. We say Easter, you say lamb. We say Fourth of July, you say barbecue. We say that everyone, quite obviously, is culturally programmed.

It's no different for wine, though in American society our responses are considerably narrower in this department. There's only one great occasional wine on these shores . . . but it's a biggie: just try to have a New Year's party, a wedding toast, or a pennant celebration in a crowded locker room without the benefit of buckets of bubbles. The festivity will fizzle faster than you can say Dom Pérignon.

It's not that these occasional foods and wines *taste* better on these occasions than they do at other times. And it's not that seasonally, or otherwise, they're the best things you could choose. From a gustatory perspective, duck at Thanksgiving and 1945 la Tâche on New Year's Eve would both probably be superior to the "clichés" that are normally served. But you don't feel right without the proper "clichés" at the proper times . . . and this is yet another demonstration of the gustatory being at least partially eclipsed by the psychological.

Since the psychological is so strongly at play, we reason, why not make it work for you? We feel strongly that occasionality—since it's such a powerful determinant of food and wine pleasure—can be pushed even further than it normally is in the selection of food and wine. Moreover, you can combine food and wine in such a way as to make the pleasure and the meaning of any occasion even stronger.

Consider the following foods for the following occasions, each of which is selected more subtly than, say, the turkey that everyone picks for Thanksgiving:

A BIRTHDAY . . . made more special with the reprise of a favorite preparation.
A BUSINESS DEAL . . . consummated against the backdrop of refined French food.
A FIRST NIGHT IN SCANDINAVIA . . . reinforced with a plateful of open-faced sandwiches.
AN ANNIVERSARY . . . marked by a dish reminiscent of the very first one shared.

These selections are exciting enough—but if you get canny about your wine as well, the occasion soars even higher:

A BIRTHDAY . . . honored with wine from the year of the birth.
A BUSINESS DEAL . . . closed with top-quality wine, as refined as the food.
A FIRST NIGHT IN SCANDINAVIA . . . toasted with chilled aquavit.
AN ANNIVERSARY . . . noted with wine as old as the marriage.

Just as every wine or food has a dominant component, flavor, or texture that acts as a gustatory beacon in guiding us to the best match, so do special occasions contain elements suggestive of the most rewarding directions to take when standing at the wine and food crossroads. While we can't actually touch or taste them, these psychological elements are, nonetheless, every bit as valid a consideration in menu planning as are the harsh tannins of a young Hermitage or the sweet snap of a freshly boiled corn-on-the-cob.

This is not to say that you *can't* enjoy a birthday dinner or an anniversary without some appropriate wine or food reference during the course of the meal. Rather, we're simply suggesting that going the extra distance to find those references is less difficult and more rewarding than you might have thought. And, as we'll soon see, there are times when the wrong food or wrong wine *can* derail an evening's pleasure or purpose.

A HYPOTHETICAL TEST

To illustrate our point, we dreamt up the following menu, and then hypothetically served it to three very different sets of guests on three very different occasions:

SALMON CAVIAR ON CRÈME FRAÎCHE BLINI	BILLECART-SALMON ROSÉ (NONVINTAGE CHAMPAGNE)
SAUTÉED SKATE IN BEURRE BLANC	DOMAINE DE LA FOLIE (A FOUR-YEAR-OLD WHITE BURGUNDY FROM RULLY)
GRILLED DUCK BREAST IN A SHERRY VINEGAR SAUCE	BEAUNE GRÈVES, MICHEL LAFARGE (A FIVE-YEAR-OLD RED BURGUNDY)
GREEN SALAD	NO WINE
PEACH TART	BRUT DE PECHE (A NONVINTAGE SPARKLING WINE FLAVORED WITH PEACH)

Considered outside of any particular context or occasion, the menu looks fine. All the food and wine combinations play out superbly, and the course-to-course rhythm swings like a medley of tunes from the Andrews Sisters. The caviar and Champagne offers a great contrast (rich and saline to crisp and fruity); the skate course provides a lovely complement (rich on rich); the duck breast with red Burgundy is a mixture of contrast and complement (meaty and acidic to gamy and fruity); and the finale—the peach tart with peach-flavored sparkling wine—is a refreshing blend of similarities. What could possibly cause a problem? The occasions, and the guests that attend them.

HYPOTHETICAL OCCASION #1: THE BIG DEAL

Let's make the first set of guests at our make-believe meal four business associates contemplating a big merger. The atmosphere around the table is charged with a kind of high-voltage tension usually reserved for SALT talks and probate hearings. The first course—in particular, the Champagne—goes a long way toward whetting appetites and lubricating conversation. But the caviar/Champagne combination, with its overt suggestion of indulgent celebration, seems—especially in anticipation of the deal—a bit out-of-place, premature.

The second and third courses, along with their wine selections, are appreciated by all, but soon the conversation ceases to focus on merging and begins to center on matching and munching. By the time the salad plate arrives—four courses down the road, and still one away from the check—one of the guests has to leave, and the others are beginning to worry whether their spouses and kids will remember their names. When the dessert course finally arrives, it is left on the plate and in the glass. Besides, there's no merger to toast. What started out looking like a good deal ended up playing like a bad hand.

HYPOTHETICAL OCCASION #2: THE ANNIVERSARY

We fashioned our second set of fictive guests from your average extended family, gathered together to honor a clan member's fiftieth wedding anniversary. Feisty grandparents, restive grandkids, mean-spirited aunts, uncles, and cousins of every size, shape, and disposition are in attendance. The air is one of great celebration—after all, making it to the half-century mark with anyone other than your pet turtle is a milestone worthy of a grand party.

The meal starts coming undone almost from the moment the first cork is popped. The honored guests hate fish eggs with a passion usually reserved for religious jihads. The kids in attendance aren't too thrilled with half an hour of gooey, orange pancakes, minus the Aunt Jemima. Then comes the problem of the fish. Skate? Even the piscine pros balk at this one, not to mention those who *always* opt for the turf over the surf. And those darned kids! They won't touch a swimmer unless it's cooked like a charcoal briquette or fried like a Chicken McNugget. The only way to satisfy everyone in this crowd might be to give the kids the product that they really want, out of a familiar box, and announce to everyone else that the fish course is "Les Batons de Poisson à la façon de Madame Paul, RD" (recently defrosted).

The quacker runs into similar problems, offending some guests ("be kind to your web-footed friends . . .") and amusing others. The chances of finding unanimity in this crowd on the subject of rare duck breast are practically nil. By this point in the meal, the kids' blood-sugar is so low that they almost appear charming.

The salad—for better or worse—becomes the only course where everyone remains contentedly seated for more than three minutes. Who would have cast a few greens in the role of the great equalizer? Finally, the dessert arrives, and everyone enjoys at least this one course together. But there's a problem still—a peach tart seems out of place when it's a big cake you were expecting! And the toast of sparkling peach wine bubbles like Champagne, but somehow comes off as too fruity and inappropriately frivolous to honor fifty years of devotion.

HYPOTHETICAL OCCASION #3:
VALENTINE'S DAY

Lest you begin to think that we are hopeless pessimists, our third scenario finds a couple happily gazing into one another's eyes over a Valentine's Day dinner. Here the rosé Champagne seems a perfect complement, not only to the caviar, but to the evening's lovely theme, playing off the holiday's traditional color code with elegance and style. The fish is pure style, dressed in its cloak of suave beurre blanc, a silky set-up for the coming of the duck. The duck breast becomes downright sexy when accompanied by a red Burgundy that—when made well—can suggest a great many amorous things. The salad course provides a gustatory and emotional respite from too much of a good thing, and a bit of time for the couple to gather enough strength for their final assault on dessert and—let's hope—each other. Truly a lovers' feast in the very best sense of the holiday.

One menu, three occasions . . . and three very different outcomes!

Some Foods and Wines that Will Taste Better on Special Occasions:

Celebrations of voyages, vacations, places Wine or food related to the place visited

Celebrations of births, birthdays, anniversaries Wine related to the year being noted; champagne; food with special emotional significance

Celebrations of graduations, special achievements Favorite food or wine; champagne

Celebration of business successes Indulgent wine or food

Celebrations of weddings, engagements Champagne

Celebrations of holidays Traditional wine or food—let one lead in the selection of the other

Celebrations of important occasions Wine or food that doesn't distract from the purpose of the event

SUMMING UP

The businessmen came to dinner with an important task to accomplish and left the restaurant unfulfilled because the style and substance of the meal are ill-suited to the business of business. As delicious as they might have been on their own, the food and wine matches got in the way of the evening's goal: the forging of a partnership.

The anniversary party didn't fare much better. The meal is too complex for the diversity of tastes in attendance and insufficiently connected to the likes and dislikes of the honorees. Its appeal is simply too narrow and unforgiving to be enjoyed by most of the guests. Once again, the matches got in the way of the event's purpose: the communal celebration of a personal milestone.

The couple enjoyed their Valentine meal because it allowed them to connect to both the food and the wine—and one another—without a great deal of effort. The wines, especially the twin sparklers, suggest romance and affection. Exotic ingredients filled the dishes. And the length of the dinner only serves to reinforce the holiday's *raison d'être:* holding hands.

To build a great meal around an occasion you have to start with some knowledge about what makes the occasion special, but a little knowledge can go a long way toward helping you decide where to lay the best foundation. Sometimes the occasion leads directly to food (as it does on Thanksgiving), or to wine (as it does on the christening of a ship). Yet, even for occasions where the food and wine choices are not culturally predetermined, or long set in ritual—a promotion, for example—some fairly direct gustatory reference "hook" can always be found or fashioned. Once you've discovered a key wine or food element, choices for the rest of the meal will follow as naturally as the kudos.

THE

GUSTATORY-

PSYCHOLOGICAL

SCORE CARD

Rhythm	*Gustatory* not a factor	*Psychological* a strong factor; we crave variety
Quality	*Gustatory* not a factor; high-class wine can go with low-class food; low-class wine can go with high-class food	*Psychological* a strong factor; unless you get a special delight from bizarre inversions, things seem to taste better when they come from the same side of the tracks
Ethnic	*Gustatory* not a strong factor in the strategy of serving ethnic wines with ethnic foods; ethnic wines can be fabulous with nonethnic foods; it is not at all necessary to serve the wines of one country with the foods of that country	*Psychological* a powerful factor on some occasions—such as the re-creation of a memorable meal abroad; if you're trying to catch the spirit of a particular place in a meal, things will actually taste better if you serve the proper ethnic wine

Seasonality	*Gustatory* a strong factor in food itself (eating things in season), but a weak factor in food-wine matches (only Beaujolais Nouveau is a seasonal wine)	*Psychological* a strong factor in seasonal food-wine matches; an in-season food can seem even more seasonal when served with a wine that's psychologically appropriate (such as summer fruit with a light, fruity white)
Occasionality	*Gustatory* not a factor	*Psychological* a powerful factor, based on tradition, ritual, or clever correspondence between the comestibles and the occasion

There is a limit to theory, especially when the subject is food and wine. There comes a point when you must fling down your pencils and pens, and lift up your glasses and forks.

PART 3

Putting it all together

Ladies and gentlemen, we have reached that point.

This section revels unabashedly in the delights of the table. We recall for you the greatest wine-and-food matches we've ever known, paying special attention to their joyful contexts. (We leave it to you and your newly-acquired knowledge to figure out why they tasted so good.) And we finish with a sextet of palate-tingling menus that can be taken as demonstrations of everything we've posited in this book—or simply as blueprints for six great dinner parties.

CHAPTER 9

THE GASTRONOMIC HALL OF FAME: THE TEN GREATEST MATCHES WE'VE EVER KNOWN

THE MATCH
LYONNAIS GARLIC SAUSAGE AND FRUITY BEAUJOLAIS
I'd blustered for years about the joys of Lyonnais garlic sausage with fruity Beaujolais, whenever I discussed regional cuisine with regional wine. Listeners and readers absorbed my unbounded enthusiasm, I

could tell—and I could also tell that they failed to guess my dark secret: I had never eaten a garlic sausage with Beaujolais in Lyon. I admit it all now! Oh, I'd had American versions in America with Beaujolais . . . but that's not an adequate credential for a man trumpeting the joys of regional food with regional wine. So it was with great trepidation, several years ago, that I ordered the garlic sausage, Lyon-style and the one-year-old Beaujolais (from Chiroubles) at that temple of Lyonnais cuisine, Léon de Lyon. Would it be the miracle that I had described so many times? Or would I find in one mouthful and one slurp that I had betrayed thousands of ears and eyes? There was, of course, no need for concern. The sausage was bursting with fat and flavor, just as the Chiroubles was bursting with fruit. The garlic flavors and the cherry flavors ran off into the night together, creating one of the most joyous unions that this Great Pretender has ever experienced.

D.R.

THE MATCH
CAVIAR BEGGAR'S PURSES WITH NONVINTAGE KRUG CHAMPAGNE
I used to work at a small, very exclusive restaurant in New York City that would, from time to time, host elegant dinner parties for expense-account clients. One of the restaurant's signature dishes was a "beggar's purse," and, as it was one of the restaurant's most expensive items, it invariably made its way onto the menus of all but the shabbiest affairs. These purses were delectable little crêpes filled with crème fraîche and beluga caviar, and tied up with a chive. These weren't exactly the stuff of staff meals. This, of course, never prevented anyone from nabbing a few off the service plates before the guests could descend upon them. The key was to shield such munching from both the party-goers and the party-throwers. It just so happened that, by some miracle of design, the safest place to pinch a bag or two was behind the bar in the dining room. This location had the double blessing of providing adequate cover from inquisitive eyes as well as a multitude of refreshments to best wash down the filched fraîche. It was there, literally on my hands and knees, that I experienced one of the great wine and food combinations of my life. This particular party had the good sense to serve Krug Grande Cuvée, and, finding myself face to face with destiny, what else was I to do but try them together? The wine was a classic Krug—big, rich, earthy yet elegant—and formed a polished foil for the rich, saline flavors hidden

behind the crêpe. It was a sliver of heaven found beneath an earth-bound sink. Sadly, I left the restaurant soon thereafter for another which didn't have beggar's purses or Krug or the clientele that would have asked for them, but I still think about the match behind the bar.

J.W.

THE MATCH
LOBSTER AND SOLE IN TWO SAUCES WITH GERMAN PINOT BLANC

I was on the hot seat. I was surrounded by interrogative Franconians at a two-star Michelin restaurant in Werthcim, just on the edge of Franconia, in south central Germany. They wanted to know my opinion of every wine with every dish in an epic meal that featured six courses and sixteen local wines. The problem was that my opinion was not matching their opinions with great regularity, and we were all starting to feel uncomfortable. Then came the Seezunge mit Hummer (that's sole with lobster, to you), served with two sauces; one, a sublime beurre blanc based on a parsley reduction, and the other the most intense, sweet orange-brown lobster reduction imaginable. The glasses were lined up, and, with increasingly shaky hands, I sampled them, one by one. The Grauburgunder (Pinot Gris) was decent, as was the Riesling Auslese Trocken—but the night belonged to wine number three, a two-year-old Würzburger Pfaffenberg Weisser Burgunder (this means White Burgundy, but the grape is Pinot Blanc) Spätlese Trocken, Burgenspital Weingut Würzburg. Its finish was even longer than its name. Fabulous pineapple-fruit poured from a tight, nervy, acidic structure, rendering it the perfect wine for this dish. Its lusciousness matched the lusciousness on the plate, but its terrific acidity kept everything honest. It furnished a life-long answer to the question of wine with lobster (Chardonnay flavors are great, but usually too intense), and it made a group of Germans and one suddenly accepted American very happy.

D.R.

THE MATCH
PEPPERONI PIZZA AND YOUNG, RUSTIC CHIANTI

I was wet-nursed on Dr. Brown's Cel-Ray Soda and teethed on Mr. Chips pretzel sticks. By the time I turned eleven I had consumed enough junk food to endow a 7-Eleven chair at the local community college. Even as an aspiring adolescent sophisticate, my favorite multi-coursed menu remained a dozen White Castle hamburgers with fries and an orange drink. Perhaps my palate intuitively sensed that the acid in the soda would stand up to those cheap little pickles and still cut through the grease. Not surprisingly, my first memorable wine and food match arrived in a square cardboard box and straw-covered bottle. I had ordered a pepperoni pizza from Starlight—the toast of Essex County—and, while scouring my parent's fridge for cold beer, happened upon an unopened bottle of a young, simple Chianti. The wine was fresh and juicy, made even more appealing by its frosty state (it was hidden behind a carton of milk). Its ripe fruit and high acidity scrubbed the oil and salt off my tongue and opened the door to the sweet flavors coming from the tomato sauce and cheese. My lunch-box legacy didn't betray me after all!

J.W.

THE MATCH

GRILLED BABY LAMB WITH RIBERA DEL DUERO RED

As long days go, this had been one of the longest. I was traveling through one of Spain's great food and wine regions, the Ribera del Duero, known for its vigorous red wines and their amazing affinity for the local lamb. "Home of Red Wine and Lamb," the road signs proclaimed, and I knew I *was* home. But how much red wine and lamb can a fella take? Even an oenophilic carnivore? One group of winemakers surprised me at ten in the morning with a mixed grill of lamb, veal, and sausages over vine cuttings along with buckets of fizzy light rosé (rosé is the local breakfast wine). Another bunch ambushed me for a long, mirthful late lunch, complete with lamb in every form and some formidable red wine. Then came the *coup de grace*. After my last wine visit of the day—when I was hellbent for a glass of milk and a pillow—the hombres showed me the suckling lamb they'd slaughtered and carved in my honor. Before I could speak, the vine cuttings were ignited over the grill, and a brigade of corks were gleefully extracted from their bottles. It was not the setting for one of my greatest wine and food matches ever. I was tired. I was full. I didn't want any more lamb for at least six months. But the almost pinelike sweetness of that fire somehow stimulated the digestive machinery, and those crisp, fatty little chops and shoulders and necks combined with a luscious four-year-old Vina Pedrosa (made principally from a clone of the Rioja grape, Tempranillo) to shame any Cabernet-and-lamb combo I'd ever tasted. The contrast of flavors was insanely good—deep lamb flavors were somehow elevated to sweetness, next to wild and earthy wine flavors—and an exhausted palate was suddenly having the time of its life.

D.R.

THE MATCH

SPIT-ROASTED QUAIL WITH A NONVINTAGE TOURAINE ROUGE

Though France is better known for its three-star Michelin temples and Grand Cru vineyards than its country cooking and vin du pays, some of the most magnificent moments I can ever recall having at the dinner table took place in small villages whose names are as forgotten as the local wines that were served. However, one night endures in my memory as particularly special. I was traveling through the Loire and about to bid it farewell, when my car broke down near a little town called Mesland, just outside of Blois. I had spent the better part of the past week sipping and spitting dry, off-dry, sweet, and sparkling white wines, and was in no mood to be marooned in a region that—except for a few renegade villages—frowned upon drinking red wine with anything but the meanest livestock. I found a garage and decided to dilute my frustration with some dinner at the nearest relais. It was the kind of restaurant that didn't have a menu, but served whatever the chef-proprietor felt like. That night the chef felt like a little bird and served up a plate of quail roasted over an open hearth. I had a choice of seven wines—six whites and a red—and grabbing my chance to undo the damage wrought by too much Sauvignon and Chenin Blanc, I ordered the nonvintage Touraine Rouge, a blend of Gamay, Cabernet Franc, and Mourvèdre. I had to fight with the waiter to get him to open it. "Surely monsieur would prefer a Vouvray?" No, monsieur wanted that damn Touraine! My color war proved more than worthwhile, for when the quail arrived, they seemed to sing a very happy song. Less profound than a Bordeaux but more complex than a Beaujolais, the red Cuvée was just what the simple birds called for. A little smoky, a little sweet, the dish seemed just right next to the country red which proceeded to echo the quail's flavors without demanding too much thought or energy. Quite a lucky break(down).

J.W.

THE MATCH

A CHEESE COURSE WITH FOUR WINES

I remember clearly the day that I became convinced of the gastronomic need to find exactly the right wine for the right food. For years,

I'd been content to make sure my matches were good enough—for acceptable matches offer a great deal of pleasure. But the sommelier at Lucas-Carton in Paris turned me into a fiend for perfection when he served four wines that matched four cheeses with a precision that can only be described as surgical. It was the cheese course of my life, and I'll never forget it. First there was a creamy, mild, not particularly goaty chevre with a two-year-old Vouvray; the wine was mostly dry, but its slight mellowness was a perfect echo of the cheese's mild character. Then—as if to show that when you're matching chevre you'd better consider which chevre it is—a dry, barnyardy chevre was offered with a two-year-old Pouilly-Fumé; here, the grassy flavors of Sauvignon Blanc were a delicious contrast to the earthy flavors of the cheese, and the high acidity of both items brought them into a more perfect union. Next up was an oily, sensuous hunk of Roquefort, and it found its mate in an unctuous Sauternes that was five years old, still quite sweet, still bursting with youthful fruit, but showing a bit of aged character just to put it in the same league with the cheese. Last and certainly not least—for this was the match that stayed with us all night—was the meanest, most fulsome fromage on earth, the great Burgundian stinker, Époisses. Which wine can match the awesome ooze of flavors that is Époisse? Which wine can top a rich Sauternes in this sequence? We didn't know. The sommelier knew. No wine could—so he served a Marc de Bourgogne, a fiery spirit distilled from grape pomace that wrestled the Époisses to the ground, and rounded off a perfect gastronomic circle.

D.R.

THE MATCH
BLUE CORN CHIP AND AVOCADO–SWEET PEPPER SALAD WITH A TWO-YEAR-OLD SANFORD CHARDONNAY
Family gatherings fueled by contributions from friends and relatives don't usually make for gustatory greatness, so I was more than a bit surprised to discover greatness cloaked in the guise of a potluck birthday dinner. A buddy of mine in the restaurant business had just turned thirty and an appropriate celebration was planned in honor of his mortal lurch toward middle-age. All the attendees were given the task of bringing something eminently edible and I—of course—was put in charge of the wines. Now, pairing in the blind can be fun, but the prospect of finding a common taste denominator for twenty-five different pots, pans, and plates can confound even the most knowl-

edgeable wine guy. Admitting confusion, I decided the easiest way out would be to line up some food-friendly whites and reds and hope for the best. On the day of the party, the guests arrived and the bowls started to pile up. Everyone played match games with their wine and food, and by the end of the evening a rather remarkable consensus had developed around a blue corn chip and avocado–sweet pepper salad paired with a two-year-old Sanford Chardonnay from the Santa Ynez Valley in southern California. The match was rich and sweet, with the wine adding just enough acidity to leave me ready for another dip in the dip. Who said you can't please everyone?

J.W.

THE MATCH
VANILLA GELATO AND POACHED PEAR WITH RECIOTO DELLA VALPOLI-CELLA SPUMANTE
Food-and-wine-together is an essentially light-hearted pursuit, and every once in a while—thank goodness—a food-and-wine experience comes along that reminds you of that. I was speaking at a wine symposium in Verona, Italy, a few years ago, and my Italian hosts were anxious to know one thing: Why do Americans drink silly wines? Why do they like "pop" wines? Fruit wines? Wine coolers? Sweet and spritzy red things that no self-respecting European would offer to his pet? It was a matter of some economic concern to them, of course—but, more important, this group was earnestly trying to leap across the cultural chasm and understand that strange alien, the American palate. After much heated debate, the blessed lunch hour rolled around; as we reached the beguiling Nuovo Marconi in downtown Verona, thankfully, the serious inquiries of the morning were forgotten. Talk turned from the crippled American palate to the fabulous Italian wine and food in front of us. And it's a good thing that it did, too—for if it hadn't, no one at the table would have been able to enjoy a most ironic dessert course with such unself-conscious abandon. Irony in dessert? Well, yes . . . the vanilla gelato sprinkled with fresh coriander seeds was served next to a pear that had been poached in Recioto della Valpolicella Spumante. In other words, sweet, red fizzy stuff—which, to be sure, accompanied the delicious dessert and was consumed in great, joyful quantities by me and by the European palates all around me. What a fabulous match! And what a fabulous moment when one of my gracious hosts, in the midst of the mid-afternoon hoopla, caught the irony in the moment, locked my

eyes, and offered a silent toast with his glass of fizz across the table. Maybe they ought to serve food and wine at the United Nations.

D.R.

THE MATCH
FRUIT RAITA WITH A TWO-YEAR-OLD ALSATIAN GEWÜRZTRAMINER
Have you ever traveled to a foreign country, anxious to sample as many culinary offerings as you could stuff under your belt, only to discover that none of them tasted as good as the less-than-indigenous cooking from some retired colonial outpost? I did—on a recent trip to London in search of great fish 'n' chips—and learned that visiting a fallen imperialist can have some unexpectedly tasty benefits. I had crossed the Atlantic in search of a more perfect union of swimmer and spud, but found only disappointment lurking beneath the layers of Fleet Street paper used to drain fat from flounder. Conceding defeat to Mrs. Paul's, I decided to take in a final meal at the Bombay Brasserie, a much-vaunted outpost of Indian cooking located in the fashionable Kensington section of town. The restaurant's setting was regal and the food was indeed splendid, but—having more or less given up on fair Albion—I wasn't expecting any gustatory epiphanies from my vegetable samosas. It was the end of the meal and I was enjoying the final sips of a two-year-old Alsatian Gewürztraminer when an unordered fruit raita (pieces of fruit marinated in a lightly spiced yoghurt) arrived at my table. I picked out a slice of pineapple and casually knocked back the last drops of wine. In an instant, the Gewürz fractured on my palate into a thousand tiny shards of tropical-fruit flavors. At the same time, the yoghurt held in check the wine's slight bitterness and heat, and cooled the tongue with its soft, creamy texture. So profound was the resonance that I ordered a second bottle just to finish the dish. My only regret is that I didn't order another dish to finish the bottle.

J.W.

CHAPTER 10

IN WHICH

WE EMBRACE

THE

GASTRONOMIC

PRINCIPLES

HEREIN

AND

TURN OUT

SOME

MEAN CHOW

A number of ideas came together for this hale and hearty wintertime banquet for eight. Rich Italian food—based on ideas from all over Italy—is the star performer. To emphasize the earthy nature of this feast, we suggest that you serve the dishes family style—place large amounts of food on platters, then pass around the table. And, to emphasize the Italian-ness of the proceedings, we've selected a quartet of wines from four different Italian regions that adds even more gaiety, warmth, and ethnic character.

An Italian Wintertime Feast

WARM SCALLOP SALAD WITH FENNEL AND WILTED SWISS CHARD
one-year-old Boscaini Pinot Grigio, Castel Firmiano Vigneti di Cornaiano (Alto Adige)

POLENTA WITH PROSCIUTTO AND MASCARPONE
four-year-old Gaja Chardonnay (Piemonte)

ROASTED CALF'S LIVER WITH BALSAMIC VINEGAR AND ROSEMARY
five-year-old Salice Salentino Rosso, Dr. Cosimo (Apulia)

ORANGE SALAD WITH AMARETTI
four-year-old Torcolato, Maculan (Veneto)

WARM SCALLOP SALAD WITH FENNEL AND WILTED SWISS CHARD

⅓ cup fresh lemon juice

⅓ cup red wine vinegar

1¼ teaspoons finely minced garlic

Make the dressing: Combine the lemon juice, the vinegar, 1 teaspoon of the garlic, and the anchovies in the bowl of a food processor. Blend for 10 seconds. With the motor running, add 2 cups of olive oil in a thin stream. Process until blended. Reserve.

Heat a cast-iron skillet over a high flame.

When the pan is hot, scatter the fennel seeds over it. Cook for about 5 minutes, stirring occasionally, until the seeds start to turn dark-brown. Remove seeds, sprinkle with salt to taste, and reserve.

Place the remaining ¼ cup of olive oil in a large sauté pan over high heat. When the oil is hot, add the scallop slices in a single layer. Cook for about 30 seconds per side, or just until the scallops have browned. Do this in two batches if necessary. Remove scallops, and place on paper towels. Meanwhile, toss the Swiss chard leaves with the remaining ¼ teaspoon of garlic in the sauté pan until the leaves are barely wilted, about 10 seconds. Season with salt and pepper. Place the leaves on a large serving platter. Toss together the fennel slices and the chicory leaves, and scatter them over the Swiss chard. Arrange the scallop slices on the fennel and chicory leaves. Sprinkle with the toasted fennel seeds. Drizzle half of the dressing over the salad, and pass the rest in a sauceboat. Garnish with tops of fennel. Serve immediately.

Serves 8

40 anchovies, about 4 tins (packed in olive oil)

2 cups virgin olive oil, plus ¼ cup for sautéing

1 teaspoon fennel seeds

Salt, to taste

1 pound sea scallops, cut into thin rounds

24 Swiss chard leaves, stalks discarded, rinsed

Freshly ground black pepper, to taste

2 cups thinly sliced fennel bulbs (reserve frilly green fennel tops for garnish)

1½ cups chicory leaves, rinsed

The Match
Contrast of components
(sweet scallops, acidic wine)

	COMPONENTS	FLAVORS	TEXTURES
SIMILARITY			
CONTRAST	■		

The single-vineyard Pinot Grigio that we've selected comes from Italy's most northerly wine-growing region, the Alto Adige—guaranteeing a bracing acidity that will, along with the crisp fennel, cut the richness of the sweet scallops. Its pearlike flavors also provide an exciting flavor contrast.

POLENTA WITH PROSCIUTTO AND MASCARPONE

5 cups water

2 teaspoons salt

1⅓ cups coarse-grained polenta

2 tablespoons melted sweet butter

4 tablespoons (6 ounces) plus 8 heaping tablespoons mascarpone, softened to room temperature

1 cup warmed milk

Pinch of freshly grated nutmeg

2 ounces very thinly sliced prosciutto

Place the water and the salt in a large, heavy-bottomed saucepan. Bring to a boil, then reduce to a bare simmer. Begin adding the polenta in a thin stream, stirring constantly. It will take about 10 minutes to add all of the polenta, after which the mixture will be fairly thick. Cook over low heat for another 20 minutes, stirring constantly.

Add the melted butter, 4 tablespoons mascarpone, the warmed milk, and the freshly grated nutmeg. Stir well. Cut each prosciutto slice into four pieces, add to the polenta, and stir gently.

Make sure the polenta mixture is warm, and pour quickly into a very wide, warmed serving bowl. Top decoratively with eight heaping tablespoons of mascarpone, and immediately pass the bowl at table. Pass a pepper mill, and a bowl of extra mascarpone if desired.

Serves 8

The Match
Similarity of textures (rich polenta, rich wine)

There's plenty of richness in this stick-to-the-soul winter dish, and Gaja's magnificent Chardonnay—more like great French Burgundy than anything we've ever tasted from Italy—stands up beautifully to every delicious molecule of cholesterol. Additionally, the wine's buttery flavors echo the flavors of corn, and the hint of clove in the wine engages the hint of nutmeg in the dish. Notice that this second match in the menu, based on similarity, differs from the first match, based on contrast.

	COMPONENTS	FLAVORS	TEXTURES
SIMILARITY			■
CONTRAST			

ROASTED CALF'S LIVER
WITH BALSAMIC VINEGAR AND ROSEMARY

Preheat oven to 550 degrees F. Place the sugar, ½ cup of balsamic vinegar, the pepper, and the rosemary in a small, heavy, nonreactive saucepan. Boil for about 5 minutes, or until the mixture just starts to become syrupy. Do not reduce it significantly.

Place the calf's liver in a roasting pan, smooth-side up. Brush it evenly on top with about two-thirds of the balsamic vinegar mixture. Place in the oven. After 10 minutes, remove the pan from the oven. Some of the sugar will have run off the liver and begun to brown in the pan. Add just enough stock to the pan to form a thin layer of liquid, scraping the browned sugar into the liquid. Brush the remaining balsamic glaze onto the top of the liver. Continue roasting for another 10 minutes, or until a meat thermometer reads 120 degrees F at the thickest part.

When done, place the liver on a cutting board and let it rest for 5 minutes. Meanwhile, add the remaining veal stock to the roasting pan, and, over high heat on top of the range, incorporate any browned bits remaining in the pan into the liquid. Reduce to 1 cup of liquid. Add the tomato puree, and the remaining tablespoon of balsamic vinegar. Season with salt and pepper.

To serve, either thinly slice the liver, arrange it on a serving platter, and pour the sauce around the slices—or, bring the whole liver on a carving board to the table, carve onto individual plates, and spoon on some sauce from a sauceboat. In either case, gar-

3 tablespoons granulated sugar

½ cup balsamic vinegar plus 1 tablespoon

½ teaspoon freshly ground black pepper

2 teaspoons fresh rosemary, chopped, or 1 teaspoon dried rosemary, crumbled

3 pound piece of calf's liver*

About 1¼ cups veal stock or chicken stock

½ cup tomato puree

Salt and freshly ground black pepper to taste

GARNISH

Sprigs of fresh rosemary, or substitute fresh parsley

---

* A whole calf's liver is about 5–6 pounds. It is tapered at one end; ask the butcher to remove a piece from that end, leaving a 3-pound piece with fairly uniform thickness.

nish with sprigs of fresh rosemary if available. You can substitute fresh parsley.

Serves 8

The Match
Similarity of components
(sweet and sour sauce,
sweet and sour wine)

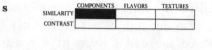

	COMPONENTS	FLAVORS	TEXTURES
SIMILARITY	■		
CONTRAST			

This highly unusual roasted liver is accented by its *agro-dolci* (sweet and sour) glaze, and the sweet and sour flavors in the sauce. A southern red wine from a ripe vintage—such as the Apulian Salice Salentino that we chose—also features an impression of sweetness and a good backbone of acidity. Dr. Cosimo's wine—five years old, but barely aged at all—is a velvety mouthful of fruit, with a lingering sweetness that meets the liver perfectly. And its cherry-red fruit flavors form an interesting contrast with the earthy flavors of liver.

ORANGE SALAD WITH AMARETTI

12 navel oranges

6 tablespoons granulated sugar

1/4 cup fresh lemon juice

1 1/2 teaspoons Frangelico

1/4 cup coarsely crumbled amaretti

Remove the orange peels and all the white pith down to the flesh with a sharp knife. You will now have a round orange that shows no white on the outside. Cut between the orange's membranes, removing whole segments of orange without any skin. Place the orange segments in a bowl, and refrigerate for at least one hour.

When ready to serve, drain off the orange juice that will have accumulated. Toss the orange segments gently with the sugar, lemon juice, and Frangelico. Arrange in a serving platter, and sprinkle the crumbled amaretti over the top. Pass at table, with additional amaretti cookies if desired.

Serves 8

The Match
Similarity of components
(sweet oranges, sweet wine)

	COMPONENTS	FLAVORS	TEXTURES
SIMILARITY	███		
CONTRAST			

Maculan's Torcolato—made from local Vespaiola grapes with just a hint of noble rot—is, as it should be, just a little sweeter than the orange salad. Its luscious richness contrasts with the refreshing orange slices, while simultaneously matching the richness of the amaretti. In this match, the joining of wine and food create additional flavors—honey, butter, ginger—on the palate from both the salad and the wine.

Spanish food—so wracked with clichés in America's Spanish restaurants—is lively and vital in Spain, where many chefs are creating a lighter, more modern cuisine. This menu—which can only be made when the fresh fruits and vegetables of summer are available—is based on some of those modern Spanish ideas. And, just to reinforce the notion that Spain is capable of embracing a more international style, we've selected a variety of wines from other places that blends exquisitely with the food.

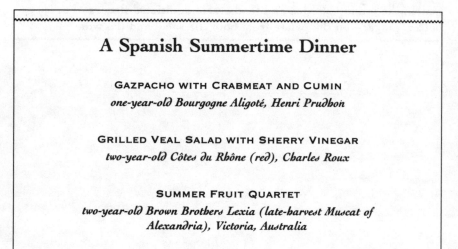

A Spanish Summertime Dinner

GAZPACHO WITH CRABMEAT AND CUMIN
one-year-old Bourgogne Aligoté, Henri Prudhon

GRILLED VEAL SALAD WITH SHERRY VINEGAR
two-year-old Côtes du Rhône (red), Charles Roux

SUMMER FRUIT QUARTET
two-year-old Brown Brothers Lexia (late-harvest Muscat of Alexandria), Victoria, Australia

GAZPACHO WITH CRABMEAT AND CUMIN

TINY CROUTONS

8 slices very, very thinly sliced white bread

3 tablespoons fruity olive oil

1 large clove garlic

Salt and freshly ground black pepper, to taste

Prepare the croutons: Dry out the white bread slices by either leaving them on a kitchen counter for 1–2 days, or by baking them in a warm oven for about 1 hour. The bread slices should be dry, but not crumbly. Cut the slices into tiny dice, place them in a colander, and shake off crumbs. Heat the olive oil in a heavy sauté pan over medium-low heat. Add 1 large clove of garlic, crushed, and sauté for 5 minutes. Add the diced bread to the pan, stirring very gently to coat croutons with oil. Cook them in a single layer over medium-low heat for about 30 minutes, stirring frequently for even browning. They're done when golden brown. Season well with salt and pepper. Let cool.

Prepare the soup: Carefully place the tomatoes into a large pot of boiling water, and cook for about ½ minute—or until the skins are starting to split. Run the tomatoes under cold water, and remove the skins. Cut the tomatoes in quarters, and remove the seeds. Place the tomatoes in a food processor, along with the green pepper, the cucumber, the garlic, the red wine vinegar, the olive oil, and the ground cumin. Blend until smooth. Season to taste with salt and pepper. Set aside in the refrigerator.

Prepare the vegetable garnish: Cut the tomato, the green pepper, the cucumber, and the onion into fine dice. Combine with the olive oil and the ground cumin. Season well with salt and pepper. Set aside in the refrigerator.

Prepare the crabmeat: Combine the crabmeat with the extra-virgin olive oil and the lemon juice. Season well with salt and pepper. Set aside in the refrigerator.

Assembly: Divide the soup among eight shallow, wide bowls. Divide the crabmeat among the bowls, placing a mound in the center of each bowl. Divide the vegetable garnish among the bowls, placing four small mounds in each bowl at 3 o'clock, 6 o'clock, 9 o'clock, and 12 o'clock. Top each vegetable garnish mound with a sprig of chervil. Pass the croutons at table.

Serves 8

SOUP

3 pounds red, ripe tomatoes

1 medium green pepper

½ cucumber, peeled

1 large clove garlic, peeled

2 tablespoons red wine vinegar

2 tablespoons virgin olive oil

1 teaspoon freshly ground cumin seed

Salt and freshly ground black pepper, to taste

VEGETABLE GARNISH

1 large, ripe tomato

1 large green pepper

½ cucumber, peeled

1 medium onion

1 tablespoon fruity olive oil

1 teaspoon freshly ground cumin seed

Salt and freshly ground black pepper, to taste

(continued)

CRABMEAT

*1 pound lump crab-
meat, picked over to
remove shells*

*1 tablespoon extra-
virgin olive oil*

*2 teaspoons fresh
lemon juice*

*Salt and freshly
ground black pep-
per, to taste*

The Match
Similarity of textures
(cold soup, cold wine)

This gazpacho is an outstanding summer
refresher, and pouring something very cold
with it reinforces its appropriateness. Of
course, there are other elements making this
match taste great: Bourgogne Aligoté is known
for nothing so much as its acidity, and—with
this salad—an
acidic wine is
just the ticket.

	COMPONENTS	FLAVORS	TEXTURES
SIMILARITY			■
CONTRAST			

GRILLED VEAL SALAD WITH SHERRY VINEGAR

*8 rib veal chops,
about ½ pound
each*

*4 medium garlic
cloves, minced*

*8 teaspoons good
sherry vinegar*

*8 teaspoons extra-
virgin olive oil*

½ teaspoon salt

*¼ teaspoon freshly
ground pepper*

*2 large red peppers,
cut into 16 broad
slices*

*2 large yellow pep-
pers, cut into 16
broad slices*

Remove the bones from the veal chops. Discard, or reserve for stock. Cut the remaining
meat from each veal chop, horizontally, into
three slices; you will have a total of twenty-
four slices. For best flavor, preserve as much
fat as possible. Blend the minced garlic, 8
teaspoons of sherry vinegar, 8 teaspoons of
olive oil, the salt, and the pepper together in
a large bowl. Add the sliced meat, and
marinate for 3–4 hours in the refrigerator.
Place the slices of red pepper, yellow pepper,
and onion on skewers.

Prepare the vinaigrette: whisk together the
6 tablespoons of sherry vinegar and the 1 cup
and 2 tablespoons of olive oil. Season well
with salt and pepper. Set aside.

Prepare a very hot charcoal fire. Grill the
peppers and onions until lightly charred on
the outside. Place in a large bowl. Grill the
veal slices for just a minute or two per side;
they should be lightly charred on the outside,
medium-rare on the inside. Place in the bowl

with the peppers and onions. Crush the olives with the side of a heavy knife, and add to the bowl. Add the lettuce leaves, and toss everything with the vinaigrette. Divide among eight plates and serve immediately.

Serves 8

The Match
Contrast of flavors
(smoky meat and vegetables,
fruity wine)

This luscious Côtes du Rhône—made in Sablet, by one of the area's best producers—is bottled joy with the grilled veal salad. The flavor complement is sublime, but the wine also has the acid to match the salad's acid—as well as sweet reserves of raspberrylike fruit to ride over everything.

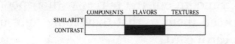

	COMPONENTS	FLAVORS	TEXTURES
SIMILARITY			
CONTRAST		■	

SUMMER FRUIT QUARTET

Prepare four fruit purees: Peel and stone the ripe peaches, and place them in a food processor with the Grand Marnier and 1 tablespoon of sugar. Process until smooth. Set aside in refrigerator. Clean out the work bowl, and place the raspberries in it along with the framboise and 3 tablespoons of sugar. Process until smooth. Set aside in refrigerator. Clean out the work bowl, and place the bananas in it along with the Spanish brandy, the lemon juice, and 1 tablespoon of sugar. Process until smooth. Set aside in refrigerator. Clean out the work bowl. Peel the kiwis and place them in the work bowl

1 large Spanish onion, about ½ pound, cut into 32 1½-inch square slices

VINAIGRETTE

6 tablespoons good sherry vinegar

1 cup plus 2 tablespoons extra-virgin olive oil

Salt and freshly ground black pepper, to taste

32 marinated olives (oil, vinegar, herbs)

8 cups red leaf lettuce, rinsed, dried, torn in large pieces

PUREES

⅔ pound ripe peaches

1 tablespoon plus 1 teaspoon Grand Marnier

6½ tablespoons granulated sugar

½ pound fresh raspberries

(continued)

2 tablespoons framboise

½ pound bananas

2 tablespoons Spanish brandy

1 teaspoon lemon juice

½ pound kiwis

1 teaspoon fresh lime juice

GARNISH

24 raspberries

1 large peach, peeled and thinly sliced

2 large kiwis, peeled and thinly sliced

1 banana, peeled and thinly sliced

along with the lime juice and 1½ tablespoons of sugar. Process until smooth. Set aside in refrigerator.

Prepare a separator by cutting two pieces of cardboard, each with a straight edge that is exactly the width of the inner, flat part of a dinner plate. Cut a slit in the center of one piece of cardboard, and fit the two pieces together at a right angle so that they form an "X" that fits into the flat part of a dinner plate.

When ready to serve, place the cardboard "X" in the flat part of a dinner plate. Spoon about 2 tablespoons of the raspberry puree into one of the sections on the plate created by the cardboard "X." Directly across from the raspberry section, spoon out 2 tablespoons of peach puree. Fill up the two remaining sections with 2 tablespoons of banana puree, and 2 tablespoons of kiwi puree. Smooth out the purees with a spoon, and spread them so that they come right up to the cardboard.

Place three raspberries in the section of peach puree. Arrange a few peach slices in the section of raspberry puree, a few kiwi slices in the section of banana puree, and a few banana slices in the section of kiwi puree. Remove the cardboard. Repeat with the remaining seven plates.

Serves 8

The Match
Similarity of components (sweet fruit, sweet wine)

We've chosen a lightly sweet wine (about 5 percent residual sugar), vio-
lating a pretty firm principle: Make sure that the wine is sweeter than
the dessert. In this case, the dessert is a bit sweeter. But there's a good
reason for this deviation. There are so many different flavors at play in
this unusual dessert, a wine with covering sweetness would obliterate
some of the distinctions. This light and lovely Australian Muscat is very
refreshing with the fruit, to be sure . . . but throws the spotlight of the
match on the dessert itself.

	COMPONENTS	FLAVORS	TEXTURES
SIMILARITY	■		
CONTRAST			

When it comes to lavish, multi-platter holiday celebrations with a crowd, the possibilities diminish for the careful matching of wines and dishes. That's when you need to find a good all-purpose wine, understand its properties, and build an entire meal around it. That's exactly what we've done here, in this joyous Thanksgiving feast: Every dish was created with Riesling Kabinett Halbtrocken in mind. A Riesling of this type features a little more alcohol than most, so we knew we could include some richer food items. And the Halbtrocken (half-dry) tells you that the wine has only a touch of sweetness—so we prepared some dishes that also feature just a hint of sweetness. It's easy to bring together many dishes for one wine, once you understand what's important for food in that wine.

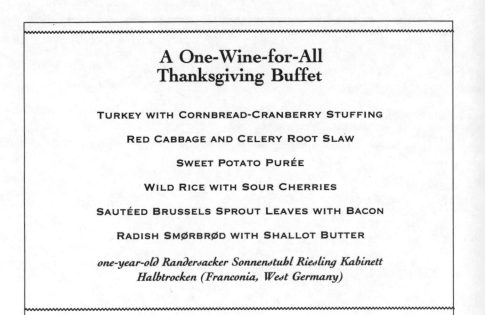

A One-Wine-for-All Thanksgiving Buffet

TURKEY WITH CORNBREAD-CRANBERRY STUFFING

RED CABBAGE AND CELERY ROOT SLAW

SWEET POTATO PURÉE

WILD RICE WITH SOUR CHERRIES

SAUTÉED BRUSSELS SPROUT LEAVES WITH BACON

RADISH SMØRBRØD WITH SHALLOT BUTTER

one-year-old Randersacker Sonnenstuhl Riesling Kabinett Halbtrocken (Franconia, West Germany)

TURKEY WITH CORNBREAD-CRANBERRY STUFFING

STUFFING

Commercial cornbread mix sufficient for 1½ pounds of bread stuffing

Make the stuffing: Preheat the oven to 350 degrees F. Prepare the cornbread according to instructions. When done, crumble into a bowl, then spread the crumbs onto an ungreased cookie sheet. Bake for approximately 10 minutes or until dry. In a large bowl combine the cornbread, boiled broth, butter, and cranberries. Stir until all the butter and broth is absorbed by the bread. Salt and pepper to taste.

Prepare the turkey: Melt 8 tablespoons of butter in a small pan. Let cool slightly, then soak the cheesecloth thoroughly in it. Preheat oven to 325 degrees F. Rub the turkey, inside and out, with lemon. Dry with paper towels. Season with salt and pepper. Stuff the bird and truss it, both at the neck and the tail. Place the turkey, breast-side up, on a rack in a roasting pan and cover with the fat-moistened cheesecloth. Roast for approximately 5 hours, basting every hour, until the leg joint almost separates from the body. Let sit for 10 minutes, then carve at table.

Prepare the gravy: In a saucepan, combine chicken broth and skimmed pan drippings. Reduce by one-third. Remove from the heat, and swirl in the butter. Season with salt and pepper to taste, and serve in a sauceboat.

Serves 12

1 cup hot chicken broth (low salt is best)

2 sticks sweet butter, softened to room temperature

12 ounces fresh, rinsed cranberries

Salt and freshly ground black pepper, to taste

TURKEY

8 tablespoons sweet butter, softened to room temperature (1 stick)

Enough cheesecloth to drape over the bird

1 16-pound turkey

1 lemon, cut in half

Salt and freshly ground black pepper, to taste

GRAVY

2 cups unsalted chicken broth

8 tablespoons sweet butter (1 stick)

Salt and freshly ground black pepper, to taste

RED CABBAGE AND CELERY ROOT SLAW

1 pound celery root

1½ teaspoons salt

4 tablespoons plus 2 teaspoons cider vinegar

2 pounds red cabbage

4 large egg yolks

¾ cup mayonnaise

4 teaspoons mustard

2 tablespoons granulated sugar

2 teaspoons celery seeds

Salt and freshly ground black pepper, to taste

Peel the celery root, and cut into long, thin julienne strips. Mix well with 1 teaspoon of salt and 2 tablespoons of cider vinegar. Let sit for at least 1 hour.

When ready to serve, shred the cabbage (it must be cut into very thin strands, with the core and thick white parts removed) and blend with the julienne of celery root. In a separate bowl, beat the egg yolks into the mayonnaise until just blended. Add the mustard, the sugar, the celery seeds, and the remaining 2 tablespoons and 2 teaspoons of cider vinegar. Blend well. Season heavily with salt and pepper to taste.

Serves 12

SWEET POTATO PUREE

12 large sweet potatoes

12 tablespoons sweet butter, softened to room temperature (1½ sticks)

1 teaspoon salt

1 teaspoon freshly ground black pepper

1 teaspoon freshly grated nutmeg

Preheat oven to 400 degrees F. Bake sweet potatoes until the flesh is fork-tender, 45 minutes to 1 hour. Let cool slightly, and scoop out the flesh into a large bowl. Add the butter, salt, pepper, and nutmeg. Hand mash until smooth, or, if a finer puree is desired, run the mixture once through a food mill. Reheat gently and serve.

Serves 12

WILD RICE WITH SOUR CHERRIES

Add the salt to the boiling water. Rinse the rice well and stir into the water. Reduce to simmer, and cook for 30 minutes over medium-low heat, covered. Add the dried cherries and cloves. Cover partially, and cook for another 15 minutes or until the water has almost all evaporated. Drain (if necessary) and toss with butter and black pepper. Serve immediately.

Serves 12

2 teaspoons salt

8 cups boiling water

1 pound wild rice

4 ounces dried sour cherries

6 whole cloves

4 tablespoons sweet butter, softened to room temperature (½ stick)

Freshly ground black pepper, to taste

SAUTÉED BRUSSELS SPROUT LEAVES WITH BACON

Cut away the root end of each sprout, and carefully separate the leaves (this is a fairly laborious task). Set aside. Sauté the bacon pieces and the smashed garlic cloves in a large pan over medium-high heat for 5 minutes. Remove the garlic, and add the Brussels sprout leaves. Mix well with the bacon fat, season with a bit of nutmeg, and sauté the leaves for 2–3 minutes—just until they wilt. The leaves should retain a bright green color. Season to taste with salt and pepper and serve.

Serves 12

1 pound Brussels sprouts

8 thin slices bacon, each cut into about eight pieces

4 smashed garlic cloves

Freshly grated nutmeg

Salt and freshly ground black pepper, to taste

Radish Smørbrød with Shallot Butter

1/2 pound sweet butter, softened to room temperature

4 medium shallots, finely minced

24 slices pumpernickel bread, trimmed to 2 1/2 inch x 2 1/2 inch

3 pounds radishes, cleaned and cut in very thin rounds

Salt and freshly ground black pepper, to taste

1/4 cup very finely chopped fresh parsley

Cream the butter with a fork in a bowl. Add the shallots, and blend well. Lay out the slices of pumpernickel on a counter, and spread the shallot butter on them, dividing evenly. Divide the radish slices, topping each bread slice with 2 or 3 neat rows of radish slices (the radish slices in each row should overlap each other). Season well with salt and black pepper, and top each open-faced sandwich with 1/2 teaspoon of parsley, placed right at the center.

Serves 12

The Match
Contrast of flavors
(spicy-fruity food, flowery wine)

	COMPONENTS	FLAVORS	TEXTURES
SIMILARITY			
CONTRAST		■	

Similarity of components
(slightly sweet food,
slightly sweet wine)

	COMPONENTS	FLAVORS	TEXTURES
SIMILARITY	■		
CONTRAST			

The Riesling goes well with every dish on this buffet table—usually because the flowery flavors of the wine form a lovely contrast with the fruity and spicy elements of the food, or because the slight sweetness of the wine is similar to the slight sweetness of the food.

People get nervous about wine selection when the subject is chile peppers, and with good reason. Too much heat from the capsicum can scorch the palate and neutralize the efforts of the finest winemaker. However, this doesn't mean that hot food always guarantees a cool reception to wine. If you keep the heat down to a moderate level, and if you refrain from serving elegant and subtle wines, you can have your chile pancake and drink wine with it too. We've put together a trio of lively, rustic wines that responds beautifully to an internationally inspired array of spicy dishes.

A Spicy Evening with Wine

SPICY THAI MELON SALAD WITH DRIED SHRIMP AND
PEANUTS
one-year-old Alveleda Vinho Verde

LENTIL-CHILE PANCAKES WITH CORIANDER SAUCE
one-year-old Ménétou-Salon, Le Petit Clos, Jean-Max Roger

BONED CHICKEN STUFFED WITH PAPADS AND HOT
SAUSAGE
three-year-old Qupé Syrah, Central Coast (California)

SPICY THAI MELON SALAD
WITH DRIED SHRIMP AND PEANUTS

Cut the onion in half, separate into broad pieces, and grill over an open flame until just browned and slightly softened. Remove from grill, and cut into strips, about ¼ by 2 inch. Carefully remove the seeds from the chile peppers, and grill the peppers over an open flame until just browned. Chop coarsely. Combine the onion and chile pepper with the melon, cucumber, and mint leaves. Toss well.

Prepare the dressing: Combine the lime

1 small Bermuda onion (about ¼ pound)

2–5 medium-hot chile peppers, enough to make 4 teaspoons of chopped chile peppers
(continued)

2 cups of very thin peeled and seeded melon slices, each slice about 1 x 2 inch

48 very thin cucumber slices, about 1 cucumber; remove alternating bands of the cucumber peel to create a striped effect

½ cup fresh mint leaves, whole

DRESSING

⅓ cup fresh lime juice

8 teaspoons oriental fish sauce, such as nam pla or nuoc man

8 teaspoons peanut oil

2 teaspoons granulated sugar

4 soft lettuce leaves (Bibb, Boston, etc.)

¼ cup dried shrimp, finely chopped

¼ cup dry-roasted peanuts, crushed with a heavy knife

juice, fish sauce, peanut oil, and sugar, whisking to blend. Pour over the melon mixture, and mix well. Place a lettuce leaf on each of four plates, and divide the melon mixture among the plates. Top with the dried shrimp and the crushed peanuts.

Serves 4

The Match
Similarity of components
(sweet melon slices, sweet wine)

Though Vinho Verde is a dry wine in Portugal, the versions that get shipped to the U.S. are usually slightly sweet. This means that you can match it with dishes, like this one, that are slightly sweet. If you make sure that the melon in this dish is not very sweet, you'll have a lovely similarity of components. Also, the slight sparkle in the Vinho Verde works wonders: It refreshes the palate from the saltiness of the peanuts and dried shrimp, and the bubbles act as a great texture contrast to the heat you feel from the chiles.

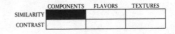

	COMPONENTS	FLAVORS	TEXTURES
SIMILARITY	■		
CONTRAST			

LENTIL-CHILE PANCAKES WITH CORIANDER SAUCE

Peel the potatoes, and cook until just tender. Mash well with a fork, add, and blend in the cooked lentils. Add the chopped chiles, the ground coriander, and the corn meal. Blend well. Season to taste with salt and pepper. Roll into a ball, cover, and refrigerate until ready to use.

Prepare the sauce: Combine the sour cream, yoghurt, diced tomato, and shredded coriander leaves. Mix well. Season to taste with salt and pepper. Keep cool until ready to use.

Fry the pancakes: Heat about ¼ inch of vegetable oil in a heavy frying pan, over medium-high heat. Meanwhile, divide the potato-lentil ball into twelve smaller balls. Flatten each one with a smooth surface (like the back of a heavy knife) to form twelve thin discs, each about 3 inches in diameter. As soon as the oil begins to smoke, fry the pancakes in a single layer. You may need to do this in several shifts, depending on the size of your pan. Flip the pancakes after 1–2 minutes, or just as they become golden-brown on the underside. Fry for another 1 minute. Remove to paper towels to absorb as much oil as possible.

On each of four dinner plates, place three pancakes, centered, in a single layer. Toward the rim of the plate, place a dab of coriander sauce on each pancake. Sprinkle the coriander sauce with a little hot chile powder. At the center of the plate (in the hole between the pancakes), garnish with fresh coriander leaves and a small slice of tomato. Serve immediately.

Serves 4

⅜ *pound potatoes, about 2 small potatoes*

¾ *cup cooked lentils, still slightly firm*

¾ *teaspoon finely chopped fresh hot chiles*

1 *tablespoon freshly ground coriander seeds*

6 *tablespoons corn meal*

Salt and freshly ground black pepper, to taste

¾ *cup sour cream*

3 *tablespoons plain yoghurt*

6 *tablespoons diced tomato*

¼ *cup coarsely shredded fresh coriander leaves*

Vegetable oil for deep-frying

GARNISH

Hot chile powder

Fresh coriander leaves

4 *tomato slices*

The Match
Similarity of flavors
(Herbaceous Pancakes,
Herbaceous Wine)

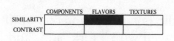

Ménétou-Salon is made right near Sancerre, and is just like the wines of
Sancerre: light, white, with bright herbaceous fruit and wonderful
acidity. In this match, it cuts the heaviness of the pancakes and the sour
cream. But what you notice even more is the terrific interplay between
herbaceous coriander and herbaceous Sauvignon Blanc (the grape from
which this wine is made). It's a welcome switch at this point in the meal;
terrific as the first match was, it didn't feature a flavor interplay between
food and wine.

BONED CHICKEN STUFFED WITH PAPADS AND HOT SAUSAGE

1 3½-pound chicken

Salt and freshly ground black pepper, to taste

3 large cloves of garlic, mashed

2 tablespoons ghee (Indian clarified butter) or substitute sweet butter

2 carrots, cut in chunks

1 small green pepper, cut in chunks

4 scallions, rinsed

1 cinnamon stick

Boning the chicken will take about 20 minutes and a great deal of patience. Cut open the back of the chicken with poultry shears, then spread the chicken out, butterfly-fashion, on a cutting board, skin-side down. With a small, very sharp knife, begin cutting the meat away from the bone, with the ultimate purpose of extracting the entire carcass—leaving behind a boneless chicken. Cut out the breast bones first, reserving the bones. Then work on extracting the back bone. Make a slit in each leg and thigh, then remove the leg and the thigh bones. As you work on these bones, be careful not to cut through the skin (which would create holes later in the stuffed bird). Finally, cut off the wings where they join the body. When you're finished, smooth out the chicken—still skin-side down—and you will have a lovely, boneless chicken, with skin and meat intact, ready for stuffing. Sprinkle the inside with salt and pepper, rub well with one of the garlic cloves, brush with 1 tablespoon of ghee, and refrigerate until ready to use.

Prepare the sauce: Place the bones in a roasting pan and place in a preheated 500-degree F oven. Cook for 30 minutes, turning once, or until the bones are golden-brown. Drain all fat from the roasting pan. Add the carrots, the green pepper, the scallions, the cinnamon stick, and the remaining two cloves of garlic to the pan, scattering them over the bones. Cook for an additional 30 minutes, then drain all fat from the roasting pan. Add the bones, vegetables, and cinnamon stick to a heavy saucepan. Pour ½ cup of water into the roasting pan and, over medium-high heat on top of the range, scrape up the browned bits in the bottom of the roasting pan. Add this liquid to the saucepan, along with an additional 1½ cups of water. Bring to a boil, then simmer gently for 1 hour. Pass the sauce through a sieve, taking care to squeeze all liquid out of the vegetables and bones with the back of a wooden spoon. Discard the vegetables and bones; set aside the sauce.

Prepare the stuffing: Remove the sausage meat from the casings, and discard casings. Break the meat into chunks, and sauté in a skillet for about 10 minutes over medium-high heat, or until the chunks are golden-brown. Remove the sausage chunks, drain on absorbent towels, and place in a bowl. Cook the four papads over an open flame (the jets on your range are fine), for about 1 minute each, or until they are crisp and lightly browned. Let the papads rest for about 2 minutes (they'll become even crisper), then break them up with your fingers until they resemble oat meal. Add the papad flakes to the sausage meat. Work them together with your fingers. Add the eggs, the bread crumbs, and the nutmeg. Mix thoroughly

STUFFING

½ pound Italian hot sausage

4 papads (spicy Indian bean wafers)

2 large eggs

5 tablespoons bread crumbs

Dash of nutmeg

12 sprigs of watercress

The Match
Contrast of
flavors

	COMPONENTS	FLAVORS	TEXTURES
SIMILARITY			
CONTRAST		■	

It's hard to get away from flavors as a theme for wine-matching when there are this many of them in the food. We chose for this dish a spectacular red wine from California—the Qupé Syrah—made from the famous Rhône Valley grape. It's a medium-rich wine, with great acidity and balance, that delivers a payload of earthy flavors. This contrasts beautifully with the poultry-cinnamon-fennel flavors of the dish.

with your hands, to form a slightly wet mass that holds its shape well.

When ready to cook, spread the boned chicken out on a board, skin-side down, with the neck side to your left. Spread the papad mixture over the half of the chicken nearest to you, then roll up the chicken—starting with the half that is covered with the papad mixture, and rolling away from you. When finished rolling, it should be one long roll, with the papad stuffing well contained. Tie with string in about six different places; it will now look like a long chicken sausage. Season the outside well with salt and pepper, and brush with the remaining tablespoon of ghee. Place in a roasting pan, and place the pan in a preheated 500-degree F oven. Cook for 30 minutes, until the outside is golden-brown and the inside is just cooked.

Remove the chicken to a cutting board, and let rest for 5 minutes. Meanwhile, pour out all fat from the roasting pan, add the reserved sauce to the roasting pan, and, over medium-high heat on top of the range, scrape up any browned bits clinging to the pan. Bring the sauce to a boil, then add 6 sprigs of watercress. Cook for about 15 seconds, or until just wilted. Slice the chicken into ¼-inch-thick rounds, distribute them among dinner plates, surround with the hot sauce, and top the chicken rounds with the remaining 6 sprigs of watercress.

Serves 4

California—blessed with a natural bounty of foodstuff unmatched outside France or Italy—has, over the past ten years, developed a culinary reputation for juxtaposing wildly different flavors and textures without sacrificing freshness and simplicity. Our California menu for four honors many of these new traditions through the use of typical Californian ingredients and methods of preparation. Of course, a California menu wouldn't be complete without a sampling of the state's vinous bounty as well, so we've paired these dishes with a variety of wines from a range of California wine-growing regions.

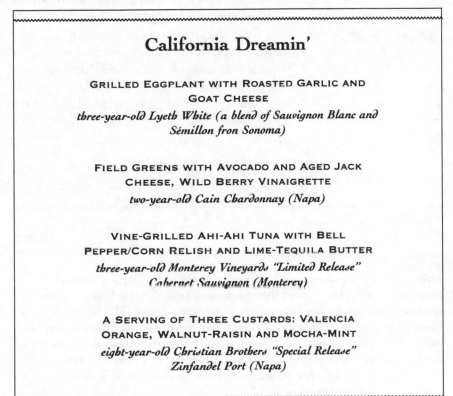

California Dreamin'

GRILLED EGGPLANT WITH ROASTED GARLIC AND GOAT CHEESE

three-year-old Lyeth White (a blend of Sauvignon Blanc and Sémillon fron Sonoma)

FIELD GREENS WITH AVOCADO AND AGED JACK CHEESE, WILD BERRY VINAIGRETTE

two-year-old Cain Chardonnay (Napa)

VINE-GRILLED AHI-AHI TUNA WITH BELL PEPPER/CORN RELISH AND LIME-TEQUILA BUTTER

three-year-old Monterey Vineyards "Limited Release" Cabernet Sauvignon (Monterey)

A SERVING OF THREE CUSTARDS: VALENCIA ORANGE, WALNUT-RAISIN AND MOCHA-MINT

eight-year-old Christian Brothers "Special Release" Zinfandel Port (Napa)

GRILLED EGGPLANT WITH ROASTED GARLIC AND GOAT CHEESE

Preheat oven to 350 degrees F, and prepare a wood or charcoal fire. Rinse the eggplant and slice it into twelve ⅓-inch thick pieces. Heat 3 tablespoons of the olive oil in a heavy skillet

1 medium eggplant, unpeeled

(continued)

¼ cup virgin olive oil

6 cloves garlic

6 ounces fresh soft chevre

12 sun-dried tomatoes, pounded flat, soaked in olive oil

Salt and freshly ground black pepper, to taste

and sauté each eggplant slice over moderate heat for 2 minutes per side. Set aside.

Peel the garlic cloves and place them, along with the goat cheese, in a small roasting pan. Drizzle the remaining tablespoon of olive oil over all, place the pan in the preheated oven, and bake until the garlic is easily pierced by a fork, about 10 minutes. Remove from oven, and mash the garlic cloves in a bowl.

When the grill is ready, cook each eggplant slice for 3 minutes per side, layering a dab of garlic paste, a dab of goat cheese, and a pounded tomato on the grilled side when the eggplant is turned over. Salt and pepper to taste. Serve immediately on a plate lightly covered with olive oil, in portions of three per person.

Serves 4

The Match
Similarity of textures
(creamy cheese, creamy wine)

	COMPONENTS	FLAVORS	TEXTURES
SIMILARITY			■
CONTRAST			

This eggplant appetizer, so Californian in its use of garlic, sun-dried tomatoes, fresh chevre, and the ubiquitous grill, finds a lovely partner in the aged Sauvignon Blanc/Sémillon wine from Lyeth. Having traded in most of its youthful fruit and zest for the more complex flavors and textures of an older Graves-like white wine, the rich Lyeth seems just right next to the rich goat cheese. A slight bitterness in the wine's finish completes the match, echoing an inherent bitterness in the eggplant's skin, in a pleasant, palate-cleansing way.

FIELD GREENS WITH AVOCADO AND AGED JACK CHEESE, WILD BERRY VINAIGRETTE

DRESSING

3 ounces extra-virgin olive oil

Make the dressing: Combine the extra-virgin olive oil, blackberry vinegar, salt, and pepper in a small bowl, and blend with a whisk until smooth.

Tear the sorrel leaves, red leaf lettuce and green leaf lettuce into medium-size pieces. Rinse and dry the leaves and arrange on individual plates. Grate the cheese over each salad. Finish the plates with avocado slices and berries. Whisk the dressing one last time, then pour over the salads. Serve immediately.

Serves 4

~~~~~~

The Match
Similarity of components
(acidic dressing,
acidic wine)

	COMPONENTS	FLAVORS	TEXTURES
SIMILARITY	■		
CONTRAST			

This composed salad gets its assertive personality from the sharp, yet ripe berry-fruit dressing. Many California Chardonnays lack the requisite acid to stand up to the acid in salads, but this one—a fresh, young, fairly acidic Chardonnay made from high-mountain fruit grown in a cool pocket of the Napa Valley— has more than enough crisp apple fruit to match the lively dressing. An intriguing subplot in this sophisticated match is the texture affinity of the rich avocado for the rich Chardonnay.

~~~~~~

5 tablespoons wild blackberry vinegar

1/4 teaspoon salt

1/2 teaspoon freshly ground black pepper

GREENS

1 medium bunch sorrel leaves

1 head red leaf lettuce

1 head green leaf lettuce

4 ounces dry (hard) Jack cheese

1 medium avocado

2 ounces fresh blackberries

VINE-GRILLED AHI-AHI WITH BELL PEPPER/CORN RELISH AND LIME-TEQUILA BUTTER

Place the tuna steaks in a bowl with 1 tablespoon of the basil, and ½ cup of the olive oil. Marinate overnight.

Prepare the lime-tequila butter by combining the softened butter in a bowl with 1 tablespoon of lime juice, the tequila, and 1 tablespoon of basil. Salt and pepper to taste, and place the butter on a sheet of wax paper.

2 pounds fresh ahi-ahi tuna (or any fresh tuna), cut into 4 steaks

3 tablespoons chopped fresh basil
(continued)

¾ cup extra-virgin olive oil

8 tablespoons sweet butter, softened (1 stick)

Juice of one lime

Salt and freshly ground black pepper, to taste

2 teaspoons anejo (aged gold) tequila

2 cups fresh corn kernels, uncooked

1 small red bell pepper, seeded and diced

1 small green bell pepper, seeded and diced

1 small orange bell pepper, seeded and diced

1 small yellow bell pepper, seeded and diced

1 clove garlic, chopped

4 scallions, chopped

1 tablespoon red wine vinegar

Roll it up to form a long cylinder. Cover tightly, and freeze until hard, approximately 2 hours.

When ready to cook, prepare a hot wood or charcoal fire. Prepare the relish by sautéing the corn, the peppers, the garlic, the scallions, and the remaining tablespoon of basil in the remaining ¼ cup of olive oil. Cook over low heat for 5 minutes, stirring often. To finish add the vinegar and the remaining lime juice. Salt and pepper to taste, and divide equally among four plates.

When the grill is ready, cook the tuna steaks for 3 minutes per side (for medium-rare fish). Place the steaks next to the bell pepper/corn relish, top each steak with a slice of the lime-tequila butter, and serve immediately.

Serves 4

The Match
Similarity of flavors
(bell peppers,
wine tasting of bell peppers)

	COMPONENTS	FLAVORS	TEXTURES
SIMILARITY		■	
CONTRAST			

Some fish don't work well with red wine, especially if they're oily or the wine is overly tannic. Tuna, however, is one of the most versatile fish to enjoy with red wine—and never is this combination more satisfying than when the tuna is cut into steaks and grilled over aromatic wood or vine cuttings. Because tuna takes on a steaklike quality when it is grilled medium-rare, it often can be paired with fairly meaty Cabernets or Cabernet/Merlot blends. Here we added a bit of bell pepper to the dish to round out the match—Monterey Cabernet is known for its herbal, bell pepper flavors.

A Serving of Three Custards:
Valencia Orange, Walnut-Raisin,
and Mocha-Mint

Preheat oven to 350 degrees F. Combine the eggs, sugar, vanilla, and salt in a large bowl and beat for three minutes, or until smooth and light yellow in color. Pour the scalded milk into the bowl and continue beating until completely mixed. Divide the mixture into three separate bowls and reserve.

Put the orange juice in a small pan and reduce by two-thirds. When fully reduced, add it to one of the three bowls containing the custard base. Now divide that bowl of custard among four ramekins (scalloped porcelain baking dishes), 3 inches in diameter and 1½ inches deep. Add the walnuts and raisins to the second bowl of custard, and divide the contents of that bowl among four small ramekins.

Combine the chocolate and espresso in a double boiler and cook for 5 minutes. Add the chocolate/espresso mixture to the remaining custard bowl, stir well, and pour into four small ramekins. Place the filled ramekins in a medium-sized roasting pan and surround them with hot water, to a depth of approximately one-half inch. Bake for 20 minutes, or until a fork is clean when withdrawn from the custard.

Chill and serve cold, three to a portion.

Serves 4

5 large eggs

½ cup granulated sugar

1 teaspoon vanilla extract

Pinch of salt

2½ cups milk, scalded

Juice of 2 Valencia oranges

2 ounces chopped walnuts

2 ounces raisins

1 ounce fresh-brewed espresso

1 ounce bittersweet chocolate

The Match
Contrast of flavors
(orange, raisin-walnut, mocha-mint custards, and pruny wine)

	COMPONENTS	FLAVORS	TEXTURES
SIMILARITY			
CONTRAST		■	

When paired with this aged, mildly tannic Zinfandel Port, each of the custards does something different, something wild. The orange makes the wine less pruny. The raisin-walnut does just the opposite, it makes the wine taste incredibly ripe; it would be too much, if not for the walnut's moderating astringence. And the mocha-mint makes the wine just plain stand on its head. How much more deliciously Californian can you get?

How do you plan a wine menu for a Chinese banquet? Since there are no historic traditions to draw from, no lists of time-honored do's and don'ts, you truly enter the gastronomic twilight zone as soon as they start firing up the woks. And the nature of Chinese food—salty here, sweet there, sometimes spicy, sometimes pulsing with other strong flavors—doesn't make things easy for the wine-lover. However, if you're a creative chef, you can tailor your Chinese meal so that wine will play a more compelling role—which is exactly what we've done in this banquet for four. We toned down the brasher elements of Chinese cooking, added a few Western ideas and techniques, and managed to preserve some authentically Chinese textures and flavors. And, of course, we've blended in a quartet of wines that, we think, represents a big improvement over the beer and tea we usually quaff with this cuisine.

A Modern Chinese Banquet

OYSTER CUSTARDS WITH STAR ANISE
nonvintage Mumm de Cramant Champagne

SQUID NOODLES WITH GINGER
two-year-old Schloss Groenesteyn Kiedricher Sandgrub Riesling, Halbtrocken

CRUNCHY LAMB WITH RED PEPPERS, WILD MUSHROOMS AND LEEKS
four-year-old J. Carey Cabernet Sauvignon, Santa Ynez Valley, La Cuesta Vineyard

LYCHEE AND COCONUT MILK SORBET
three-year-old Chateau St. Jean Late-Harvest Gewürztraminer, Belle Terre Vineyard

OYSTER CUSTARDS WITH STAR ANISE

Preheat oven to 350 degrees F. Beat the eggs well, then beat in the half-and-half, the five-spice powder, the sugar, and the chopped chive. Divide the oysters and the bean curd

2 large eggs

2/3 cup half-and-half

(continued)

*¼ teaspoon five-spice
powder*

*½ teaspoon granu-
lated sugar*

*1 teaspoon finely
chopped fresh chive*

*4 freshly shucked,
medium-sized oys-
ters*

*2 ounces bean curd,
cut into ½-inch dice*

*10 ounces unsalted
chicken broth*

4 star anise

*2 tablespoons shao
hsing (rice wine)*

GARNISH

8 whole cloves

among four 2-ounce ramekins, then divide the egg mixture among the ramekins. Place the ramekins in a roasting pan, then pour 1 inch of boiling water in the bottom of the pan. Place the pan in the oven, and bake for about 15 minutes, until the custards are just set. If you remove the custards at the right moment, they'll be creamy and soft; just a few moments' overcooking will make them watery and/or hard.

While the custards are cooking, place the chicken broth in a saucepan along with the star anise. Bring to a boil, and add the *shao hsing*. Boil for 30 seconds, then turn off the heat.

To assemble, carefully remove the custards from the ramekins, placing each one—browned-side up—in a wide, shallow bowl. Pour the hot broth around the custards (there'll be only about a ¼ cup in each bowl). Place one star anise in each bowl, and cross two chives on top.

Serves 4

The Match
Similarity of textures
(delicate custard,
delicate wine)

	COMPONENTS	FLAVORS	TEXTURES
SIMILARITY			
CONTRAST			

Mumm de Cramant is a type of Champagne known as *crémant*—that is, it contains less forceful bubbles than other Champagnes. This gentleness, we feel, usually makes *crémant* easier to match with food than other Champagnes. And, in this case—when it partners a custard, which contains an oyster, set in a puddle of delicate broth—the serenity of the cumulative effect would likely delight a Zen master.

SQUID NOODLES WITH GINGER

Cut the squid into the shape of noodles. First, separate the tentacles—cutting them so that each strand stands by itself, resembling a noodle. Then, open the squid sacs on one side with a scissor, and spread each sac out on a cutting board. Cut the sacs *horizontally*—*not* the long way—into long, thin strips. (If you cut the long way the squid will curl up when cooking.) Set aside the squid strips in the refrigerator.

Boil the noodles according to package directions. In most cases, this will be in a large quantity of salted boiling water for about 6 minutes, or until just tender. Rinse under cold water and set aside.

When ready to cook, add the vegetable oil to a large, hot wok over very high heat. Salt the squid strips liberally, and add to the wok when the oil is hot. Stir in 1 tablespoon of garlic. Within 2 minutes or so a few tablespoons of liquid from the squid will appear in the bottom of the wok. Remove the squid, and boil away the liquid. Return the squid to the wok, and stir-fry over very high heat for 1 minute more. Remove squid and set aside.

Add a little more vegetable oil to the wok if it's dry. With the heat still high, add the scallions, the carrot, and the ginger root. Stir well. Add the remaining 2 tablespoons of garlic and ¾ teaspoon sugar. Stir-fry for about 2 minutes, or until the vegetables are just cooked and lightly brown. Add the soy sauce and the fish sauce. Stir to blend. Return the squid to the wok, leaving behind any accumulated liquid; add the reserved noodles. Stir-fry over high heat for 30 seconds. Remove to platter, and toss with sesame oil.

Working quickly, add the spinach leaves to

1 pound squid, cleaned

2 ounces dried Chinese wheat-flour noodles

3 tablespoons vegetable oil, or more

Salt, to taste

3 tablespoons finely chopped garlic

4 scallions, cut into long julienne strips

1 medium carrot, cut into long julienne strips (about ⅓ cup altogether)

½ cup long julienne strips of fresh ginger root

¾ teaspoon granulated sugar, plus more to taste

2 teaspoons soy sauce

1½ teaspoons oriental fish sauce (such as **nam pla** *or* **nuoc man**)

½ teaspoon sesame oil

About 50 spinach leaves, rinsed

the wok along with a sprinkling of salt and sugar. Stir-fry for 5 seconds or so—until the spinach is barely wilted. Divide the spinach among four dinner plates, and divide the squid mixture among the plates—placing the squid just on the edge of the spinach, so that most of the spinach is not covered.

Serves 4

The Match
Contrast of components
(salty squid, sweet wine)

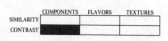

Actually, this match has many elements working simultaneously. In addition to the overall salty-sweet impression, the match features a delicious subplot based on ginger. Since Halbtrocken wines have more alcohol than most other German wines, this wine's a little hot. The heat of the fresh ginger easily meets that challenge. And the fruity flavor of the ginger teases the wine, drawing out an even deeper, more complex fruitiness.

CRUNCHY LAMB WITH RED PEPPERS, WILD MUSHROOMS, AND LEEKS

LAMB

3/4 pound boneless lamb, cut from the leg

1 teaspoon baking soda

2 large egg whites

1/2 teaspoon salt

4 teaspoons cornstarch

Cut the lamb into broad slices, no more than 1/4-inch thick. Place the baking soda in a bowl, and blend well with 1/4 cup water. Add the lamb slices, coating well with the baking soda mixture. Refrigerate for 4–5 hours.

When ready to prepare dish, mix the lamb with the egg whites, the salt, 4 teaspoons of cornstarch, 2 teaspoons of minced garlic, 2 teaspoons of peanut oil, and 2 tablespoons of *shao hsing*. Stir well to blend using chopsticks.

Prepare the sauce: Mix together the brown stock, 3 tablespoons of *shao hsing*, the black vinegar, the oyster sauce, the soy sauce, the sesame oil, and 1/2 teaspoon of sugar. In a separate bowl, mix 1 tablespoon of cornstarch with 2 tablespoons cold water to form a milky paste. When the cornstarch is dissolved, add the liquid to the sauce, stirring well to blend. Set aside.

To prepare the dish: Heat the sunflower oil in a deep fryer, large Dutch oven, or a wok over very high heat. When the oil reaches 375 degrees F, add the coated lamb slices, stirring quickly to keep them separate. Deep-fry for 1 minute, and remove to paper towels. Let the oil return to 375 degrees F. Separate any lamb slices that have clung together. When the oil is reheated, add the lamb and cook for an additional 1–2 minutes, until the lamb is brown and crunchy. Drain on paper towels.

Remove 2 tablespoons of oil from the deep-frying vessel, and place in a large wok over very high heat. Add the mushrooms, and stir-fry for about 30 seconds. Add the leek and stir-fry for 30 seconds. Add the corn, the peppers, and the garlic. Blend well and stir-fry for 30 seconds. Add the lamb slices and blend well. Push all ingredients to the side of the wok and, still over very high heat, add the sauce mixture. Stir well, and as soon as the sauce starts to thicken (10–15 seconds) return the ingredients to the center of the wok, mixing well with the sauce. Immediately remove from the wok, toss with the coriander leaves and the hot chili oil.

Serves 4

2 teaspoons minced garlic

2 teaspoons peanut oil

2 tablespoons shao hsing *(rice wine)*

SAUCE

½ cup brown stock (or canned beef broth, low salt is best)

3 tablespoons shao hsing *(rice wine)*

3 tablespoons black vinegar

2 tablespoons oyster sauce

1 teaspoon soy sauce

1 teaspoon sesame oil

½ teaspoon sugar

1 tablespoon cornstarch

STIR-FRY

1 quart sunflower oil

2 ounces wild mushrooms, broadly sliced

1 medium leek, white part only, rinsed and cut in very thin rounds

8 pickled baby corns

(continued)

2 medium red peppers, roasted, skinned, and cut in strips

4 teaspoons minced garlic

1/3 cup loosely packed fresh coriander leaves, coarsely minced

2 tablespoons hot chili oil

The Match
Similarity of flavors
(vegetal coriander
and red pepper, vegetal wine)

	COMPONENTS	FLAVORS	TEXTURES
SIMILARITY		■	
CONTRAST			

This is a tough dish to match, with its blend of sweet, salty, and hot ingredients. But the green-tasting parts of this dish—fresh coriander and roasted bell peppers—give a pleasantly green-tasting Cabernet Sauvignon from California's south central coast something to grab on to. Lighter wines wash away; heavier wines collide unpleasantly with the fury of flavors in this dish. This particular Cabernet—mid-range all the way, well-balanced, graceful, and with good acidity—negotiates the match like a career diplomat.

LYCHEE AND COCONUT MILK SORBET

1 10-ounce can lychee nuts, packed in heavy syrup

1 cup unsweetened coconut milk, fresh or bottled

3 tablespoons fresh lime juice

4 ounces commercial sugar syrup or a homemade syrup of 2 parts sugar to 3 parts water

Separate the canned lychees from the heavy syrup; set the lychees aside. Place half of the syrup into a small saucepan and reduce by one third. Reserve.

Place the remaining syrup in a bowl, and add the coconut milk, the lime juice and the commercial sugar syrup. Mix in the reduced syrup.

Prepare sorbet in an ice-cream machine according to the manufacturer's instructions. Just before the sorbet is ready, mix in the reserved lychees.

Serves 4

	COMPONENTS	FLAVORS	TEXTURES
SIMILARITY		■	
CONTRAST			

The Match
Similarity of flavors
(lychee flavor, lychee-flavored wine)

We've always rejected the notion that Gewürztraminer tastes "spicy." That's far too general . . . and, in almost every case, inaccurate. Rose water and lychees are flavor images that we find much more acceptable. So at long last we've confronted a Gewürztraminer with a lychee nut— with predictably delicious results. Other things contribute to the success of this pairing, but it's the lychee-meets-lychee pas de deux that makes this match dance.

PART 4

lists
and
index

GLOSSARY

OF WINEMAKING

AND

WINETASTING

TERMS

. . . AND HOW

THEY APPLY

TO WINE WITH

FOOD

ACIDITY. An important component when considering wine for food. Acidity in wine comes from natural acids in the grape—or from the addition of acid by the winemaker—and is the element that makes wine taste lively, refreshing, crisp. The acidity helps with many foods: it cuts heavy foods (like roast pork with acidic German Riesling/component contrast); it relieves salty foods (like briny oysters with Chablis/component contrast); it matches acidic foods (like a tart, off-vintage red Burgundy with a crouton-and-chicken-liver salad/component similarity). Low acidity can make wine dull-tasting, and more difficult to match with food. Generally, wines from northerly growing regions feature the liveliest natural acidity.

ALCOHOL. The critical component that separates wine from grape juice. During fermentation, the natural sugar of grapes is converted into alcohol. Most of the world's wines contain around 12 percent alcohol. The extent to which a wine is above or below that average is important when considering wine for food. Low-alcohol wines are lighter in body; high-alcohol wines are richer in body, sometimes featuring an impression of sweetness, and sometimes leaving a "hot" sensation on the palate. Wines with a low level of alcohol—such as German Rieslings at around 8 percent—are easy to match with a wide variety of light foods. Wines with a high level of alcohol—such as southern French wines, or some California wines that contain 13–14 percent alcohol—are good with coarse, rustic food, but can be tricky with a wide range of dishes.

AGING. An important factor in determining a wine's appropriateness with food. Most wines are not meant to age; you enjoy them at one or two years old for the vibrancy of young fruit. When that fresh fruit flavor has faded, there's usually nothing left to enjoy. However, a small percentage of the world's wines has the ability to develop new flavors and aromas once the fruit has faded. Sometimes referred to as "bottle character," these qualities are often subtle and complex. Generally, it's easier to match the buoyant fruit of young wine with a wide variety of dishes. The subtle flavors of age usually require subtler dishes, carefully chosen to show off the qualities of the aged wine.

ASTRINGENT. A puckery, mouth-drying feeling caused by tannin. See **Tannin**.

AUSTERE. An imprecise taster's term used to describe wines that are either hard (see **Tannin**), very dry, thin, or high in acid. The general impression is that the wine is *not* fleshy, rich, generous. Often, austere wines are improved by serving them with the right dish. A hard, tannic wine tastes better with fatty meats. A thin wine seems richer with sharp, dry cheeses. An acidic wine seems softer when served with acidic foods. Austere wines often improve with age.

BALANCE. The harmony of ingredients in wine. When you taste a balanced wine, no single element—such as sweetness, or acidity, or tannin, or alcohol—stands out; they are all integrated into a pleasing whole. Balanced wines have a head start in food matching; food qualities that compensate for wine deficiencies are not needed. Balanced wines fit nicely with a wide variety of foods.

BARREL FERMENTATION. A throwback to an older style of winemaking, wherein the wine is fermented in small oak barrels, usually holding fifty-five gallons. The winemaker has less control over fermentation (more things can go wrong), but the perceived advantages are greater complexity and greater body in the wine. Most of the world's wines today are fermented in large stainless steel tanks. In recent years barrel fermentation is more popular as a means of producing high-quality (usually expensive) Chardonnay around the world. The resulting Chardonnay wines—which in California may be indicated by "barrel-fermented" on the label—usually exhibit an earthier, spicier range of aromas and flavors. Barrel-fermented Chardonnays are rarely simple whites that go well with simple seafood; they usually require richer, more complex dishes (lest the wines overwhelm the food).

BERRYLIKE. A taster's term for the hints of raspberry, blackberry, mulberry, strawberry, or other berry that appears in the aromas and flavors of wine (usually red). Young Zinfandel in particular is often described as berrylike, but young Cabernet and young Pinot Noir can also fit the description. It's a quality in red wine that fades with time. Generally, berrylike red wines are good flavor matches with a whole range of simply grilled or simply roasted red meats.

BITTERNESS. An unpleasant taste in wine caused by a number of factors: hard pressing on grape seeds and stems that contribute bitter oils to the wine; a very hot summer which turns the grape skins bitter; prolonged contact with bitter wood barrels. Bitterness in wine almost always presents difficulties for food; no matter what you serve (except for very sweet dishes), the wine will still taste bitter. Serving bitter food with bitter wine usually doesn't help either; each bitterness tends to reinforce rather than cancel the other.

BODY. Refers to the weight of a wine. You can judge a wine's body by "weighing" it on your palate; does it feel heavy? Medium? Light?

Usually, heavier body is a function of higher alcohol—and since high alcohol is a difficult element for food matching, heavy-bodied wines usually require special care in food selection. Heavy-bodied wines can overwhelm food very easily. On the other hand, light-bodied wines require lighter foods; they can be overwhelmed by foods with heavy textures. Another element that can increase body in wine is sugar, which is much more manageable in food-matching than alcohol. Heavy-bodied sweet wines are easy to match with desserts, as long as the desserts are a little less sweet and a little less rich than the wine.

BOTRYTISED. Refers to a wine whose grapes were affected on the vine by botrytis, a form of rot called "noble rot" by winemakers. When botrytis forms on grapes, the grapes shrivel and intensify in flavor. The percentage of sugar content increases, and a flavor similar to the flavor of honey develops. Botrytised wines are usually sweet (though sometimes dry Chardonnay and other wines can have a botrytised character), usually rich, and usually taste of honey. The most famous of all are the Sauternes of France, but botrytis also works to splendid effect on the sweet wines of the Loire (Vouvray, Montlouis, Coteaux du Layon), on the Sélection de Grains Nobles wines of Alsace, on the late-harvest wines of Germany and Austria (Beerenauslese and Trockenbeerenauslese), on the late-harvest wines of California (usually from the Riesling grape or the Gewürztraminer grape), and on others. Serve sweet botrytised wines by themselves, with foie gras, or with desserts that are a little less sweet than the wines.

CARBONIC MACERATION. A type of grape crushing/fermentation arrangement used to create light red wines with vivid fruit character, but very little ability to age. Beaujolais wines, for example, undergo a variation of carbonic maceration. If a wine undergoes carbonic maceration, its odds for food-matching are improved. Carbonic maceration reds are usually free of the tannin, high alcohol, or bitterness that causes problems for food. They are lovely with a wide range of meat and vegetable dishes and—since they're so light—they often blend harmoniously with seafood as well. Look for wines labeled "Nouveau;" they have usually undergone carbonic maceration.

CHAPTALIZATION. A process, invented by the Frenchman J. A. Chaptal, which boosts the alcoholic strength of a wine through the addition of sugar at the time of fermentation. (The extra sugar gets fermented into alcohol, leaving a higher alcohol content.) It is employed in cold, northerly regions where the grapes fail to reach high sugar levels on the vine due to the lack of sunshine. Chaptalization doesn't affect food-matching, though the life-expectancy of these wines is somewhat short. Menu-planners should be cautious when approaching older red Burgundy, for example (Burgundy wines are almost always chaptalized); sometimes these wines show a sweet-and-sour character that is tricky at the table.

CLOYING. A taster's term for a wine that is *too* sweet without having compensating acidity. Cloying wines, however, are fine with sweet desserts that are a little less sweet than the wines.

COLD FERMENTATION. The modern method of fermenting white wine; the grape juice is placed in tanks that have a temperature control, and fermentation proceeds between about 45 and 60 degrees F. This method preserves the fresh-fruit character in wine, leading to simple flavors and aromas that suggest pears, apples, peaches, melons. Sometimes, when these wines are very young, they have such an extremely fruity character that they become difficult to match with food.

COMPLEX. Term for a wine that has many layers of flavor. It's always used in a positive sense: the more complexity, the better. This doesn't always hold, however, when it comes to food matching. On some occasions, and with some food—notably food with strong complex flavors, like Indian food—brash, simple wines are more appropriate than venerable, complex ones. The fear is that the exquisite complexity of the wine will be lost against a riot of food flavors. Of course, a dish with subtly complex flavors that fits in perfectly with a subtly complex wine is an exquisite thing.

CRISP. Term for a wine with good acidity. See **Acidity**.

DELICATE. A positive term, usually applied to light- or medium-bodied wines with great balance and subtlety. Delicate wines are easy to match with food—due to their balance—as long as you don't select dishes that overwhelm them. A good example of a lovely, delicate match is the Oyster Custards with Star Anise, see page 203, with a bottle of Mumm de Cramant (a lightly sparkling Champagne).

DOSAGE. A technical term in the production of Champagne and other sparkling wines. When a bottle of Champagne is ready for release by a winery, its cork is removed, along with all the dead yeast cells that are clinging to the cork (see **Methode Champenoise**). At this time, most Champagne houses add a solution called dosage to the wine. Dosage is a combination of sugar and, usually, old wine. It is designed to replace the liquid lost when the cork is removed, and to add a little sweetness and balance to the Champagne. Levels of dosage vary widely from house to house; because of high dosage, some basic Brut Champagnes—such as Taittinger's Brut La Française—are surprisingly sweet. This is important information for menu-planners, since a glass of sweet Champagne will definitely not go with caviar. If you become familiar with the various house styles in Champagne, you'll know which houses to rely on for dry wines (better for caviar and other before-dessert delights), and which for sweeter wines (better for sweet dishes and dessert).

DRY. One of the most important considerations in choosing wine for food. Dry simply means "not sweet"—and dry wines are the natural partners for foods that are not sweet. (Consider the alternative: steak with Sauternes, or sushi with cream sherry.) Occasionally, a sweet wine seems correct with a "dry" food—just like adding a fruit sauce to duck is sometimes correct—but, generally, think "dry" wine when the food is "dry."

DUMB. A term applied to wines that have yet to develop their full flavor. Often, a wine is dumb when it has lost its youthful fruit (say, after two or three years) but has not yet developed a bottle character (which may not set in until seven or eight years). Due to their low-profile flavors, dumb wines may not be exciting with food, but there's no reason why they can't fit harmoniously with it.

EARTHY. An aroma and/or flavor sometimes found in aged wines. The description is quite literal: An earthy wine tastes of earth, of soil. It's a quality that makes a lovely flavor similarity with earthy foods (such as black truffles) or an exciting flavor contrast with other foods (such as an earthy, aged red Burgundy with sweet, meaty prime ribs).

ELEGANT. A much-used, perhaps overused, taster's term for a quality that's difficult to pin down. An elegant wine is balanced, above all—but also seems to possess qualities of refinement. Its flavors and textures are not obvious or meretricious. Tasters who use the word "elegant" may have you believe that it takes discernment on the part of the taster to recognize elegance in a wine. "Elegant" is most often used for Champagne, since it's a good term for discriminating between the finesse of the sparkling wine that comes from the Champagne region of France, and the coarseness of the sparkling wine that comes from most other places. For food, elegant wines must be approached as delicate (see **Delicate**) or balanced (see **Balanced**) wines are approached: A wide range of quiet foods will work, but full-flavored, brash foods may drown out the beauty of the wine.

FINISH. Refers to the sensation on the palate as you swallow a sip of wine. Some wines seem harmonious when you first put them in your mouth, but suddenly bite you with a harsh "finish" as you swallow. Other wines finish smoothly. For food, a wine that finishes harshly—often a function of tannin (see **Tannin**) or too much wood, which both can make a wine bitter—can cause problems. A smooth-finishing wine is almost always preferable. Another aspect of "finish" is length; some wines keep registering on your palate for many moments after you've swallowed them. This is the "long finish" that is much appreciated among winetasters. Length of finish has little effect on the compatibility of wine and food, though a match that features a long-finishing wine will also be more exciting just because it goes on longer.

FLABBY. Describes a wine that lacks sharp definition. A key structural element—such as tannin or acid—is probably in short supply. Flabby is never a positive description of a wine, but flabby wines can be decent refreshment with certain foods—particularly when they're flowing freely at barbecues.

FLOWERY. A term commonly used for the aroma of some young white wines, usually northern in origin, particularly wines made from the Riesling grape. This flowery quality works beautifully with food, since not many foods have flowery flavors. Therefore, pairing a flowery wine with, say, a spicy food (like clove-scented fresh ham) makes an exciting flavor contrast.

FORTIFIED. A technical term. Fortified wines are those with alcohol added in the winemaking process. They rise far above the average alcohol level of table wines, which normally contain 12 percent alcohol. Some of the most famous fortified wines are sherry, Port and Madeira, all of which contain between 17 and 20 percent alcohol. Fortified wines are usually sweet, and go best with cheese, nuts, and desserts that are less sweet than the wines. Fino sherry, one of the few fortified wines that's dry, goes well with a range of foods—such as ham, asparagus, almonds, olives.

FOXY. A word used to describe the very grapy flavor that's found in wines made from Vitis Labrusca, a native American vine. Most of the world's grapes are grown on Vitis Vinifera vines (an old world vine), but Vitis Labrusca yields wines with a flavor not unlike the familiar flavor of grape jam. Most wine-lovers look down on "foxy" wines, but at the table there's no reason to regard them as second-class citizens. Dry foxy wines can provide wonderful flavor contrast to many main-course dishes, and sweet foxy wines—particularly sparkling wines from the Finger Lakes in New York—can be lovely dessert wines.

FRUITY. A confusing descriptive term. The word "fruity" suggests things that it doesn't actually mean to winetasters. When wine is young, its aroma resembles the aroma of the freshly crushed grapes that made the wine; this is the "fruit" that is described in the word "fruity." But this aroma may not resemble the aroma we normally associate with grapes; "fruity"—except in the case of Vitis Labrusca (see Foxy)—does not normally refer to the grape aroma that's recognizable from grape juice or grape jam. A fruity wine may smell like strawberries, or melons, or peaches, or pineapples—this will vary from wine to wine—but the descriptive term for a wine smelling of young fruit is always "fruity." Usually, the term "fruity" helps to distinguish young wine from old wine; as wines age, they lose their fruitiness. Fruity reds—which may smell like strawberries, raspberries, cassis—are easy to match with a wide range of foods (grilled meats, hard cheeses, even fish dishes if the wine is light as well as fruity). Fruity whites—which may smell like melons, pineapples—are usually trickier to match with food (their fruitiness tends to have a slightly sweeter character).

GRASSY. This taster's term is usually reserved for herbaceous white wines made from the Sauvignon Blanc grape. The "grassiest" examples of all are Sancerre, Pouilly-Fumé, and the Sauvignon Blancs of New Zealand. Wines made from Sauvignon Blanc in Bordeaux, in California, in Italy, and in other places tend to be less grassy. Grassy wines (which do taste like vegetables—perhaps a hint of asparagus—but rarely like grass) are wonderful complements to dishes featuring herbs. Fresh coriander, in particular, is great with grassy white wines—which is why Sauvignon Blanc is a good choice for Mexican and Indian dishes flavored with coriander.

LENGTH. See **Finish.**

MADERIZED. A term usually reserved for white wines exposed to too much oxygen, taking on the old taste of Madeira and perhaps turning brown in the process. Maderized wines are always flawed from a pure wine perspective, but—if you drop your technical prejudices—they can work nicely with foods such as cheese and nuts.

MALOLACTIC FERMENTATION. An event in the life of a wine with enormous implications for food-matching. After wine undergoes its first fermentation—caused by yeast, and leading to the production of alcohol—it may or may not undergo a second fermentation. This second fermentation is caused by bacteria, and its most significant result is the conversion of malic acid into lactic acid (hence the term "malolactic"). Malic acid, the acid of apples, is much sharper and more sour than lactic acid, the acid of milk. A wine that has undergone malolactic fermentation will be softer, and will have additional complexity. Malolactic fermentation is a good thing for wines with abundant acid; it's a bad thing for wines short on acid. Since acid helps wine as a partner for food, the winemaker's decision on this subject will have a profound effect at the table.

METHODE CHAMPENOISE. This is the method invented in Champagne, France, for the production of sparkling wine. Carbon dioxide is trapped inside a tightly corked bottle, producing the bubbles of Champagne. By twisting the bottle daily in a precise fashion for several months, the resulting dead yeast cells are forced to gather around the cork of the bottle. Finally, the yeast-covered cork is removed, the bottle is recorked, and Methode Champenoise sparkling wine is presented to the public in the same bottle. There are other, less labor-intensive ways to produce sparkling wine, but none produce wine with the finesse of Methode Champenoise sparkling wine. The resulting wines—such as Champagne—are your only options when considering Champagne in its traditional gastronomic guises, i.e., with caviar, smoked salmon, foie gras. Most sparkling wines produced from other methods are usually too coarse for these luxury foods, and should be saved for thirsty gulps on summer days, or for duty with spicy foods.

NUTTY. A very interesting quality in wine, usually associated with sherry—which, predictably enough, makes a lovely flavor similarity with nuts. Nonfortified wines can also be nutty; the great white Burgundy called Meursault is often said to have a hazelnut character. This can serve as an exciting flavor contrast to fish dishes, for example. Aged Champagne occasionally has a nutty character as well—a great flavor contrast to dry, sharp cheese.

OAKY. A quality derived from a wine's sojourn in oak barrels. See **Wood**.

OVERRIPE. Usually a negative description. If a wine is overripe, technically, the grapes that went into the wine stayed on the vine past the ideal stage of ripeness. This usually brings a baked character to the wine, reminiscent of raisins (sometimes of macaroons and almonds). It also contributes bitterness (from the scorched skins), and too much alcohol (which comes from the high sugar content of overripe grapes). Most noble grape varieties produce bizarre wines when the grapes are overripe (like Cabernet, Pinot Noir, Chardonnay). But Zinfandel, and red grape varieties from warm-weather regions (Grenache from the Rhône Valley, for example) can produce interesting wines if the grapes are only moderately overripe. Overripe wines are usually problematic for dishes with elegance, subtlety, or great balance; but slightly overripe Zinfandel, Amarone, Châteauneuf-du-Pape can be superb with barbecued foods, and with lusty sweet-and-sour meat dishes.

OXIDIZED. Refers to a wine that has been exposed to too much oxygen, either in the winemaking process, or during its stay in bottle, or after its bottle has been opened. See **Maderized**.

PETILLANCE. A slight sparkle in wine, but not forceful enough to classify the wine as a sparkling wine. Simple whites with petillance (like Portugal's Vinho Verde) are very refreshing, and can work well with a wide range of dishes. Try with light seafood dishes that have some heat (such as Spicy Thai Melon Salad with Dried Shrimp and Peanuts, see page 191).

RESIDUAL SUGAR. Another key element in matching wine with food. All grapes contain a certain amount of sugar. During fermentation, the sugar is converted into alcohol. Usually, all of the grape's sugar is converted, leaving a completely dry wine of about 12 percent alcohol. Sometimes, for various reasons, some of the original grape sugar is not converted to alcohol. This sugar that remains in the finished wine is called "residual sugar," and is apparent to the palate if it reaches about 0.5 percent of the wine. Between 0.5 percent residual sugar and 1.5 percent, a wine seems off-dry. Between that level and about 3 percent residual sugar, a wine seems medium sweet. From about 3 percent to 6 percent residual sugar, a wine seems decidedly sweet. There are many dessert wines that have above 6 percent residual sugar, and these seem very sweet and usually almost syrupy. Residual sugar in wine is not a problem for food, if you know how sweet the wine is, and if you choose your food carefully. For example, wines with a little residual sugar—like German Kabinett Rieslings, which have great compensating acidity—go beautifully with certain fatty foods, such as smoked fish and all types of pork preparations. If there's more sugar in the wine—as there may be in Spätlese Rieslings, Vouvrays, mildly sweet Chenin Blancs from California—the key is finding a way to incorporate some sweetness into the food. If done properly, the levels of sweetness in wine and food will seem very natural together. Fruit sauces and fruit accompaniments, of course, are the easiest ways to accomplish this. Very sweet wines go with dessert, but be careful to serve a dessert that's less sweet than the wine; the lusciousness of a good dessert wine gets wiped out by sweeter food. And then there's that odd strategy of pairing sweet, viscous wines with meal-opening velvety food: Sauternes with foie gras, or with oysters, for example. Most people don't like the thought of starting a meal with a sweet wine, but if you can prepare yourself mentally there is something sinfully lavish about it.

SILKY. A textural quality in wine that usually comes from glycerine and/or alcohol. A thin, low-alcohol wine cannot be described as silky. Silky wines present lovely opportunities for textural similarity; if everything else matches up (such as components and flavors), a silky Corton-Charlemagne with Dover sole in a silky beurre blanc can be exquisite.

SMOKY. A taster's term for a widely appreciated quality in wine. Sometimes a smoky taste in wine comes from the charred insides of barrels with which the wine has had contact, and sometimes it comes from a combination of grape variety and soil. It's usually whites that are described as smoky (like Pouilly-Fumé, like some aged white Burgundies, or, more specifically, like an aged Bernkasteler Doktor from the Mosel). Reds can also have a smoky character (usually from charred barrels). In any event, it's often a positive description—unless the wine is smoky to excess. A smoky flavor furnishes a great opportunity for matches based on flavor contrast. It's a foodlike flavor that works very nicely as a foil for many nonsmoky foods—a whole range of things from meaty, to earthy, to fishy, to spicy. Usually, a smoky wine does not work as a flavor similarity with smoky foods, since the pronounced smokiness of smoked foods will drown out the subtler smokiness of a smoky wine.

SOFT. Means a wine lacks acidity. This can be a real problem for food, since acidity helps so much in the matching of wine and food (see **Acidity**). Soft reds can handle a range of simply grilled or roasted meat dishes, but soft whites are very tricky for food. Occasionally, "soft" is used by tasters in a positive sense—denoting a balanced wine with no rough edges sticking out.

SPICY. A very imprecise tasting term, since spice is not a very specific description. Most often, the "spiciness" refers to flavors in the clove-cinnamon-nutmeg range, affording menu-planners a wonderful opportunity for flavor contrast matches. Barrel-fermented Chardonnays (see **Barrel Fermentation**) often have this quality, as do some young Cabernet Sauvignons. A range of northern whites can have the "spice" of spice-scented gumdrops (something like allspice). Riesling heads this list, particularly wines from Ürziger Würzgarten (this vineyard name means "spice garden"). Muscat is another grape with this type of spiciness. The most famous grape of all for spicy flavors is the Gewürztraminer ("spiced Traminer"), but the aromas and flavors of the white wines made from Gewürztraminer are actually more reminiscent of lychee nuts and rose water. Reds can be spicy as well, with wines from the Zinfandel grape most often mentioned in this regard; big young spicy wines such as these are great with barbecued ribs. Young Pinot Noir wines taste spicy; these lighter reds are interesting with fish and light meat dishes.

STRUCTURE. An imprecise taster's term that most often refers to the way that tannin has influenced the feel of a wine in the mouth. It's actually a metaphoric concept; when tasters discuss "structure," they're visualizing the wine as if it were a building (or something built), and discussing its structural components. Other elements aside from tannin also contribute to the wine's "structure": acid, glycerine, alcohol. A wine with "firm structure" will probably be quite tannic (for food, see **Firm** and **Tannin**). A wine with "weak structure" will probably lack tannin and/or acid (for food, see **Tannin** and **Acidity**).

TANNIN. A most important element when considering wine for food. Nothing affects the feel of a wine in the mouth as much as tannin. If a wine contains a lot of tannin, as you begin to swallow it you will notice an abrasive, astringent scrape on your gums, tongue, teeth, palate. It's like drinking very strong tea, eating the papery part of a walnut, or licking a chalked-up blackboard. You can expect to find tannin in forceful young reds. Whites don't usually contain noticeable tannin, and old wines usually have lost theirs. Tannin comes from a range of things; it appears naturally in grape skins (more in some grapes than others; more in riper vintages). It appears naturally in grape stems and seeds (some winemakers ferment the wine with stems and seeds, leading to greater tannin extraction; some winemakers press their grapes very hard, leading to greater tannin extraction). Tannin is also found in oak barrels, and long contact with new wood (fresh barrels) will increase a wine's tannin levels. Tannin is not usually a pleasant sensation, but it does act as a preservative while the wine is aging and reaching new heights of flavor. And, young, tannic reds present a terrific opportunity for menu-planners: Tannin cuts through the fattiness of meats and cheese. A brawny, tannic red is sometimes just the wine to render a fatty steak or leg of lamb more digestible. Also, red wines are usually flattened by soft cheeses— unless the wines contain a lot of tannin. Big, fruity, tannic reds—such as young Rhône wines, or young Zinfandel—are your best red wine bets for many cheeses. A word of caution: If a dish is delicate to any degree, keep it away from tannic wines.

THIN. Wines that are lacking body, and may even be watery. Normally, it's best to keep these wines away from rich foods, heavy foods, or full-flavored foods. But they may be perfectly in line with simple, light foods—such as a thin Muscadet with a sautéed, unsauced flounder fillet (texture similarity).

VANILLA. A lovely quality in wine usually derived from the vanillin-rich wood of oak barrels. Chardonnays in particular—since the inherent flavors of Chardonnay are not that pronounced—seem to pick up vanilla most prominently. There was a vogue, for a time, of matching vanilla-scented California Chardonnays and white Burgundies with foods in vanilla sauce (such as Alain Senderens' lobster with vanilla sauce). However, you must exercise caution—since vanilla-scented wines are also apt to be big wines, and big wines can be too much for big creamy, vanilla-scented sauces. So, despite the flavor similarity, you might have an unpleasant match. It's safer to use vanilla-scented wines as a flavor contrast to grilled chicken, fish.

VARIETAL. Refers to a wine's grape variety; use as either an adjective or a noun. (Either, "This wine isn't showing much varietal character." Or, "What's the varietal in this wine?") No factor influences the flavor of a wine as much as its grape variety. Gamay wines will taste like strawberries, Cabernet wines like mint or herbs, Riesling wines like flowers and peaches, Gewürztraminer wines like lychee nuts. This is obviously important information for menu-planners, especially when looking for matches based either on flavor similarity or flavor contrast. Often, however, the varietal flavors of a wine are not as important in food-matching as are the levels of acid, sugar, alcohol, and tannin in the wine—and these factors have more to do with geography, weather, and winemaking than they have to do with varietals.

VEGETAL. A taster's term for an herbaceous quality in wine. See **Grassy**.

VINTAGE. The year in which a wine was made. Knowing a wine's vintage can tell you much about the kind of wine. But menu-planners make the common mistake of paying attention only to the quality ratings that vintages receive on vintage charts; they assume that only top-rated vintages are suitable for drinking with food. Nothing could be further from the truth. Very often, a wine from a lesser vintage—which usually means less sun, less richness, less striking individuality—will behave itself better at table than a wine from a top-rated vintage. A 1980 red Bordeaux, for example—a thin, low-rated vintage—can be paired with a wide range of food items, including fish. But red Bordeaux from 1982—a super-rich, extremely well-regarded vintage—have more limited applicability with food.

You can save a lot of money—and elicit a lot of pleasure and surprise—by serving off-vintage wines with your meals.

VITIS LABRUSCA. A native American vine. See **Foxy**.

VITIS VINIFERA. A vine native to the Old World. Most of the world's great wines come from grapes grown on Vitis Vinifera vines (Chardonnay, Cabernet, Riesling, Pinot Noir, Chenin Blanc, Zinfandel, Gamay, are all Vitis Vinifera). Generally, the wines from Vitis Vinifera are subtler and more elegant than wines from other vine types, such as labrusca, and have become the accepted standards when considering wine for food.

WOOD. The amount of time a wine spent in wood, and what kind of wood it was stored in, are key factors when considering wine for food. Rich Chardonnays, top-rated red Bordeaux, California Cabernet, red Burgundy, California Pinot Noir, red Rhônes, California Zinfandel, an increasing number of serious Italian reds, and other wines of the world spend a good deal of time in small, new, oak barrels. These wines pick up oaky flavors (like vanilla, cedar, and spice), but they also pick up tannic harshness. Be careful with food: Over-oaked wines may have unpleasant finishes that clash with food. Other wines of the world—such as white and red Spanish wines, such as German whites—also spend time in wood, but in these cases the wood is usually not new. The wines will not pick up much flavor or tannin; the barrels are just used as storage containers in which the wines can slowly age and reduce. These barrel-aged wines—even if they've been in barrels for decades—do not pose any special problems for food.

The Big List is a guide to basic wine characteristics, vintage distinctions, and producer styles. Its purpose is to help you find an appropriate wine match for whatever dish—or menu—is at hand. The list itself is based on the food-and-wine-matching experiments found throughout this book; it naturally evolved from them. While it is not meant to be a comprehensive guide, The Big List does cover most of the world's major wine-producing regions.

The listing of components, flavors, and textures for each wine entry follows the categories established in Chapter 3 (see page 66). Vintage considerations refer to annual climatic conditions that might affect these key elements. Producer styles suggest differences in winemaking that could influence the way a wine tastes and interacts with food. A wine described as "lighter" may have lower alcohol, or less tannin, or less concentration. A wine described as "fuller" may have higher alcohol, or more tannin, or greater concentration, or some combination of these factors. The categorizing of a producer's style as either lighter or fuller has nothing to do with wine quality.

WINE(S): Aloxe-Corton; Pernand-
Vergelesses; Savigny-Les-Beaune;
Beaune-Red
COUNTRY: France

REGION: Burgundy
SUB-REGION: Côte de Beaune

COMPONENT(S): Moderate acidity,
dry

FLAVOR(S): Black cherry, raspberry, blackberry, plum, smoke, violets, game, earth, oak, spice, burning leaves, licorice

TEXTURE(S): Medium bodied

VINTAGE CONSIDERATIONS:
1980 • Fairly light; balanced
1981 • Fairly light; acidic
1982 • Fairly light; balanced
1983 • Very rich; alcoholic
1984 • Fairly light; acidic
1985 • Rich; balanced
1986 • Moderately rich; acidic
1987 • Moderately rich; balanced

PRODUCER STYLES:
Lighter • Bonneau du Martray, Bize, Boillot, Chanson, Delagrange, Chandon de Briailles, Jadot, Drouhin, Guyon, Prince de Mérode, Senard, Voarick
Fuller • Bouchard Père et Fils, Cornu, Dubreuil-Fontaine, Gaunoux, Lafarge, L. Latour, Leroy, Moillard, Morey, Morot, Prieur, Rapet, Remoissenet, Rollin

---

WINE(S): Amontillado and Oloroso Sherry
COUNTRY: Spain
REGION: Andalusia
SUB-REGION: Jerez

COMPONENT(S): Moderate acidity, dry
FLAVOR(S): Roast nuts, wheat biscuit, fresh dough, vanilla, oak
TEXTURE(S): Medium bodied, alcoholic

VINTAGE CONSIDERATIONS:
Blended from many different vintages by the solera system (casks triangularly stacked and connected)

PRODUCER STYLES:
Lighter • Osborne, Croft, Gonzalez Byass, Duff Gordon, Williams and Humbert
Fuller • Harvey and Sons, Sandeman, Domecq, Lustau, Díez-Merito

---

WINE(S): Arneis
COUNTRY: Italy
REGION: Piedmont
SUB-REGION: Roeri

COMPONENT(S): Moderate acidity, dry
FLAVOR(S): Pears, honeysuckle, spice, rose petal, peach, green apple, almond
TEXTURE(S): Light to medium bodied

VINTAGE CONSIDERATIONS:
1983 • Rich; balanced
1984 • Thin; acidic
1985 • Very rich; alcoholic
1986 • Moderately rich; balanced
1987 • Moderately rich; balanced

PRODUCER STYLES:
Lighter • Bruno Giacosa, Ceretto
Fuller • Castello di Neive, Vietti, Fratelli Rabino

WINE(S): Bairrada
COUNTRY: Portugal
REGION: Lower Beira
SUB-REGION: N/A

COMPONENT(S): Moderate acidity, dry
FLAVOR(S): Plum, blackberry, cedar, tobacco, smoke, leather
TEXTURE(S): Medium to full bodied

VINTAGE CONSIDERATIONS:
1983 • Rich; balanced
1984 • Fairly light; balanced
1985 • Rich; balanced

1986 • Fairly light; acidic
1987 • Fairly light; fruity

PRODUCER STYLES:
Lighter • Caves Aliança
Fuller • Caves São João, Messias, Central da Chavinha, Luiz Pato, Buçaco

~~~~~~~~~~~~~~~~~~~~~~~~~~~~~

WINE(S): Bandol (Red)
COUNTRY: France
REGION: Provence
SUB-REGION: N/A

COMPONENT(S): Low to moderate acidity, dry
FLAVOR(S): Blackberry, raspberry, plum, smoke, truffles, oak, black pepper, leather, nutmeg, herbs
TEXTURE(S): Medium to full bodied

VINTAGE CONSIDERATIONS:
1982 • Very rich; balanced
1983 • Rich; balanced
1984 • Fairly light; balanced
1985 • Rich; low in acid
1986 • Fairly light; balanced
1987 • Fairly light; balanced

PRODUCER STYLES:
Lighter • de Frégate, Mas de la Rouvière
Fuller • de L'Hermitage, de Pibarnon, Ott, Tempier, Château Vannières

~~~~~~~~~~~~~~~~~~~~~~~~~~~~~

WINE(S): Barbaresco
COUNTRY: Italy
REGION: Piedmont
SUB-REGION: N/A

COMPONENT(S): Moderate acidity, dry
FLAVOR(S): Tar, oak, plum, earth, smoke, leather, tobacco, black cherry, spice, orange peel (riservas are less fruity and more com-

plex than nonriservas)
TEXTURE(S): Medium to full bodied

VINTAGE CONSIDERATIONS:
1979 • Rich; balanced
1980 • Moderately rich; balanced
1981 • Fairly light; acidic
1982 • Rich; balanced
1983 • Moderately rich; balanced
1984 • Thin; diluted
1985 • Very rich; balanced
1986 • Moderately rich; balanced

PRODUCER STYLES:
Lighter • Pio Cesare, Giovannini Moresco, Angelo Gaja-Costa Russi, Marchesi di Gresy, Roagna
Fuller • Castello di Neive, Bruno Ceretto, Bruno Giacosa, Produttori di Barbaresco, Angelo Gaja-Sorí Tilden, Deforville, Scarpa, Giuseppe Mascarello, Fontanafredda, La Spinona, Vietti

~~~~~~~~~~~~~~~~~~~~~~~~~~~~~

WINE(S): Barbera D'Alba
COUNTRY: Italy
REGION: Piedmont
SUB-REGION: Alba

COMPONENT(S): Moderate acidity, dry
FLAVOR(S): Black cherry, plum, oak, tar, toast, plum, earth
TEXTURE(S): Medium bodied

VINTAGE CONSIDERATIONS:
1982 • Rich; balanced
1983 • Rich; balanced
1984 • Thin; acidic
1985 • Very rich; balanced
1986 • Moderately rich; balanced
1987 • Rich; fruity

PRODUCER STYLES:
Lighter • Aldo Conterno, Luigi Pia, Scarpa
Fuller • Ceretto, Angelo Gaja, Pio Cesare, Vietti, Castello di Neive,

Bruno Giacosa, Giacomo Conterno

WINE(S): Bardolino
COUNTRY: Italy
REGION: Veneto
SUB-REGION: N/A

COMPONENT(S): Moderate to high acidity, dry and bitter
FLAVOR(S): Black cherry, red grape, cherry blossom, bitter almond
TEXTURE(S): Light bodied

VINTAGE CONSIDERATIONS:
Drink the youngest vintage possible

PRODUCER STYLES:
Lighter • Aldegheri, Bolla, Bertani, Santa Sofia, Tre Colline, Tommasi, Guerrieri Rizzardi
Fuller • Villa Girardi, Lamberti, Masi, Cantina Sociale di Soave, Zonin, Tedeschi, Anselmi, Boscaini

---

WINE(S): Barolo
COUNTRY: Italy
REGION: Piedmont
SUB-REGION: N/A

COMPONENT(S): Moderate acidity, dry
FLAVOR(S): Tar, oak, plum, earth, smoke, leather, tobacco, black cherry, blackberry, spice, orange peel (riservas are less fruity and more complex than nonriservas)
TEXTURE(S): Medium to full bodied, tannic when young

VINTAGE CONSIDERATIONS:
1979 • Rich; balanced
1980 • Moderately rich; balanced
1981 • Fairly light; acidic
1982 • Rich; balanced
1983 • Moderately rich; balanced

1984 • Thin; diluted
1985 • Very rich; balanced
1986 • Moderately rich; balanced

PRODUCER STYLES:
Lighter • Aldo Conterno, Bruno Ceretto, Cogno-Marcarini, Luigi Einaudi, Pio Cesare
Fuller • Carretta, Clerico, Fontanafredda, Bruno Giacosa, Giuseppe Rinaldi, L. Sandrone, Giacomo Conterno, Giuseppe Mascarello, Prunotto, Renato Ratti, Valentino, Vietti, Scarpa, Gianfranco Bovio

---

WINE(S): Beaujolais; Beaujolais-Villages; Cru Beaujolais (red)
COUNTRY: France
REGION: Burgundy
SUB-REGION: N/A

COMPONENT(S): Moderate acidity, dry
FLAVOR(S): Cherry, raspberry, blackberry, plum, strawberry, violets, banana, spice, gumdrop
TEXTURE(S): Light (Beaujolais-Villages; Brouilly; Chiroubles; Côte de Brouilly; Fleurie; Regnié; St-Amour) to medium bodied (Chénas; Juliénas; Morgon; Moulin-à-Vent)

VINTAGE CONSIDERATIONS:
1985 • Rich; balanced
1986 • Fairly light; balanced
1987 • Fairly light; balanced
1988 • Moderately rich; balanced

PRODUCER STYLES:
Lighter • Bedin, Chanut, Depagneux, Ferraud, S. Fessy, Jadot, Marchand, Piat, Tête
Fuller • Berrod, Château de la Chaize, Dalicieux, Duboeuf, Gonon, Lapierre, L. Latour, Patissier, Thivin, Trenel

WINE(S): Brunello di Montalcino
COUNTRY: Italy
REGION: Tuscany
SUB-REGION: Montalcino

COMPONENT(S): Moderate acidity, dry
FLAVOR(S): Black cherry, plum, oak, cedar, smoke, spice, leather, tobacco, orange peel (riservas have less fruit and more complexity than nonriservas)
TEXTURE(S): Medium to full bodied

VINTAGE CONSIDERATIONS:
1982 • Rich; balanced
1983 • Rich; alcoholic
1984 • Very thin; acidic
1985 • Very rich; balanced
1986 • Moderately rich; fruity
1987 • Fairly light; balanced

PRODUCER STYLES:
Lighter • Col d'Orcia, Capanna, Camigliano, San Filippo, la Fortuna, Val di Suga
Fuller • Altesino, Campogiovanni, Costanti, Caparzo, Lisini, Caprili, Biondi-Santi, Pertimali, Barbi, il Poggione, Poggio Antico, il Greppone Mazzi

WINE(S): Cabernet Sauvignon
COUNTRY: Chile
REGION: Central Valley and Secano
SUB-REGION: N/A

COMPONENT(S): Moderate acidity, dry
FLAVOR(S): Cassis, raspberry, blackberry, tobacco, plum, bell pepper, vanilla, oak, tar, herbs, cedar
TEXTURE(S): Medium bodied

VINTAGE CONSIDERATIONS:
1984 • Rich; balanced
1985 • Moderately rich; balanced
1986 • Fairly light; acidic

PRODUCER STYLES:
Lighter • José Canepa, Unduragga, Viña Linderos, Concha y Toro
Fuller • Viña Cousiño Macul, Viña Santa Rita, Miguel Torres

WINE(S): Cabernet Sauvignon
COUNTRY: USA
REGION: Washington
SUB-REGION: Columbia Valley

COMPONENT(S): Moderate acidity, dry
FLAVOR(S): Cassis, blackberry, raspberry, herbs, rhubarb, earth, oak
TEXTURE(S): Light to medium bodied

VINTAGE CONSIDERATIONS:
1983 • Very rich; balanced
1984 • Rich; tannic
1985 • Rich; tannic
1986 • Moderately rich; low acidity

PRODUCER STYLES:
Lighter • Arbor Crest
Fuller • Ste. Michelle, Haviland, Columbía, Kiona, Quilceda Creek, Snoqualmie, Woodward Canyon

WINE(S): Cabernet and blends of Cabernet
COUNTRY: Australia
REGION: New South Wales
SUB-REGION: Hunter Valley

COMPONENT(S): Low to moderate acidity, dry
FLAVOR(S): Cassis, raspberry, blackberry, tobacco, plum, bell pepper, vanilla, oak, tar, herbs, cedar
TEXTURE(S): Medium to full bodied, alcoholic

VINTAGE CONSIDERATIONS:
1982 • Very rich; balanced
1983 • Rich; balanced
1984 • Rich; alcoholic
1985 • Rich; balanced
1986 • Rich; balanced
1987 • Rich; balanced

PRODUCER STYLES:
Lighter • Rothbury, Robson Vineyard, Arrowfield, Peacock Hill
Fuller • Lake's Folly, Brokenwood, Tyrrell's, Elliott's, Lindeman's, Tulloch, Rosemount Estate

---

WINE(S): Cabernet and blends of Cabernet
COUNTRY: Australia
REGION: South Australia
SUB-REGION: Clare and Barossa

COMPONENT(S): Low to moderate acidity, dry
FLAVOR(S): Cassis, raspberry, blackberry, tobacco, plum, bell pepper, vanilla, oak, tar, herbs, cedar
TEXTURE(S): Medium to full bodied, alcoholic

VINTAGE CONSIDERATIONS:
1982 • Moderately rich; balanced
1983 • Moderately rich; balanced
1984 • Rich; balanced
1985 • Rich; balanced
1986 • Rich; forward
1987 • Very rich; balanced

PRODUCER STYLES:
Lighter • Seppelt, Orlando, Taylors Wines, Pewsey Vale
Fuller • Thomas Hardy, Seppelt, Wendouree, Leasingham, Orlando, Coriole, Henschke

---

WINE(S): Cabernet and blends of Cabernet
COUNTRY: Australia
REGION: South Australia
SUB-REGION: Coonawarra

COMPONENT(S): Moderate acidity, dry
FLAVOR(S): Cassis, raspberry, blackberry, tobacco, plum, bell pepper, vanilla, oak, tar, herbs, cedar
TEXTURE(S): Medium bodied

VINTAGE CONSIDERATIONS:
1982 • Rich; balanced
1983 • Fairly light; acidic
1984 • Very rich; balanced
1985 • Very rich; balanced
1986 • Rich; forward
1987 • Rich; balanced

PRODUCER STYLES:
Lighter • Bowen, Rouge Homme, Wynn
Fuller • Brand's Laira, Wolf Blass, Hardy's, Katnook Estate

WINE(S): Cabernet and blends of Cabernet
COUNTRY: Australia
REGION: Victoria
SUB-REGION: Central Districts

COMPONENT(S): Low to moderate acidity, dry
FLAVOR(S): Cassis, raspberry, blackberry, tobacco, plum, bell pepper, vanilla, oak, tar, herbs, cedar
TEXTURE(S): Medium to full bodied, alcoholic

VINTAGE CONSIDERATIONS:
1982 • Moderately rich; balanced
1983 • Rich; tannic
1984 • Moderately rich; balanced
1985 • Rich; balanced
1986 • Very rich; alcoholic
1987 • Rich; balanced

PRODUCER STYLES:

Lighter • Mt. Helen Vineyard, Roseburg, Mitchelton, Lindeman's, Wirra Wirra

Fuller • Chateau Tahbilk, Virgin Hills, Taltarni, Balgownie, Chateau le Amon, Tisdall, Mt. Avoca

---

WINE(S): Cabernet and blends of Cabernet
COUNTRY: Australia
REGION: Victoria
SUB-REGION: Yarra Yarra

COMPONENT(S): Moderate acidity, dry
FLAVOR(S): Cassis, raspberry, blackberry, tobacco, plum, bell pepper, vanilla, oak, tar, herbs, cedar
TEXTURE(S): Medium bodied

VINTAGE CONSIDERATIONS:
1982 • Rich; balanced
1983 • Moderately rich; balanced
1984 • Rich; balanced
1985 • Rich; forward
1986 • Very rich; alcoholic
1987 • Moderately rich; balanced

PRODUCER STYLES:

Lighter • Yarra Yering, St. Huberts, Yeringberg, Mount Mary, Seville Estate

Fuller • Wantirna Estate, Middleton, Coldstream Hills

WINE(S): Cabernet, Cabernet Franc, Merlot
COUNTRY: Italy
REGION: Friuli-Venezia Giulia
SUB-REGION: N/A

COMPONENT(S): Moderate to high acidity, dry
FLAVOR(S): Berry-fruit, cassis, bitter almond, spice, tea, herbs, rhubarb, beetroot, black olive
TEXTURE(S): Light to medium bodied

VINTAGE CONSIDERATIONS:
1986 • Rich; balanced
1987 • Moderately rich; balanced

PRODUCER STYLES:

Lighter • Pighin, Plozner, il Gallo

Fuller • Borgo Conventi, Eno Friulia, Farra, Ronco del Gnemiz, Vigne dal Leon, Volpe Pasini Schiopetto, Abbazia di Rosazzo

---

WINE(S): Cabernet, Cabernet Franc, Merlot
COUNTRY: Italy
REGION: Trentino-Alto Adige
SUB-REGION: N/A

COMPONENT(S): Moderate to high acidity, dry
FLAVOR(S): Berry-fruit, cassis, bitter almond, herbs, rhubarb, black olive, beetroot
TEXTURE(S): Light to medium bodied

VINTAGE CONSIDERATIONS:
1986 • Rich; balanced
1987 • Moderately rich; balanced

PRODUCER STYLES:

Lighter • San Michele, Tenuta San Leonardo, Josef Brigl, Kellereigenossenschaft Terlan, Lageder, Hirschprunn

Fuller • Giorgio Gray, Joseph Hofstätter

WINE(S): Cabernet Sauvignon and Cabernet blends
COUNTRY: USA
REGION: California

SUB-REGION: Central Coast–
Monterey

COMPONENT(s): Low to moderate
acidity, dry
FLAVOR(s): Cassis, raspberry, blackberry, tobacco, bell pepper,
plum, herbs, chocolate, cedar,
vanilla, toast, smoke, tar
TEXTURE(s): Medium to full bodied

VINTAGE CONSIDERATIONS:
1982 • Fairly light; acidic
1983 • Moderately rich; fruity
1984 • Rich; tannic
1985 • Very rich; concentrated
1986 • Rich; fruity

PRODUCER STYLES:
Lighter • Congress Springs,
Roudon-Smith, San Saba, Cor-
bett Canyon, Firestone, Miras-
sou, Almadén, San Martin,
Monterey Vineyard, Paul Mas-
son, Zaca Mesa
Fuller • David Bruce, Mount
Eden, Ridge-Montebello, Santa
Cruz Mountain, Martin Ray,
Durney, Jekel

WINE(s): Cabernet Sauvignon and
Cabernet blends
COUNTRY: USA
REGION: California
SUB-REGION: Napa

COMPONENT(s): Low to moderate
acidity, dry
FLAVOR(s): Cassis, raspberry, blackberry, tobacco, bell pepper,
plum, herbs, chocolate, cedar,
vanilla, toast, smoke, tar, mint
TEXTURE(s): Medium to full bodied

VINTAGE CONSIDERATIONS:
1982 • Moderately rich; uneven
1983 • Fairly light; soft
1984 • Very rich; alcoholic

1985 • Rich; balanced
1986 • Very rich; balanced

PRODUCER STYLES:
Lighter • Neyers, Rutherford Hill,
Round Hill, Cakebread, Tre-
fethen, Vichon, Shafer, Sterling,
Martini, Silverado, Flora
Springs, Robert Mondavi, Heitz,
Inglenook, Freemark Abbey,
Christian Brothers, Belvedere,
Stag's Leap, Sequoia Grove,
Beaulieu-Beau Tour and Ruther-
ford, Clos du Val, William Hill-
Silver label
Fuller • Newton, Long, Dunn,
Conn Creek, Burgess, Girard,
Buehler, Diamond Creek,
Caymus-Special Selection,
Phelps-Insignia and Eisele,
Dominus, Opus One, Beaulieu-
Private Reserve, Spottswoode,
Carneros Creek, Frog's Leap,
Johnson Turnbull, Forman,
Groth, Heitz-Martha's Vineyard,
William Hill-Gold label, Nie-
baum Coppola-Rubicon,
Sterling-Reserve, Mayacamas
Vineyards, Robert Mondavi-
Reserve, Chateau Montelena,
Inglenook-Reserve, Monticello
Cellars, Silver Oak, Stag's Leap-
Cask 23, Flora Springs-Trilogy,
Cuvaison, Ridge-York Creek and
Howell Mountain

WINE(s): Cabernet Sauvignon and
Cabernet blends
COUNTRY: USA
REGION: California
SUB-REGION: Sonoma

COMPONENT(s): Low to moderate
acidity, dry
FLAVOR(s): Cassis, raspberry, blackberry, tobacco, bell pepper,
plum, herbs, chocolate, cedar,

vanilla, toast, smoke, tar, mint
TEXTURE(s): Medium to full bodied

VINTAGE CONSIDERATIONS:
1982 • Moderately rich; balanced
1983 • Fairly light; soft
1984 • Very rich; tannic
1985 • Very rich; balanced
1986 • Rich; forward

PRODUCER STYLES:
Lighter • Glen Ellen, Sebastiani,
Sonoma Vineyards, Pedroncelli,
Kenwood, Fisher, Dry Creek,
Zellerbach, Iron Horse,
Beringer-Knight's Valley, Simi
Fuller • Lyeth, Carmenet, Kistler,
Laurel Glen, Jordan, Clos du
Bois, Alexander Valley,
Kenwood-Jack London,
Sebastiani-Eagle label, Simi-
Reserve, Gundlach Bundschu,
Haywood, Sam Sebastiani,
Ravenswood

WINE(s): Cahors
COUNTRY: France
REGION: Southwest
SUB-REGION: N/A

COMPONENT(s): Low to moderate
acidity, dry
FLAVOR(s): Blackberry, raspberry,
cherry, plum, oak, leather, herbs
TEXTURE(s): Medium to full bodied

VINTAGE CONSIDERATIONS:
1982 • Very rich; balanced
1983 • Rich; balanced
1984 • Fairly light; acidic
1985 • Rich; balanced
1986 • Rich; tannic
1987 • Fairly light; balanced

PRODUCER STYLES:
Lighter • Clos Triguedina, Côtes
d'Olt, Paillas, Quattre
Fuller • Château de Cayrou,

Château de Chambert, Château
de Haute-Serre, Clos la Coutale

WINE(s): Carmignano
COUNTRY: Italy
REGION: Tuscany
SUB-REGION: N/A

COMPONENT(s): Moderate acidity,
dry
FLAVOR(s): Black cherry, tobacco,
spice, earth, oak, cedar, smoke,
orange peel (riservas have less
fruit and more complexity than
nonriservas)
TEXTURE(s): Medium bodied

VINTAGE CONSIDERATIONS:
1982 • Very rich; balanced
1983 • Rich; alcoholic
1984 • Thin; acidic
1985 • Very rich; balanced
1986 • Moderately rich; fruity
1987 • Thin; acidic

PRODUCER STYLES:
Lighter • Artimino, Bacchereto
Fuller • Capezzana, Trefiano, il
Poggiolo

WINE(s): Chablis
COUNTRY: France
REGION: Burgundy
SUB-REGION: Yonne

COMPONENT(s): Moderate to high
acidity, dry
FLAVOR(s): Green apple, lemon,
minerals (chalk), slate, straw, vanilla, oak, earth, smoke
TEXTURE(s): Medium to full bodied

VINTAGE CONSIDERATIONS:
1983 • Very rich; alcoholic
1984 • Fairly light; acidic
1985 • Rich; low in acid

1986 • Moderately rich; balanced
1987 • Fairly light; acidic

PRODUCER STYLES:
Lighter • Beaubassin, Chauvenet, la Chablisienne, Château de Maligny, Domaine de l'Eglantiere, Thevenin, Lavantureux, J. Moreau, Pic, Laroche, Regnard, Domaine servin, Simmonet-Febvre, Y. Febvre
Fuller • Billaud-Simon, Bourée, Collet, J. Dauvissat, R. Dauvissat, Dauvissat-Camus, Drouhin, Droin, Fevre, L. Michel, R. Moreau, Pinson, Raveneau, G. Robin, Tremblay, Vocoret, Long-Depaquit

WINE(S): Chambolle-Musigny
COUNTRY: France
REGION: Burgundy
SUB-REGION: Côte de Nuits

COMPONENT(S): Moderate acidity, dry
FLAVOR(S): Black cherry, raspberry, blackberry, plum, smoke, violets, game, earth, oak, spice, burning leaves, licorice
TEXTURE(S): Medium bodied

VINTAGE CONSIDERATIONS:
1980 • Moderately rich; balanced
1981 • Fairly light; acidic
1982 • Fairly light; balanced
1983 • Very rich; alcoholic
1984 • Fairly light; acidic
1985 • Rich; balanced
1986 • Moderately rich; balanced
1987 • Fairly light; balanced

PRODUCER STYLES:
Lighter • Delaunay, Drouhin, Drouhin-Laroze, Groffier
Fuller • B. Amiot, Bertheau, Bourée, Barthod-Noëllat, Clair-Daü (Jadot), G. Lignier, Roumier,

Serveau, Domaines des Varoilles, Comtes de Vogüé

WINE(S): Champagne (nonvintage Brut)
COUNTRY: France
REGION: Champagne
SUB-REGION: N/A

COMPONENT(S): Moderate to high acidity, dry
FLAVOR(S): Green apple, lemon, yeast, wheat biscuit, butter, vanilla, allspice, roast nut, earth
TEXTURE(S): Light to full bodied, effervescent

VINTAGE CONSIDERATIONS:
Buy the freshest bottles available (nonvintage Champagne does not benefit from aging)

PRODUCER STYLES:
Light bodied • Piper Heidsieck, Larmandier, Alfred Rothschild, Legras, Nicholas Feuillatte, Besserat de Bellefon, Beaumet, Jacquesson, H. Germain, Lanson, Launois, Bruno Paillard, Perrier-Jouët, Bonnaire, Charbaut, Lasalle
Medium bodied • Cattier, Billecart-Salmon, Gosset, Lechere, Pommery, Pol Roger, Moët and Chandon, Laurent-Perrier, Taittinger, Taillevent, Ayala, Deutz, Charles Heidsieck, Joseph Perrier, Philipponat, Mumm, Oudinot, Jacquart, Heidsieck Monopole, Salon
Full bodied • Paul Bara, Barancourt, Alfred Gratien, Louis Roederer, Veuve Clicquot, Bollinger, Krug, Henriot

WINE(S): Champagne (vintage Brut)

COUNTRY: France
REGION: Champagne
SUB-REGION: N/A

COMPONENT(S): Moderate to high acidity, dry
FLAVOR(S): Green apple, lemon, yeast, butter, wheat biscuit, vanilla, ginger, toasted oat, allspice, roast nut, earth, truffle
TEXTURE(S): Light to full bodied, effervescent

VINTAGE CONSIDERATIONS:
1978 • Very rich, balanced
1979 • Moderately rich; balanced
1980 • Fairly light; acidic
1981 • Moderately rich; balanced
1982 • Very rich; low in acid
1983 • Rich; balanced
1984 • Light; acidic
1985 • Rich; balanced

PRODUCER STYLES:
Light bodied • Piper Heidsieck, Pommery et Greno, Alfred Rothschild, Nicholas Feuillatte, Besserat de Bellefon, Beaumet, Jacquesson, H. Germain, Cattier, Lanson, Launois, Bruno Paillard, Perrier-Jouët, Taittinger, Billecart-Salmon, Bonnaire, Charbaut, Lechere, Lasalle
Medium bodied • Pol Roger, Moët and Chandon, Laurent-Perrier, Ayala, Deutz, Charles Heidsieck, Joseph Perrier, Philipponat, Mumm, Oudinot, Jacquart, Larmandier, Heidsieck Monopole
Full bodied • Paul Bara, Barancourt, Alfred Gratien, Gosset, Louis Roederer, Veuve Clicquot, Bollinger, Krug, Henriot

WINE(S): Champagne (nonvintage Extra Dry)
COUNTRY: France

REGION: Champagne
SUB-REGION: N/A

COMPONENT(S): Moderate to high acidity, off-dry
FLAVOR(S): Green apple, lemon, yeast, wheat biscuit, butter, vanilla, allspice, roast nut, burnt sugar, honey
TEXTURE(S): Light to full bodied, effervescent

VINTAGE CONSIDERATIONS:
Buy the freshest bottles available

PRODUCER STYLES:
Light bodied • Piper Heidsieck, Besserat de Bellefon, Lanson
Medium bodied • Pommery, Pol Roger, Moët and Chandon, Laurent-Perrier, Ayala, Deutz, Mumm, Oudinot, Jacquart
Full bodied • Louis Roederer, Veuve Clicquot

WINE(S): Champagne (nonvintage and vintage Rosé)
COUNTRY: France
REGION: Champagne
SUB-REGION: N/A

COMPONENT(S): High acidity, dry
FLAVOR(S): Raspberry, strawberry, black cherry, yeast, clove, allspice, chocolate, truffle
TEXTURE(S): Light to full bodied, effervescent

VINTAGE CONSIDERATIONS:
(If nonvintage, buy the freshest bottles available)
1978 • Very rich; balanced
1979 • Moderately rich; balanced
1980 • Fairly light; acidic
1981 • Moderately rich; balanced
1982 • Very rich; low in acid
1983 • Rich; balanced
1984 • Light; acidic
1985 • Rich; balanced

PRODUCER STYLES:
Light bodied • Piper Heidsieck, Pommery et Greno, Alfred Roth-schild, Nicholas Feuillatte, Besserat de Bellefon, Beaumet, Jacquesson, Lanson, Bruno Pail-lard, Perrier-Jouët, Charbaut, Lasalle
Medium bodied • Cattier, Billecart-Salmon, Pol Roger, Moët and Chandon, Laurent-Perrier, Taittinger, Ayala, Deutz, Charles Heidsieck, Joseph Perrier, Philipponat, Mumm, Jacquart, Heidsieck Monopole
Full bodied • Barancourt, Alfred Gratien, Gosset, Louis Roederer, Veuve Clicquot, Bollinger, Krug

~~~~~~~~~~~~~~~~~~~~~~~~~~~~~~~~~~~~

WINE(S): Chardonnay
COUNTRY: Australia
REGION: New South Wales
SUB-REGION: Hunter Valley

COMPONENT(S): Low to moderate acidity, dry
FLAVOR(S): Vanilla, oak, butter, lemon
TEXTURE(S): Medium to full bodied

VINTAGE CONSIDERATIONS:
1982 • Very rich; alcoholic
1983 • Moderately rich; balanced
1984 • Light
1985 • Rich; fruity
1986 • Very rich; balanced
1987 • Moderately rich; balanced

PRODUCER STYLES:
Lighter • Tulloch, Allandale, Sutherland
Fuller • Rothbury, Robson Vine-yard, Lindeman's, Huntington Estate, Lake's Folly, Tyrrell's, Rosemount Estate, Peacock Hill Estate

~~~~~~~~~~~~~~~~~~~~~~~~~~~~~~~~~~~~

WINE(S): Chardonnay

COUNTRY: Australia
REGION: South Australia
SUB-REGION: Clare, Barossa, and Southern Districts

COMPONENT(S): Moderate acidity, dry
FLAVOR(S): Vanilla, oak, butter, lemon, green apple
TEXTURE(S): Medium to full bodied

VINTAGE CONSIDERATIONS:
1982 • Moderately rich; balanced
1983 • Fairly light; acidic
1984 • Rich; balanced
1985 • Moderately rich; balanced
1986 • Very rich; alcoholic
1987 • Rich; balanced
1988 • Moderately rich; balanced

PRODUCER STYLES:
Lighter • Angoves, Krondorf, Or-lando, Thomas Hardy, Hill Smith Estate, Heggies Vineyard, Wirra Wirra
Fuller • Seppelt, Petaluma, Tol-ley, Scott

~~~~~~~~~~~~~~~~~~~~~~~~~~~~~~~~~~~~

WINE(S): Chardonnay
COUNTRY: Australia
REGION: Victoria
SUB-REGION: Yarra Yarra

COMPONENT(S): Moderate acidity, dry
FLAVOR(S): Vanilla, oak, butter, lemon, green apple
TEXTURE(S): Medium bodied

VINTAGE CONSIDERATIONS:
1982 • Moderately rich; balanced
1983 • Moderately rich; balanced
1984 • Rich; balanced
1985 • Moderately rich; balanced
1986 • Very rich; alcoholic
1987 • Rich; balanced
1988 • Rich; balanced

PRODUCER STYLES:
Lighter • St. Huberts, Seville Es-

tate, Coldstream Hills
Fuller • Yarra Yering, Middleton

~~~~~~~~~~~~~~~~~~~~~~~~~~~~~~~~~~~

WINE(S): Chardonnay
COUNTRY: Italy
REGION: Trentino-Alto Adige
SUB-REGION: N/A

COMPONENT(S): Moderate to high acidity, dry
FLAVOR(S): Green apple, lemon, green herbs, honeysuckle, bitter almond
TEXTURE(S): Light bodied

VINTAGE CONSIDERATIONS:
1986 • Rich; fruity
1987 • Moderately rich; balanced

PRODUCER STYLES:
Lighter • Bollini, Pojer and Sandri, Zeni, Tiefenbrunner, Santa margherita
Fuller • None

~~~~~~~~~~~~~~~~~~~~~~~~~~~~~~~~~~~

WINE(S): Chardonnay
COUNTRY: USA
REGION: California
SUB-REGION: Mendocino

COMPONENT(S): Low to moderate acidity, dry
FLAVOR(S): Green apple, vanilla, oak, butter, butterscotch, papaya, pineapple, mango, coconut, toast, lemon
TEXTURE(S): Light to medium bodied

VINTAGE CONSIDERATIONS:
1982 • Fairly light; balanced
1983 • Moderately rich; alcoholic
1984 • Moderately rich; balanced
1985 • Rich; balanced
1986 • Rich; fruity
1987 • Moderately rich; balanced

PRODUCER STYLES:
Lighter • William Baccala, Fetzer-Sundial, Guenoc, Hidden Cellars, Parducci, Willow Creek
Fuller • Dolan Vineyards, Fetzer Vineyard-Barrel Select, Milano, Husch, Kendall-Jackson, Navarro

~~~~~~~~~~~~~~~~~~~~~~~~~~~~~~~~~~~

WINE(S): Chardonnay
COUNTRY: USA
REGION: California
SUB-REGION: Monterey

COMPONENT(S): Low to moderate acidity, dry
FLAVOR(S): Green apple, vanilla, oak, butter, butterscotch, papaya, pineapple, mango, coconut, toast, lemon
TEXTURE(S): Medium to full bodied

VINTAGE CONSIDERATIONS:
1982 • Fairly light; acidic
1983 • Fairly light; balanced
1984 • Rich; forward
1985 • Rich; balanced
1986 • Rich; balanced
1987 • Moderately rich; balanced

PRODUCER STYLES:
Lighter • J. Lohr, Mirassou, Charles Lefranc (Almadén), Monterey Vineyard
Fuller • Morgan, Chalone, Jekel-Reserve, Robert Talbott, Ventana

~~~~~~~~~~~~~~~~~~~~~~~~~~~~~~~~~~~

WINE(S): Chardonnay
COUNTRY: USA
REGION: California
SUB-REGION: Napa

COMPONENT(S): Low to moderate acidity, dry
FLAVOR(S): Green apple, vanilla, oak, butter, butterscotch, papaya, pineapple, mango, coco-

nut, toast, lemon
TEXTURE(S): Medium to full bodied

VINTAGE CONSIDERATIONS:
1982 • Moderately rich; balanced
1983 • Fairly light; fruity
1984 • Very rich; alcoholic
1985 • Rich; balanced
1986 • Rich; balanced
1987 • Moderately rich; balanced

PRODUCER STYLES:
Lighter • St. Clement, Silverado, Beringer, Acacia, Saintsbury, Cronin-Napa Valley, Cuvaison, Shafer, William Hill-Silver label, Girard, Flora Springs, Neyers, Burgess, St. Andrews, Folie a Deux, Sterling, Stratford
Fuller • Ritchie Creek, ZD, Robert Mondavi-Reserve, Chateau Montelena-Napa, Acacia-Carneros, Marina and Winery Lake, Grgich-Hills, Trefethen, Beringer-Private Reserve, Forman, Stag's Leap Wine Cellars, Long, Monticello, Raymond, William Hill-Gold label, Groth, Anderson, Flora Springs-Barrel fermented, Stony Hill, Far Niente

WINE(S): Chardonnay
COUNTRY: USA
REGION: California
SUB-REGION: North Central Coast

COMPONENT(S): Low to moderate acidity, dry
FLAVOR(S): Green apple, vanilla, oak, butter, butterscotch, papaya, pineapple, mango, coconut, toast, lemon
TEXTURE(S): Medium to full bodied

VINTAGE CONSIDERATIONS:
1982 • Rich; alcoholic
1983 • Fairly light; balanced

1984 • Rich; balanced
1985 • Rich; balanced
1986 • Rich; balanced
1987 • Moderately rich; balanced

PRODUCER STYLES:
Lighter • San Martin, Paul Masson
Fuller • Mount Eden, Congress Springs, Martin Ray, Bonny Doon, Calera, Cronin, Fogarty, David Bruce

WINE(S): Chardonnay
COUNTRY: USA
REGION: California
SUB-REGION: Sonoma

COMPONENT(S): Low to moderate acidity, dry
FLAVOR(S): Green apple, vanilla, oak, butter, butterscotch, papaya, pineapple, mango, coconut, toast, lemon
TEXTURE(S): Medium to full bodied

VINTAGE CONSIDERATIONS:
1982 • Fairly light; balanced
1983 • Thin; diluted
1984 • Very rich; alcoholic
1985 • Very rich; balanced
1986 • Rich; balanced
1987 • Moderately rich; balanced

PRODUCER STYLES:
Lighter • St. Francis, Glen Ellen-Proprietor Reserve, Sonoma-Cutrer-Russian River Ranches, Dehlinger, Simi, Mark West, Pedroncelli, Souverain, Hacienda, Belvedere, Balverne, Dry Creek, Domaine Laurier, Geyser Peak, Rodney Strong-Sonoma, Iron Horse
Fuller • Sonoma-Cutrer-les Pierres and Cutrer, Simi-Reserve, Hacienda, Matanzas Creek, DeLoach, Kistler, Clos du Bois, Chateau

St. Jean, la Crema Vinera, Chateau Montelena-Alexander Valley, Landmark, Stemmler

---

WINE(S): Chardonnay
COUNTRY: USA
REGION: California
SUB-REGION: South Central Coast

COMPONENT(S): Low to moderate acidity, dry
FLAVOR(S): Green apple, vanilla, oak, butter, butterscotch, papaya, pineapple, mango, coconut, toast, lemon
TEXTURE(S): Medium to full bodied

VINTAGE CONSIDERATIONS:
1982 • Rich; alcoholic
1983 • Moderately rich; balanced
1984 • Rich; forward
1985 • Rich; balanced
1986 • Rich; balanced
1987 • Moderately rich; balanced

PRODUCER STYLES:
Lighter • Creston Manor, Gainey, Au Bon Climat, Zaca Mesa, Firestone, Corbett Canyon, Vega
Fuller • Edna Valley, Sanford, Chamisal, Leeward Winery

WINE(S): Chardonnay
COUNTRY: USA
REGION: New York
SUB-REGION: Long Island

COMPONENT(S): Moderate acidity, dry
FLAVOR(S): Green apple, lemon, vanilla, oak
TEXTURE(S): Light to medium bodied

VINTAGE CONSIDERATIONS:
1985 • Moderately rich; balanced

1986 • Fairly light; acidic
1987 • Rich; balanced

PRODUCER STYLES:
Lighter • Bedell, le Reve, Peconic Bay, Pindar, Bridgehampton
Fuller • Hargrave, Lenz, Palmer

WINE(S): Chardonnay
COUNTRY: USA
REGION: New York
SUB-REGION: Finger Lakes

COMPONENT(S): Moderate acidity, dry
FLAVOR(S): Green apple, lemon, vanilla, oak
TEXTURE(S): Light to medium bodied

VINTAGE CONSIDERATIONS:
1985 • Moderately rich; balanced
1986 • Fairly light; acidic
1987 • Modeately rich; balanced

PRODUCER STYLES:
Lighter • Finger Lakes Wine Cellars, Glenora, Heron Hill, Vinifera Wine Cellars, Woodbury (Lake Erie), Casa Larga, Great Western
Fuller • Knapp, Wagner, Plane's Cayuga

WINE(S): Chardonnay
COUNTRY: USA
REGION: Oregon
SUB-REGION: Eugene–Salem

COMPONENT(S): Moderate to high acidity, dry
FLAVOR(S): Butter, butterscotch, vanilla, toast, oak, spice, green apple, pineapple
TEXTURE(S): Light to medium bodied

VINTAGE CONSIDERATIONS:
1982 • Moderately rich; balanced
1983 • Very rich; balanced
1984 • Fairly light; acidic
1985 • Rich; balanced
1986 • Rich; balanced

PRODUCER STYLES:
Lighter • Alpine, Henry Estate, Hinman, Valley View
Fuller • None

WINE(S): Chardonnay
COUNTRY: USA
REGION: Oregon
SUB-REGION: Yamhill–Tualatin

COMPONENT(S): Moderate to high acidity, dry
FLAVOR(S): Butter, butterscotch, vanilla, toast, oak, spice, green apple, pineapple
TEXTURE(S): Light to medium bodied

VINTAGE CONSIDERATIONS:
1982 • Moderately rich; balanced
1983 • Very rich; balanced
1984 • Fairly light; acidic
1985 • Rich; balanced
1986 • Fairly light
1987 • Rich; balanced

PRODUCER STYLES:
Lighter • Elk Cove, Oak Knoll, Ponzi, Shafer, Forgeron, Knudsen Erath, Veritas
Fuller • Peter F. Adams, Adelsheim, Amity, Eyrie, Tualatin

WINE(S): Chardonnay
COUNTRY: USA
REGION: Washington
SUB-REGION: Columbia Valley

COMPONENT(S): Moderate to high acidity, dry
FLAVOR(S): Green apple, vanilla, oak, butter, toast, lemon
TEXTURE(S): Light to medium bodied

VINTAGE CONSIDERATIONS:
1983 • Rich; balanced
1984 • Fairly light
1985 • Moderately rich; balanced
1986 • Fairly light; balanced
1987 • Very rich; fruity

PRODUCER STYLES:
Lighter • Columbia, Hogue, Ste. Michelle, Covey Run
Fuller • Arbor Crest, Kiona, Woodward Canyon

WINE(S): Chardonnay and Chardonnay blends
COUNTRY: Italy
REGION: Friuli-Venezia Giulia
SUB-REGION: N/A

COMPONENT(S): Moderate acidity, dry
FLAVOR(S): Green apple, citrus fruit, honeysuckle, toasted hazelnut, butter, herbs
TEXTURE(S): Light to medium bodied

VINTAGE CONSIDERATIONS:
1986 • Very rich; balanced
1987 • Moderately rich; balanced

PRODUCER STYLES:
Lighter • Plozner, Pighin, Leoni, Villanova
Fuller • EnoFriulia, Abbazia di Rosazzo, Gravner, Collavini, Ronco del Gnemiz, Jermann-Vintage Tunina, Borgo Conventi

---

WINE(S): Chassagne-Montrachet and Puligny-Montrachet (White)
COUNTRY: France

REGION: Burgundy

SUB-REGION: Côte de Beaune

COMPONENT(s): Moderate acidity, dry

FLAVOR(s): Green apple, lemon, toasted oat, butter, vanilla, oak, roast nut, earth, truffle, smoke, spice

TEXTURE(s): Medium to full bodied

VINTAGE CONSIDERATIONS:

1983 • Very rich; alcoholic
1984 • Fairly light; balanced
1985 • Rich; low in acid
1986 • Moderately rich; balanced
1987 • Fairly light; balanced

PRODUCER STYLES:

Lighter • Roux, Gagnard-Delagrange, P. Bouzereau, Chanson, Drouhin, Patriarche, Jadot, Latour, Bouchard Père et Fils, Henri de Villamont,

Fuller • Sauzet, F. Colin, M. Colin, M. Colin-Deleger, G. Deleger, B. Morey, J.M. Morey, P. Morey, Ramonet, Bachelet, Leroy, Niellon, O. Leflaive, Marquis de la Guiche, Château de la Maltroye

WINE(s): Châteauneuf-du-Pape; Gigondas (Red)

COUNTRY: France

REGION: Rhône

SUB-REGION: Southern Rhône

COMPONENT(s): Low to moderate acidity, dry

FLAVOR(s): Blackberry, raspberry, plum, smoke, coffee, oak, black pepper, roast nut, licorice, leather, fennel

TEXTURE(s): Medium to full bodied

VINTAGE CONSIDERATIONS:

1980 • Fairly light; balanced
1981 • Moderately rich; balanced
1982 • Rich; alcoholic
1983 • Very rich; balanced
1984 • Moderately rich; balanced
1985 • Rich; low in acid
1986 • Moderately rich; balanced
1987 • Fairly light; balanced

PRODUCER STYLES:

Lighter • Caves des Vignerons, Chapoutier, Château du Trignon, Clos de l'Oratoire, Delas, Jaboulet, Longue-Toque, Mont-Redon, Père Caboche, Père Anselme

Fuller • Beaucastel, Bosquet des Papes, les Cailloux, Clos des Cazeaux, Clos des Papes, les Clefs d'Or, Cayron, Fortia, les Goubert, Grand Tinel, Guigal, la Nerthe, les Pallières, Chateau Raspail, Rayas, Saint Gayan, Vieux Télégraphe

WINE(s): Chianti

COUNTRY: Italy

REGION: Tuscany

SUB-REGION: Classico, Rufina, Colli Fiorentini, Colli Senesi

COMPONENT(s): Moderate to high acidity, dry

FLAVOR(s): Black cherry, tobacco, spice, earth, oak, cedar, smoke, orange peel (riservas have less fruit and more complexity than nonriservas)

TEXTURE(s): Light to medium bodied

VINTAGE CONSIDERATIONS:

1982 • Very rich; balanced
1983 • Rich; alcoholic
1984 • Thin; acidic
1985 • Very rich; balanced
1986 • Moderately rich; fruity
1987 • Thin; acidic

PRODUCER STYLES:

Lighter • Antinori, Nozzole,

Ruffino-Riserva Ducale, Castello di Nipozzano, Berardenga, Castello di Gabbiano, Brolio, la Querce, Villa Banfi

Fuller • Capannelle, Monsanto, Fontodi, Castello dei Rampolla, Badia a Coltibuono, Isole e Olena, Castello di Volpaia, Villa Cafaggio, Selvapiana, Castellare di Castellina, Fossi, il Poggiolino, Rocca delle Macie, Savignola Paolina

---

WINE(S): Chinon and Bourgueil
COUNTRY: France
REGION: Loire
SUB-REGION: Touraine

COMPONENT(S): Moderate acidity, dry
FLAVOR(S): Tobacco, licorice, prune, red cherry, violet, earth, oak
TEXTURE(S): Medium bodied

VINTAGE CONSIDERATIONS:
1983 • Rich; alcoholic
1984 • Fairly light; acidic
1985 • Rich; balanced
1986 • Moderately rich; balanced
1987 • Fairly light; balanced

PRODUCER STYLES:
Lighter • Jean-Marie Dozon, Calsot-Galbrun
Fuller • Couly-Dutheil, Charles Joguet, Olga Raffault, Robert Caslot

---

WINE(S): Condrieu; Château Grillet
COUNTRY: France
REGION: Rhône
SUB-REGION: Northern Rhône

COMPONENT(S): Low to moderate acidity, dry
FLAVOR(S): Apricot, honeysuckle, pear, peach, melon, almond, spice
TEXTURE(S): Medium bodied

VINTAGE CONSIDERATIONS:
1985 • Rich; low in acid
1986 • Fairly light; balanced
1987 • Fairly light; balanced

PRODUCER STYLES:
Lighter • Cuilleron, Delas, Jaboulet, Vernay
Fuller • Château Grillet, Guigal, Pinchon, Château du Rozay

WINE(S): Cortese di Gavi
COUNTRY: Italy
REGION: Piedmont
SUB-REGION: Gavi

COMPONENT(S): Moderate acidity, dry
FLAVOR(S): Lemon, hay, slate, green apple, earth
TEXTURE(S): Light to medium bodied

VINTAGE CONSIDERATIONS:
1982 • Rich; balanced
1983 • Rich; balanced
1984 • Thin; acidic
1985 • Very rich; balanced
1986 • Moderately rich; balanced
1987 • Rich; fruity

PRODUCER STYLES:
Lighter • Pio Cesare, Granduca, Fontanafredda, Principessa, Banfi
Fuller • Broglia, Contratto, La Guistiniana, Villa Sparina, la Scolca, la Raia, Tenuta San Pietro

---

WINE(S): Coteaux du Layon, Bonnezeaux, Quarts de Chaume
COUNTRY: France

REGION: Loire
SUB-REGION: Anjou-Saumur

COMPONENT(S): Moderate acidity, semi-sweet to sweet
FLAVOR(S): Melon, green apple, pear, quince, honey, acacia, fig
TEXTURE(S): Medium to full bodied, fairly soft

VINTAGE CONSIDERATIONS:
1983 • Rich; balanced
1984 • Fairly light; acidic
1985 • Rich; alcoholic
1986 • Moderately rich; balanced
1987 • Moderately rich; balanced

PRODUCER STYLES:
Lighter • Château de Fesles, Logis du Prieuré, Château du Brieul
Fuller • Jacques Beaujeau, Château de Plaisance, Château de Fesles, Château de l'Echarderie, Domaine de la Croix de la Mission

WINE(S): Côtes de Provence; Coteaux d'Aix-en-Provence (Red)
COUNTRY: France
REGION: Provence
SUB-REGION: N/A

COMPONENT(S): Low to moderate acidity, dry
FLAVOR(S): Blackberry, raspberry, plum, smoke, truffles, oak, black pepper, leather, nutmeg, herbs
TEXTURE(S): Medium to full bodied

VINTAGE CONSIDERATIONS:
1982 • Very rich; balanced
1983 • Very rich; balanced
1984 • Fairly light; balanced
1985 • Rich; low in acid
1986 • Fairly light; balanced
1987 • Fairly light; balanced

PRODUCER STYLES:
Lighter • Château Bas, Château de Beaulieu, Commanderie de la Bargemone, l'Estandon, Mas de la Dame, Gavoty
Fuller • Commanderie de Peyrassol, Ott, Trevallon, Château Vignelaure

WINE(S): Côtes du Rhône; Côtes du Rhône-Villages (Red)
COUNTRY: France
REGION: Rhône
SUB-REGION: Southern Rhône

COMPONENT(S): Low to moderate acidity, dry
FLAVOR(S): Blackberry, raspberry, plum, smoke, coffee, oak, black pepper, roast nut, licorice
TEXTURE(S): Medium to full bodied

VINTAGE CONSIDERATIONS:
1980 • Fairly light; balanced
1981 • Moderately rich; balanced
1982 • Rich; alcoholic
1983 • Very rich; balanced
1984 • Moderately rich; balanced
1985 • Rich; low in acid
1986 • Moderately rich; balanced
1987 • Fairly light; balanced

PRODUCER STYLES:
Lighter • All Côtes du Rhône-Village Coopérative Wines, Château d'Aigueville, Château de Ruth, Delas, Jaboulet, la Vieille Ferme, Mont Redon
Fuller • Brusset, Pelaquie, Charavin, Château du Trignon, Caves St. Pierre, Clos des Cazeaux, Château de Fonsalette, Cru de Coudoulet, Château de Montmirail, Guigal, Ste. Anne, St. Estève, St. Gayan, St. Roch

WINE(S): Côte Rôtie
COUNTRY: France

REGION: Rhône
SUB-REGION: Northern Rhône

COMPONENT(S): Low to moderate acidity, dry
FLAVOR(S): Blackberry, raspberry, plum, game, smoke, coffee, oak, black pepper, almond, tar
TEXTURE(S): Medium to full bodied

VINTAGE CONSIDERATIONS:
1980 • Moderately rich; balanced
1981 • Fairly light; acidic
1982 • Rich; low in acid
1983 • Very rich; balanced
1984 • Moderately rich; balanced
1985 • Rich; low in acid
1986 • Fairly light; balanced
1987 • Moderately rich; balanced

PRODUCER STYLES:
Lighter • Chapoutier, Gerin, Jaboulet
Fuller • Barge, Dervieux-Thaize, Gentaz-Dervieux, Guigal, Jasmin, Rostaing

~~~~~~~~~~~~~~~~~~~~~~~~~~~~~~~~~~~

WINE(S): Crémant d'Alsace
COUNTRY: France
REGION: Alsace
SUB-REGION: N/A

COMPONENT(S): Moderate acidity, dry
FLAVOR(S): Green grape, green apple, honeysuckle, lemon, yeast

TEXTURE(S): Light to medium bodied, effervescent

VINTAGE CONSIDERATIONS:
Buy the youngest vintage available, or the freshest nonvintage blend

PRODUCER STYLES:
Lighter • Aussay, Laugel
Fuller • Muré, Willm, Kuentz-Bas, Dopff "au Moulin"

~~~~~~~~~~~~~~~~~~~~~~~~~~~~~~~~~~~

WINE(S): Dão

COUNTRY: Portugal
REGION: Upper Beira
SUB-REGION: N/A

COMPONENT(S): Moderate acidity, dry
FLAVOR(S): Blackberry, cedar, tobacco, smoke, leather, earth, spice
TEXTURE(S): Medium to full bodied

VINTAGE CONSIDERATIONS:
1983 • Rich; balanced
1984 • Fairly light; balanced
1985 • Very rich; balanced
1986 • Fairly light; acidic
1987 • Fairly light; acidic

PRODUCER STYLES:
Lighter • Rittos Irmãos, Caves Velhas, Grão Vasco, Vinícola do Vale do Dão
Fuller • Caves Aliança, Conde de Santar

~~~~~~~~~~~~~~~~~~~~~~~~~~~~~~~~~~~

WINE(S): Dolcetto d'Alba
COUNTRY: Italy
REGION: Piedmont
SUB-REGION: Alba

COMPONENT(S): Moderate acidity, dry
FLAVOR(S): Black cherry, plum, berry-fruit, smoke, oak, earth
TEXTURE(S): Light to medium bodied

VINTAGE CONSIDERATIONS:
1982 • Rich; balanced
1983 • Fairly light; acidic
1984 • Thin; acidic
1985 • Very rich; balanced
1986 • Rich; balanced
1987 • Rich; balanced

PRODUCER STYLES:
Lighter • Valentino, L. Sandrone, Aldo Conterno, Renato Ratti
Fuller • Castello di Neive, Luigi

Einaudi, Bruno Ceretto, Gianfranco Bovio, Giacomo
Conterno, Alfredo Prunotto, Vietti

WINE(S): Fino and Manzanilla
Sherry
COUNTRY: Spain
REGION: Andalusia
SUB-REGION: Jerez

COMPONENT(S): Moderate acidity,
dry
FLAVOR(S): Roast nuts, wheat biscuit, fresh dough, minerals,
straw
TEXTURE(S): Medium bodied, alcoholic

VINTAGE CONSIDERATIONS: Blended
from many different vintages by
the solera system (casks triangularly stacked and connected)

PRODUCER STYLES:
Lighter • Osborne, Croft, Gonza-
lez Byass, Duff Gordon,
Williams and Humbert
Fuller • Harvey and Sons, Sande-
man, Domecq, Lustau, Díez-
Merito

WINE(S): Fixin
COUNTRY: France
REGION: Burgundy
SUB-REGION: Côte de Nuits

COMPONENT(S): Moderate acidity,
dry
FLAVOR(S): Cherry, raspberry,
blackberry, plum, smoke, violets,
game, earth, oak, spice, burning
leaves, licorice
TEXTURE(S): Medium bodied

VINTAGE CONSIDERATIONS:
1980 • Moderately rich; balanced

1981 • Fairly light; acidic
1982 • Fairly light; balanced
1983 • Very rich; alcoholic
1984 • Fairly light; acidic
1985 • Rich; balanced
1986 • Moderately rich; balanced
1987 • Fairly light; balanced

PRODUCER STYLES:
Lighter • Derey
Fuller • Berthoud, Clair, Gelin-
Molin, P. Gelin, Joliet

WINE(S): Galestro, Vernaccia di San
Gimignano
COUNTRY: Italy
REGION: Tuscany
SUB-REGION: N/A

COMPONENT(S): Moderate acidity,
dry
FLAVOR(S): Lemon, green apple,
grapefruit, pine, straw
TEXTURE(S): Light to medium bodied

VINTAGE CONSIDERATIONS:
1986 • Rich; balanced
1987 • Fairly light; acidic

PRODUCER STYLES:
Lighter • Antinori, Quercia, Pan-
cole, Fonti, Falchini,
Frescobaldi, Ruffino, Rocca delle
Macie
Fuller • Teruzzi and Puthod,
Strozzi, Pietraserena, Ponte a
Rondolino

WINE(S): Gattinara, Spanna,
Ghemme
COUNTRY: Italy
REGION: Piedmont
SUB-REGION: N/A

COMPONENT(S): Moderate acidity,
dry

FLAVOR(S): Tar, oak, plum, earth, smoke, leather, tobacco, black cherry, blackberry, spice, orange peel

TEXTURE(S): Medium to full bodied

VINTAGE CONSIDERATIONS:
1979 • Rich; balanced
1980 • Moderately rich; balanced
1981 • Fairly light; acidic
1982 • Rich; balanced
1983 • Moderately rich; balanced
1984 • Thin; diluted
1985 • Very rich; balanced
1986 • Rich; balanced

PRODUCER STYLES:
Lighter • Agostino Brugo, Dessilani
Fuller • Guido Barra, Vallana, le Colline, Luigi Ferrando, Luigi Nervi

---

WINE(S): Gevrey-Chambertin
COUNTRY: France
REGION: Burgundy
SUB-REGION: Côte de Nuits

COMPONENT(S): Moderate acidity, dry
FLAVOR(S): Cherry, raspberry, blackberry, plum, smoke, violets, game, earth, oak, spice, burning leaves, licorice
TEXTURE(S): Medium bodied

VINTAGE CONSIDERATIONS:
1980 • Moderately rich; balanced
1981 • Fairly light; acidic
1982 • Fairly light; balanced
1983 • Very rich; alcoholic
1984 • Fairly light; acidic
1985 • Rich; balanced
1986 • Moderately rich; balanced
1987 • Fairly light; balanced

PRODUCER STYLES:
Lighter • Dujac, Rossignol, Boillot, Drouhin, Drouhin-Laroze, Pernot-Fourrier, Taupenot, Trapet, Domaines des Varoilles
Fuller • Bachelet, Bourée, Clair-Daü (Jadot), Burguet, Damoy, Faiveley, Gelin-Molin, P. Leclerc, R. Leclerc, Leroy, G. Lignier, Marchand, Ponsot, Roumier, Rousseau, Roty

---

WINE(S): Gewürztraminer
COUNTRY: France
REGION: Alsace
SUB-REGION: N/A

COMPONENT(S): Moderate acidity, dry to sweet
FLAVOR(S): Lychee, rosewater, mango, coconut, papaya, grapefruit, honeysuckle, quince, pear, peach, apricot, allspice
TEXTURE(S): Medium bodied (Gewürztraminer), medium to full bodied (Vendange Tardive Gewürztraminer), full bodied (Selection des Grains Nobles Gewürztraminer)

VINTAGE CONSIDERATIONS:
1983 • Very rich; alcoholic
1984 • Fairly light; acidic
1985 • Rich; balanced
1986 • Fairly light; balanced
1987 • Fairly light; balanced

PRODUCER STYLES:
Lighter • Aussay, Hugel, Boeckel, Schmidt, Trimbach, Ostertag, Klug
Fuller • Josmeyer, Kuentz-Bas, Weinbach, Zind-Humbrecht, Schleret, Schaetzel, Sparr, G. Lorentz, Beyer, Schlumberger, Sipp, Dopff "au Moulin," Klack, Klipfel, Gisselbrecht, Dopff and Irion, Willm

---

WINE(S): Graves (Red)

COUNTRY: France
REGION: Bordeaux
SUB-REGION: N/A

COMPONENT(S): Moderate acidity, dry
FLAVOR(S): Blackberry, cassis, black cherry, earth, smoke, tobacco, vanilla, oak, cedar, spice, minerals, herbs
TEXTURE(S): Medium to full bodied

VINTAGE CONSIDERATIONS:
1980 • Fairly light; balanced
1981 • Moderately rich; balanced
1982 • Very rich; balanced
1983 • Rich; balanced
1984 • Fairly light; tannic
1985 • Rich; balanced
1986 • Very rich; tannic
1987 • Fairly light; fruity

PRODUCER STYLES:
Lighter • Carbonnieux, Haut-Bailly, la Garde, Malartic-Lagravière, Olivier, Pape-Clément, Smith-Haut-Lafitte
Fuller • Bouscaut, Domaine de Chevalier, la Mission-Haut-Brion, Laville-Haut-Brion, Haut-Brion, la Louvière, la Tour-Haut-Brion, la Tour-Martillac, Rahoul, de Fieuzal

WINE(S): Graves (White)
COUNTRY: France
REGION: Bordeaux
SUB-REGION: N/A

COMPONENT(S): Moderate acidity, dry
FLAVOR(S): Green apple, lemon, grass, green herbs, gooseberry, oak, spice, lanolin, vanilla
TEXTURE(S): Light to medium bodied

VINTAGE CONSIDERATIONS:
1983 • Very rich; balanced

1984 • Moderately rich; balanced
1985 • Rich; low in acid
1986 • Moderately rich; balanced
1987 • Moderately rich; balanced

PRODUCER STYLES:
Lighter • Carbonnieux, la Garde, Malartic-Lagravière, Olivier, Smith-Haut-Lafitte
Fuller • Bouscaut, Laville-Haut-Brion, Haut-Brion Blanc, Domaine de Chevalier, la Louvière, la Tour-Martillac, Rahoul, de Fieuzal

WINE(S): Hermitage; Crozes-Hermitage; Cornas; St. Joseph (Red)
COUNTRY: France
REGION: Rhône
SUB-REGION: Northern Rhône

COMPONENT(S): Low to moderate acidity, dry
FLAVOR(S): Blackberry, raspberry, plum, game, smoke, coffee, oak, black pepper, almond, tar
TEXTURE(S): Medium to full bodied

VINTAGE CONSIDERATIONS:
1980 • Moderately rich; balanced
1981 • Fairly light; acidic
1982 • Rich; low in acid
1983 • Very rich; balanced
1984 • Moderately rich; balanced
1985 • Rich; low in acid
1986 • Fairly light; balanced
1987 • Fairly light; balanced

PRODUCER STYLES:
Lighter • Caves de Clairmont, Coopérative de Tain l'Hermitage, Collonge, Coursodon, Delas, Grippat
Fuller • de Barjac, Chapoutier, Chave, Delas, Clape, Fayolle, Gripa, Guigal, Jaboulet, Juge, Michel, Sorrel, Tardy and Ange, Voge

WINE(S): Hermitage; Crozes-Hermitage; St. Joseph (White)
COUNTRY: France
REGION: Rhône
SUB-REGION: Northern Rhône

COMPONENT(S): Low to moderate acidity, dry
FLAVOR(S): Apricot, honeysuckle, pear, peach, melon, almond, spice

TEXTURE(S): Medium bodied

VINTAGE CONSIDERATIONS:
1985 • Rich; low in acid
1986 • Fairly light; balanced
1987 • Fairly light; balanced

PRODUCER STYLES:
Lighter • Caves de Clairmont, Coopérative de Tain l'Hermitage, Coursodon, Delas, Jaboulet
Fuller • Chapoutier, Chave, Fayolle, Gripa, Grippat, Guigal, Sorrel, Tardy and Ange

WINE(S): Inferno, Sassella, Grumello, Valgella
COUNTRY: Italy
REGION: Lombardy
SUB-REGION: Valtellina

COMPONENT(S): Moderate acidity, dry
FLAVOR(S): Tar, violet, black truffle, red cherry, oak, smoke
TEXTURE(S): Medium bodied

VINTAGE CONSIDERATIONS:
1982 • Very rich; balanced
1983 • Fairly light; fruity
1984 • Thin; diluted
1985 • Rich; balanced
1986 • Rich; balanced
1987 • Moderately rich; balanced

PRODUCER STYLES:
Lighter • Nera, Rainoldi, Giovanni Tona, Triacca, Polatti
Fuller • Nino Negri, Enologica Valtellinese, Franco Balgera

WINE(S): Mâcon-Villages; Pouilly-Fuissé; St.-Véran
COUNTRY: France
REGION: Burgundy
SUB-REGION: Mâconnais

COMPONENT(S): Moderate acidity, dry
FLAVOR(S): Green apple, lemon, toasted oat, butter, vanilla, spice
TEXTURE(S): Medium to full bodied

VINTAGE CONSIDERATIONS:
1983 • Very rich; alcoholic
1984 • Fairly light; acidic
1985 • Rich; balanced
1986 • Moderately rich; balanced
1987 • Fairly light; balanced

PRODUCER STYLES:
Lighter • Domaine Corsin, Producteurs de Prissé, Depagneux, Prosper-Maufoux, Mommessin, Duboeuf, Delaunay, R. Cordier, Vignerons d'Igé, L. Latour, L. Jadot, Château de Viré, Piat, Drouhin, J. Thevenet
Fuller • M. Vincent, J. J. Vincent, Plumet, Goyon, Dubois

WINE(S): Madeira
COUNTRY: Portugal
REGION: Madeira
SUB-REGION: N/A

COMPONENT(S): High acidity, off-dry to sweet
FLAVOR(S): Coffee, toffee, caramel, orange peel, almond, smoke, honey
TEXTURE(S): Medium bodied (Sercial and Verdelho) to full bodied (Bual and Malmsey), alcoholic

VINTAGE CONSIDERATIONS:
Though some Madeiras are vintage-dated, most consist of blended wines and are ready to consume when purchased

PRODUCER STYLES:
Lighter • Pereira d'Oliveira, Henriques and Henriques, Barbeito, Harvey's
Fuller • Leacock, Blandy Brothers, Cossart Gordon

~~~~~~~~~~~~~~~~~~~~~~~~~~~~~~

WINE(S): Margaux
COUNTRY: France
REGION: Bordeaux
SUB-REGION: Southern Médoc

COMPONENT(S): Moderate acidity, dry
FLAVOR(S): Blackberry, cassis, black cherry, earth, smoke, chocolate, tobacco, vanilla, oak, cedar, spice, leather, minerals, herbs
TEXTURE(S): Medium to full bodied

VINTAGE CONSIDERATIONS:
1980 • Fairly light; balanced
1981 • Moderately rich; balanced
1982 • Very rich; balanced
1983 • Rich; balanced
1984 • Fairly light; tannic
1985 • Rich; balanced
1986 • Very rich; tannic
1987 • Fairly light; fruity

PRODUCER STYLES:
Lighter • Boyd-Cantenac, Brane-Cantenac, d'Angludet, Dauzac, d'Issan, Kirwan, Lascombes, Prieuré-Lichine, Rausan-Ségla, Tayac
Fuller • Cantenac-Brown, Durfort-Vivens, du Tertre, Giscours, Malescot St. Exupéry, Margaux, Palmer, Rauzan-Gassies, Siran

~~~~~~~~~~~~~~~~~~~~~~~~~~~~~~

WINE(S): Médoc

COUNTRY: France
REGION: Bordeaux
SUB-REGION: Northern Médoc

COMPONENT(S): Moderate acidity, dry
FLAVOR(S): Blackberry, cassis, black cherry, earth, smoke, chocolate, tobacco, vanilla, oak, cedar, spice, leather, minerals, herbs
TEXTURE(S): Medium bodied

VINTAGE CONSIDERATIONS:
1980 • Fairly light; balanced
1981 • Moderately rich; balanced
1982 • Very rich; balanced
1983 • Rich; balanced
1984 • Fairly light; tannic
1985 • Rich; balanced
1986 • Very rich; tannic
1987 • Fairly light; fruity

PRODUCER STYLES:
Lighter • Greysac, la Cardonne, la Tour de By, les Ormes-Sorbet, Loudenne
Fuller • Patache d'Aux, Potensac

~~~~~~~~~~~~~~~~~~~~~~~~~~~~~~

WINE(S): Mercurey; Montagny; Rully-White
COUNTRY: France
REGION: Burgundy
SUB-REGION: Chalonnaise

COMPONENT(S): Moderate acidity, dry
FLAVOR(S): Green apple, lemon, toasted oat, butter, vanilla, oak, straw, earth, almond, spice
TEXTURE(S): Medium to full bodied

VINTAGE CONSIDERATIONS:
1983 • Very rich; alcoholic
1984 • Fairly light; acidic
1985 • Rich; balanced
1986 • Moderately rich; balanced
1987 • Fairly light; balanced

PRODUCER STYLES:
Lighter • Domaine Saier, de

Launay, Arnoux, Cave des Vignerons de Buxy, Goubard, L. Latour
Fuller • Suremain, Domaine de la Folie, Michel Juillot

WINE(S): Mercurey; Rully (Red)
COUNTRY: France
REGION: Burgundy
SUB-REGION: Côte de Beaune

COMPONENT(S): Moderate acidity, dry
FLAVOR(S): Cherry, raspberry, blackberry, plum, smoke, violets, game, earth, oak, spice, burning leaves, licorice
TEXTURE(S): Light to medium bodied

VINTAGE CONSIDERATIONS:
1980 • Moderately rich; balanced
1981 • Fairly light; balanced
1982 • Fairly light; balanced
1983 • Very rich; alcoholic
1984 • Fairly light; acidic
1985 • Rich; balanced
1986 • Fairly light; acidic
1987 • Fairly light; balanced

PRODUCER STYLES:
Lighter • Suremain
Fuller • Bachelet, Domaine de la Folie, Faiveley, Juillot, de Launay, Leroy, Saier

---

WINE(S): Merlot
COUNTRY: USA
REGION: California
SUB-REGION: Napa

COMPONENT(S): Low to moderate acidity, dry
FLAVOR(S): Cassis, black cherry, plum, black olive, raspberry, blackberry, herbs, chocolate, cedar, vanilla, toast, smoke, coffee
TEXTURE(S): Medium to full bodied

VINTAGE CONSIDERATIONS:
1982 • Fairly light; uneven
1983 • Fairly light; uneven
1984 • Moderately rich; balanced
1985 • Very rich; balanced
1986 • Rich; balanced

PRODUCER STYLES:
Lighter • Rutherford Hill, Carneros Creek, Round Hill, Rombauer, Shafer, Sterling, Duckhorn, Inglenook, Clos du Val, Franciscan, Lakespring, Martini and Martini-Reserve, Stratford
Fuller • Duckhorn-Three Palms Vineyard, Chateau Chevre, Newton, Pine Ridge, Whitehall Lane, Flora Springs, Inglenook-Reserve Cask, Jaeger-Inglewood, Franciscan, Lakespring

---

WINE(S): Merlot
COUNTRY: USA
REGION: California
SUB-REGION: Sonoma

COMPONENT(S): Low to moderate acidity, dry
FLAVOR(S): Cassis, black cherry, plum, black olive, raspberry, blackberry, herbs, chocolate, cedar, vanilla, toast, smoke, coffee
TEXTURE(S): Medium to full bodied

VINTAGE CONSIDERATIONS:
1982 • Moderately rich; balanced
1983 • Fairly light; fruity
1984 • Moderately rich; balanced
1985 • Very rich; balanced
1986 • Rich; balanced

PRODUCER STYLES:
Lighter • Buena Vista-Private Reserve, Laurel Glen, Clos du Bois
Fuller • Gundlach Bundschu-

Rhinefarm, Matanzas Creek, St. Francis, Ravenswood, Alexander Valley, Dry Creek-Reserve

Fuller • Ste. Michelle, Covey Run, Arbor Crest, Haviland, Hogue

---

WINE(S): Merlot
COUNTRY: USA
REGION: New York
SUB-REGION: Long Island

COMPONENT(S): Moderate acidity, dry
FLAVOR(S): Plum, blackberry, black cherry, tar, beetroot, smoke
TEXTURE(S): Light to medium bodied

VINTAGE CONSIDERATIONS:
1985 • Moderately rich; balanced
1986 • Fairly light; acidic
1987 • Rich; balanced

PRODUCER STYLES:
Lighter • le Reve, Peconic Bay, Pindar
Fuller • Bedell, Bridgehampton, Hargrave, Lenz, Palmer

WINE(S): Merlot
COUNTRY: USA
REGION: Washington
SUB-REGION: Columbia Valley

COMPONENT(S): Moderate acidity, dry
FLAVOR(S): Black cherry, plum, black olive, beetroot, herbs, oak
TEXTURE(S): Light to medium bodied

VINTAGE CONSIDERATIONS:
1983 • Very rich; balanced
1984 • Rich; tannic
1985 • Rich; tannic
1986 • Moderately rich; fruity

PRODUCER STYLES:
Lighter • Columbía

WINE(S): Meursault (White)
COUNTRY: France
REGION: Burgundy
SUB-REGION: Côte de Beaune

COMPONENT(S): Moderate acidity, dry
FLAVOR(S): Green apple, lemon, toasted oat, butter, vanilla, oak, roast nut, earth, truffle, smoke, spice
TEXTURE(S): Medium to full bodied

VINTAGE CONSIDERATIONS:
1983 • Very rich; alcoholic
1984 • Fairly light; balanced
1985 • Rich; low in acid
1986 • Moderately rich; balanced
1987 • Fairly light; balanced

PRODUCER STYLES:
Lighter • Rougeot, H. Boillot, Monnier, Coche-Debord, Drouhin, Maufoux, Jadot, Latour, Bouchard Père et Fils, H. Bouzereau-Gruère, P. Bouzereau, Chanson, H. Germain
Fuller • Ampeau, Grivault, Château de Meursault, Michelot-Buisson, G. Michelot, Prieur-Brunet, Roulot, J. Matrot, Coche-Dury, Delagrange, Comtes Lafond, Duc de Magenta, P. Morey, Jobard, Caillot

---

WINE(S): Montepulciano d'Abruzzo
COUNTRY: Italy
REGION: Abruzzi
SUB-REGION: N/A

COMPONENT(S): Moderate acidity, dry

FLAVOR(S): Black cherry, plum, leather, spice, violet, oak
TEXTURE(S): Medium bodied

VINTAGE CONSIDERATIONS:
1983 • Moderately rich; balanced
1984 • Thin; acidic
1985 • Rich; balanced
1986 • Moderately rich; balanced

PRODUCER STYLES:
Lighter • Cantina Sociale di Tollo, Tenuta Sant'Agnese
Fuller • Lucio di Giulio, Illuminati, Valentini, Emilio Pepe

WINE(S): Morey St. Denis
COUNTRY: France
REGION: Burgundy
SUB-REGION: Côte de Nuits

COMPONENT(S): Moderate acidity, dry
FLAVOR(S): Black cherry, raspberry, blackberry, plum, smoke, violets, game, earth, oak, spice, burning leaves, licorice
TEXTURE(S): Medium bodied

VINTAGE CONSIDERATIONS:
1980 • Moderately rich; balanced
1981 • Fairly light; acidic
1982 • Fairly light; balanced
1983 • Very rich; alcoholic
1984 • Fairly light; acidic
1985 • Rich; balanced
1986 • Moderately rich; balanced
1987 • Fairly light; balanced

PRODUCER STYLES:
Lighter • Bouchard Père et Fils, Dujac, Ropiteau, Pernot-Fourrier, Serveau, Taupenot
Fuller • P. Amiot, Clair-Daü, G. Lignier, H. Lignier, Mommessin-Clos de Tart, Ponsot, Roumier, Rousseau

WINE(S): Moscato d'Asti

COUNTRY: Italy
REGION: Piedmont
SUB-REGION: Asti

COMPONENT(S): Moderate acidity, off-dry to sweet
FLAVOR(S): Peach, apricot, melon, nectarine, pear
TEXTURE(S): Medium bodied, slightly sparkling to effervescent

VINTAGE CONSIDERATIONS: Drink the youngest available vintage

PRODUCER STYLES:
Lighter • Ceretto-Santo Stefano, Braida, Bera, Fontanafredda
Fuller • Dogliotti, Bruno Giacosa, Rivetti, Vietti, Saracco

WINE(S): Moulis; Listrac; Haut-Médoc
COUNTRY: France
REGION: Bordeaux
SUB-REGION: N/A

COMPONENT(S): Moderate acidity, dry
FLAVOR(S): Blackberry, cassis, black cherry, earth, smoke, chocolate, tobacco, vanilla, oak, cedar, spice, leather, minerals, herbs
TEXTURE(S): Medium to full bodied

VINTAGE CONSIDERATIONS:
1980 • Fairly light; balanced
1981 • Moderately rich; balanced
1982 • Very rich; balanced
1983 • Rich; balanced
1984 • Fairly light; tannic
1985 • Rich; balanced
1986 • Very rich; tannic
1987 • Fairly light; fruity

PRODUCER STYLES:
Lighter • Camensac, Cantemerle, Citran, Clarke, Fourcas-Dupré, Lamarque, Larose-Trintaudon, la Tour-Carnet, Maucaillou

Fuller • Chasse-Spleen, Fourcas Hosten, la Lagune, Lanessan, Poujeaux, Sociando-Mallet, Verdignan

---

WINE(S): Müller-Thurgau
COUNTRY: Germany
REGION: Franconia
SUB-REGION: N/A

COMPONENT(S): Moderate acidity, dry
FLAVOR(S): Green apple, lemon, lime, green herb, asparagus
TEXTURE(S): Light bodied

VINTAGE CONSIDERATIONS:
1983 • Rich; balanced
1984 • Fairly light; acidic
1985 • Rich; balanced
1986 • Moderately rich; low in acid
1987 • Fairly light, acidic

PRODUCER STYLES:
Lighter • Bürgerspital, Juliusspital, H. Wirsching
Fuller • Fürst Castell, Staatl. Hofkeller, P. Schmitt, R. Schmitt

---

WINE(S): Muscadet
COUNTRY: France
REGION: Loire
SUB-REGION: Nantais

COMPONENT(S): High acidity, dry
FLAVOR(S): Green apple, lemon, minerals (chalk)
TEXTURE(S): Light to medium bodied

VINTAGE CONSIDERATIONS:
Drink the youngest available (within three years of the vintage)

PRODUCER STYLES:
Lighter • Fief de la Brie, Louis

Métaireau, Château de la Ragotière, Château de la Jannière, Château de l'Oiselinière, Domaine de la Fevrie
Fuller • Château de Chasseloir, Château la Noë, Château du Cléray, Marquis de Goulaine

---

WINE(S): Muscat
COUNTRY: France
REGION: Alsace
SUB-REGION: N/A

COMPONENT(S): Moderate acidity, dry
FLAVOR(S): Green grapes, musk, lemon
TEXTURE(S): Light to medium bodied

VINTAGE CONSIDERATIONS:
1983 • Very rich; alcoholic
1984 • Fairly light; acidic
1985 • Rich; balanced
1986 • Fairly light; balanced
1987 • Fairly light; balanced

PRODUCER STYLES:
Lighter • Schmidt
Fuller • Kuentz-Bas, Zind-Humbrecht, Schleret, Schaetzel, G. Lorentz, Beyer, Muré, Willm

---

WINE(S): Muscat de Beaumes-de-Venise
COUNTRY: France
REGION: Rhône
SUB-REGION: Southern Rhône

COMPONENT(S): Low to moderate acidity, sweet
FLAVOR(S): Apricot, honeysuckle, peach, melon, coconut, orange peel, almond, spice
TEXTURE(S): Medium bodied, alcoholic

VINTAGE CONSIDERATIONS:
Drink within two years of the
vintage
1987 • Moderately rich; balanced

PRODUCER STYLES:
Lighter • Coopérative des Vins et
Muscats Beaumes-de-Venise, Do-
maine de Coyeux, Domaine St.
Sauveur, Jaboulet
Fuller • Domaine Durban

~~~~~~~~~~~~~~~~~~~~~~~~~~~~~~

WINE(S): Navarra (Red)
COUNTRY: Spain
REGION: Navarra
SUB-REGION: N/A

COMPONENT(S): Moderate acidity,
dry
FLAVOR(S): Blackberry, black
cherry, plum, cedar, leather,
chocolate, tobacco, smoke, coffee, roast nuts

TEXTURE(S): Medium to full bodied

VINTAGE CONSIDERATIONS:
1981 • Rich; balanced
1982 • Rich; alcoholic
1983 • Moderately rich; balanced
1984 • Moderately rich; balanced
1985 • Rich; balanced
1986 • Fairly light; balanced

PRODUCER STYLES:
Lighter • las Campanas, Castillo
de Tiebas, Ochoa, Vinícola
Navarra
Fuller • Vina Magana, Señorío de
Sarria

~~~~~~~~~~~~~~~~~~~~~~~~~~~~~~

WINE(S): New Wave Reds (Sangio-
vese and Cabernet based)
COUNTRY: Italy
REGION: Tuscany
SUB-REGION: N/A

COMPONENT(S): Moderate acidity,
dry
FLAVOR(S): Black cherry, tobacco,
spice, earth, oak, cedar, smoke,
chocolate, herbs, coffee, orange
peel
TEXTURE(S): Medium to full bodied

VINTAGE CONSIDERATIONS:
1982 • Very rich; balanced
1983 • Rich; alcoholic
1984 • Thin; acidic
1985 • Very rich; balanced
1986 • Moderately rich; fruity
1987 • Thin; acidic

PRODUCER STYLES:
Lighter • Ania, Balifico, le Pergole
Torte, Ser Gioveto, Monte
Antico
Fuller • Coltassala, Fontalloro,
Grosso Senese, Palazzo Altesi,
Sangioveto, Cabreo il Borgo,
Grifi, i Sodi di San Niccolo,
Tignanello, Ghiaie della Furba,
Mormoreto, Sammarco, Ca'del
Pazzo, Cepparello, Flaccianello

~~~~~~~~~~~~~~~~~~~~~~~~~~~~~~

WINE(S): Nuits St. Georges
COUNTRY: France
REGION: Burgundy
SUB-REGION: Côte de Nuits

COMPONENT(S): Moderate acidity,
dry
FLAVOR(S): Cherry, raspberry,
blackberry, plum, smoke, violets,
game, earth, oak, spice, burning
leaves, licorice
TEXTURE(S): Medium bodied

VINTAGE CONSIDERATIONS:
1980 • Moderately rich; balanced
1981 • Fairly light; acidic
1982 • Fairly light; balanced
1983 • Very rich; alcoholic
1984 • Fairly light; acidic
1985 • Rich; balanced

1986 • Moderately rich; balanced
1987 • Fairly light; balanced

PRODUCER STYLES:
Lighter • F. Chauvenet, Drouhin
Fuller • Arnoux, J. Chauvenet, Chevillion, Faiveley, Grivot, Gouges, Jadot, H. Jayer, J. Jayer, Marchard du Gramont, Leroy, G. Mugneret, Moillard, Rion

〜〜〜〜〜〜〜〜〜〜〜〜〜〜

WINE(S): Pauillac
COUNTRY: France
REGION: Bordeaux
SUB-REGION: Northern Médoc

COMPONENT(S): Moderate acidity, dry
FLAVOR(S): Blackberry, cassis, black cherry, earth, smoke, chocolate, tobacco, vanilla, oak, cedar, spice, leather, minerals, herbs
TEXTURE(S): Medium to full bodied

VINTAGE CONSIDERATIONS:
1980 • Fairly light; balanced
1981 • Moderately rich; balanced
1982 • Very rich; balanced
1983 • Rich; balanced
1984 • Fairly light; tannic
1985 • Rich; balanced
1986 • Very rich; tannic
1987 • Fairly light; fruity

PRODUCER STYLES:
Lighter • Batailley, Croizet-Bages, Grand-Puy-Ducasse, Haut-Batailley, Lynch-Moussas, Moulin des Carruades, Mouton-Baronne-Philippe, Pichon Baron
Fuller • Duhart-Milon-Rothschild, Grand-Puy-Lacoste, Haut-Bages-Libéral, Latour, les Forts de Latour, Mouton-Rothschild, Lafite-Rothschild, Lynch-Bages, Pontet-Canet, Pichon Lalande, Clerc-Milon

〜〜〜〜〜〜〜〜〜〜〜〜〜〜

WINE(S): Penedès (Red)
COUNTRY: Spain
REGION: Catalonia
SUB-REGION: N/A

COMPONENT(S): Low to moderate acidity, dry
FLAVOR(S): Blackberry, black cherry, cassis, cedar, leather, spice, chocolate, tobacco, smoke, coffee, tar
TEXTURE(S): Medium to full bodied

VINTAGE CONSIDERATIONS:
1981 • Moderately rich; balanced
1982 • Rich; alcoholic
1983 • Moderately rich; balanced
1984 • Moderately rich; balanced
1985 • Very rich; balanced
1986 • Fairly light; balanced

PRODUCER STYLES:
Lighter • Gran Caus, René Barbier, Vina Laranda, Masía Bach
Fuller • Torres, Masía Vallformosa, Jean León

〜〜〜〜〜〜〜〜〜〜〜〜〜〜

WINE(S): Pinot Bianco
COUNTRY: Italy
REGION: Friuli-Venezia Giulia
SUB-REGION: N/A

COMPONENT(S): Moderate acidity, dry
FLAVOR(S): Green apple, apple blossom, honeysuckle, citrus fruit, hazelnut, almond toast
TEXTURE(S): Medium bodied
VINTAGE CONSIDERATIONS:
1986 • Very rich; balanced
1987 • Moderately rich; soft

PRODUCER STYLES:
Lighter • Pighin, Russolo, Marco Felluga, EnoFriulia
Fuller • Borgo Conventi, Buzzinelli, Humar, Villa Russiz, Formentini, Schiopetto, Doro

Princic, Livio Felluga, Vigne dal Leon

~~~~~~

WINE(S): Pinot Bianco
COUNTRY: Italy
REGION: Trentino-Alto Adige
SUB-REGION: N/A

COMPONENT(S): Moderate acidity, Dry
FLAVOR(S): Green apple, apple blossom, honeysuckle, citrus fruit, hazelnut, bread crust
TEXTURE(S): Medium bodied

VINTAGE CONSIDERATIONS:
1986 • Rich; balanced
1987 • Moderately rich; balanced

PRODUCER STYLES:
Lighter • Foradori, Maso Poli, San Michele, Villa Borino
Fuller • Zeni, Hofstätter, de Cles

~~~~~~

WINE(S): Pinot Blanc
COUNTRY: France
REGION: Alsace
SUB-REGION: N/A

COMPONENT(S): Moderate acidity, dry
FLAVOR(S): Lemon, green apple, honeysuckle, acacia, allspice

TEXTURE(S): Medium bodied

VINTAGE CONSIDERATIONS:
1983 • Very rich; alcoholic
1984 • Fairly light; acidic
1985 • Rich; balanced
1986 • Fairly light; balanced
1987 • Fairly light; balanced

PRODUCER STYLES:
Lighter • Aussay, Hugel, Boeckel, Schmidt, Trimbach, Ostertag, Klug
Fuller • Josmeyer, Kuentz-Bas,

Weinbach, Schleret, Schaetzel, Sparr, G. Lorentz, Beyer, Schlumberger, Sipp, Dopff "au Moulin," Klack, Klipfel, Gisselbrecht, Dopff and Irion, Willm

~~~~~~

WINE(S): Pinot Grigio
COUNTRY: Italy
REGION: Friuli-Venezia Giulia
SUB-REGION: N/A

COMPONENT(S): Moderate acidity, dry
FLAVOR(S): Green apple, lemon, pear, licorice, spice
TEXTURE(S): Light to medium bodied

VINTAGE CONSIDERATIONS:
1986 • Rich; balanced
1987 • Moderately rich; balanced

PRODUCER STYLES:
Lighter • Plozner, Pighin, Venica, Marco Felluga, EnoFriulia, Villanova
Fuller • Borgo Conventi, Buzzinelli, Jermann, Villa Russiz, Francesco Lui, Livio Felluga, Doro Princic, Furlan, Ronco del Gnemiz, Abbazia di Rosazzo, Farra

~~~~~~

WINE(S): Pinot Grigio (Rulander)
COUNTRY: Italy
REGION: Trentino-Alto Adige
SUB-REGION: N/A

COMPONENT(S): Moderate to high acidity, dry
FLAVOR(S): Green apple, citrus fruit, pear, grass, spice
TEXTURE(S): Light to medium bodied

VINTAGE CONSIDERATIONS:
1986 • Rich; balanced
1987 • Moderately rich; balanced

PRODUCER STYLES:
Lighter • Barone Fini, Càvit, La-
geder, Tiefenbrunner,
Kellereigenossenschaft-Terlan
Fuller • Boscaini, Hofstätter

~~~~~~~~~~~~~~~~~~~~~~~~~~~~~~~~

WINE(S): Pinot Gris (Tokay
d'Alsace)
COUNTRY: France
REGION: Alsace
SUB-REGION: N/A

COMPONENT(S): Moderate acidity,
dry to sweet
FLAVOR(S): Butterscotch, honey,
pear, smoke, vanilla, licorice
TEXTURE(S): Medium bodied (Pinot
Gris), medium to full bodied
(Vendange Tardive Pinot Gris),
full bodied (Selection des Grains
Nobles Pinot Gris)

VINTAGE CONSIDERATIONS:
1983 • Very rich; alcoholic
1984 • Fairly light; acidic
1985 • Rich; balanced
1986 • Fairly light; balanced
1987 • Fairly light; balanced

PRODUCER STYLES:
Lighter • Aussay, Hugel, Boeckel,
Schmidt, Trimbach, Ostertag,
Klug
Fuller • Josmeyer, Kuentz-Bas,
Weinbach, Zind-Humbrecht,
Schleret, Schaetzel, Sparr, G.
Lorentz, Beyer, Schlumberger,
Sipp, Dopff "au Moulin," Klack,
Klipfel, Gisselbrecht, Dopff and
Irion, Willm

~~~~~~~~~~~~~~~~~~~~~~~~~~~~~~~~

WINE(S): Pinot Noir
COUNTRY: USA
REGION: California
SUB-REGION: Napa

COMPONENT(S): Moderate acidity,
dry
FLAVOR(S): Black cherry, plum,
leather, berry-fruit, spice, smoke,
violet, cola
TEXTURE(S): Medium to full bodied

VINTAGE CONSIDERATIONS:
1982 • Fairly light; soft
1983 • Moderately rich; balanced
1984 • Very rich; alcoholic
1985 • Rich; balanced
1986 • Very rich, balanced

PRODUCER STYLES:
Lighter • Schug, Saintsbury,
Carneros Creek, Acacia-
Carneros, Tulocay, Martini
Fuller • Acacia—St. Clair and Ma-
donna, Robert Mondavi-Reserve,
Monticello, Beaulieu-Los
Carneros, Trefethen

~~~~~~~~~~~~~~~~~~~~~~~~~~~~~~~~

WINE(S): Pinot Noir
COUNTRY: USA
REGION: California
SUB-REGION: North Central Coast

COMPONENT(S): Moderate acidity,
dry
FLAVOR(S): Black cherry, plum,
leather, berry-fruit, spice, smoke,
violet, cola
TEXTURE(S): Medium to full bodied

VINTAGE CONSIDERATIONS:
1982 • Moderately rich; balanced
1983 • Moderately rich; soft
1984 • Rich; tannic
1985 • Very rich; balanced
1986 • Rich; balanced

PRODUCER STYLES:
Lighter • Calera-Santa Barbara,
David Bruce
Fuller • Calera-Jensen, Selleck and
Reed, Chalone, David Bruce-
Reserve, Mount Eden, Congress

Springs, Santa Cruz Mountain,
Martin Ray

WINE(S): Pinot Noir
COUNTRY: USA
REGION: California
SUB-REGION: Sonoma

COMPONENT(S): Moderate acidity,
dry
FLAVOR(S): Black cherry, plum,
leather, berry-fruit, spice, smoke,
violet, cola
TEXTURE(S): Medium to full bodied

VINTAGE CONSIDERATIONS:
1982 • Moderately rich; balanced
1983 • Fairly light; acidic
1984 • Moderately rich; balanced
1985 • Very rich; balanced
1986 • Very rich; balanced

PRODUCER STYLES:
Lighter • Stemmler, Iron Horse,
Sea Ridge, Davis Bynum, Do-
maine Laurier, Hacienda, la
Crema
Fuller • Hanzell, Belvedere, Kis-
tler, Richardson, Joseph Swan

WINE(S): Pinot Noir
COUNTRY: USA
REGION: California
SUB-REGION: South Central Coast

COMPONENT(S): Moderate acidity,
dry
FLAVOR(S): Black cherry, plum,
leather, berry-fruit, spice, smoke,
violet, cola, damp earth
TEXTURE(S): Medium to full bodied

VINTAGE CONSIDERATIONS:
1982 • Very rich; balanced
1983 • Fairly light; acidic
1984 • Rich; fruity

1985 • Rich; balanced
1986 • Rich; balanced

PRODUCER STYLES:
Lighter • Creston Manor, Santa
Lucia
Fuller • Edna Valley, Sanford
Winery, Firestone, Au Bon Cli-
mat

WINE(S): Pinot Noir
COUNTRY: USA
REGION: Oregon
SUB-REGION: Tualatin–Eugene

COMPONENT(S): Moderate to high
acidity, dry
FLAVOR(S): Black cherry, plum,
berry-fruit, leather, spice, smoke,
violet, earth, oak
TEXTURE(S): Light to medium bodied

VINTAGE CONSIDERATIONS:
1982 • Moderately rich; balanced
1983 • Very rich, alcoholic
1984 • Fairly light; balanced
1985 • Rich; balanced
1986 • Fairly light; balanced

PRODUCER STYLES:
Lighter • Alpine, Bethel Heights,
Chateau Benoit, Shafer, Henry
Estate, Hinman, Tualatin, Val-
ley View
Fuller • Ponzi Vineyards, Oak
Knoll

WINE(S): Pinot Noir
COUNTRY: USA
REGION: Oregon
SUB-REGION: Yamhill

COMPONENT(S): Moderate to high
acidity, dry
FLAVOR(S): Black cherry, plum,
berry-fruit, leather, spice, smoke,

violet, earth, oak
TEXTURE(S): Light to medium bodied

VINTAGE CONSIDERATIONS:
1982 • Moderately rich; balanced
1983 • Very rich, alcoholic
1984 • Fairly light; balanced
1985 • Rich; balanced
1986 • Fairly light; balanced

PRODUCER STYLES:
Lighter • Peter F. Adams, Adelsheim, Amity, Eyrie, Sokol Blosser, Knudsen Erath
Fuller • Elk Cove, Rex Hill, Yamhill Valley, Veritas

Fleur-Pétrus, la Gaffelière, l'Angélus, Monbousquet, Troplong-Mondot, Trottevieille
Fuller • Ausone, Beauséjour, Canon, Cap de Mourlin, Certan de May, Cheval Blanc, Clos l'Eglise, Figeac, la Croix, la Dominique, Lafleur, Larmande, l'Arrosée, Latour à Pomerol, la Tour-Figeac, le Gay, l'Evangile, Fonroque, Haut-Sarpe, Magdelaine, Nenin, Pavie, Pavie-Decesse, Petite-Village, Pétrus, Rouget, Soutard, Trotanoy, Vieux Château Certan, la Conseillante

---

WINE(S): Pomerol; St.-Emilion
COUNTRY: France
REGION: Bordeaux
SUB-REGION: Right Bank

COMPONENT(S): Moderate acidity, dry
FLAVOR(S): Blackberry, cassis, black cherry, plum, truffles, earth, smoke, tobacco, vanilla, oak, cedar, spice, minerals, herbs
TEXTURE(S): Medium to full bodied, silky

VINTAGE CONSIDERATIONS:
1980 • Light; acidic
1981 • Fairly light; balanced
1982 • Very rich; low in acid
1983 • Rich; balanced
1984 • Light, acidic
1985 • Very rich; balanced
1986 • Rich; balanced
1987 • Moderately rich; balanced

PRODUCER STYLES:
Lighter • Beauregard, Belair, Beau Séjour-Bécot, le Bon Pasteur, Canon-la-Gaffelière, Certan-Giraud, Clos des Jacobins, Clinet, Clos Fourtet, Clos René, de Sales, Fombrauge, Gazin, la

WINE(S): Pommard; Volnay
COUNTRY: France
REGION: Burgundy
SUB-REGION: Côte de Beaune

COMPONENT(S): Moderate acidity, dry
FLAVOR(S): Cherry, raspberry, blackberry, plum, smoke, violets, game, earth, oak, spice, burning leaves, licorice
TEXTURE(S): Medium bodied

VINTAGE CONSIDERATIONS:
1980 • Moderately rich; balanced
1981 • Fairly light; balanced
1982 • Fairly light; balanced
1983 • Very rich; alcoholic
1984 • Fairly light; acidic
1985 • Rich; balanced
1986 • Fairly light; acidic
1987 • Fairly light; balanced

PRODUCER STYLES:
Lighter • Ampeau, Boillot, Delagrange, Chandon de Briailles, Jadot, Drouhin, Guyon, Machard de Gramont, Marquis-d'Angerville, Parent
Fuller • Billard-Gonnet, Bitouzet-Prieur, Comte Armand, Comtes

Lafon, Bouchard Père et Fils, de
Montille, Gaunoux, Girardin,
Lafarge, L. Latour, Leroy, Re-
moissenet

~~~~~~~~~~~~~~~~~~~~~~~~~~~~~~~~~~~~

WINE(S): Ruby Port
COUNTRY: Portugal
REGION: Upper Douro
SUB-REGION: N/A

COMPONENT(S): Low to moderate
acidity, semi-sweet to sweet
FLAVOR(S): Plum, black cherry, raisin, spice
TEXTURE(S): Medium bodied, alcoholic

VINTAGE CONSIDERATIONS: Ruby
ports are not vintage-dated; drink
the freshest available

PRODUCER STYLES:
Lighter • Offley Forrester, Smith
Woodhouse, Niepoort, Croft,
Kopke, Sandeman, Churchill,
Delaforce, Ferreira
Fuller • Taylor, Ramos-Pinto,
Cockburn, Graham, Warre, Fon-
seca, Dow, Noval

~~~~~~~~~~~~~~~~~~~~~~~~~~~~~~~~~~~~

WINE(S): Tawny Port
COUNTRY: Portugal
REGION: Upper Douro
SUB-REGION: N/A

COMPONENT(S): Low to moderate
acidity, semi-sweet to sweet
FLAVOR(S): Raisin, black cherry,
cedar, spice, tobacco, smoke,
leather, chocolate, coffee, toffee,
roast nuts
TEXTURE(S): Medium bodied, alcoholic

VINTAGE CONSIDERATIONS: Though
some tawny ports are vintage-
dated, most consist of blended

wines aged for a long time in oak
casks before bottling; they are
ready to consume when
purchased

PRODUCER STYLES:
Lighter • Offley Forrester, Smith
Woodhouse, Niepoort, Croft,
Kopke, Sandeman, Churchill,
Delaforce, Ferreira
Fuller • Taylor, Ramos-Pinto,
Cockburn, Graham, Warre, Fon-
seca, Dow, Noval

~~~~~~~~~~~~~~~~~~~~~~~~~~~~~~~~~~~~

WINE(S): Vintage Port
COUNTRY: Portugal
REGION: Upper Douro
SUB-REGION: N/A

COMPONENT(S): Low to moderate
acidity, semi-sweet to sweet
FLAVOR(S): Plum, raisin, black
cherry, cedar, spice, tobacco,
smoke, leather, chocolate, coffee
TEXTURE(S): Medium to full bodied,
alcoholic

VINTAGE CONSIDERATIONS:
1977 • Very rich; balanced
1980 • Moderately rich; balanced
1982 • Fairly light; balanced
1983 • Rich; balanced
1985 • Very rich; balanced

PRODUCER STYLES:
Lighter • Offley Forrester, Smith
Woodhouse, Niepoort, Croft,
Kopke, Sandeman, Churchill,
Delaforce, Ferreira
Fuller • Taylor, Ramos-Pinto,
Cockburn, Graham, Warre, Fon-
seca, Dow, Noval

~~~~~~~~~~~~~~~~~~~~~~~~~~~~~~~~~~~~

WINE(S): Pouilly-Fumé
COUNTRY: France
REGION: Loire
SUB-REGION: Eastern Loire

COMPONENT(s): Moderate to high acidity, dry

FLAVOR(s): Green apple, musk, earth, herbs, hay, grass

TEXTURE(s): Medium to full bodied

VINTAGE CONSIDERATIONS:
1983 • Rich; alcoholic
1984 • Fairly light; acidic
1985 • Rich; alcoholic
1986 • Rich; balanced
1987 • Moderately rich; balanced

PRODUCER STYLES:
Lighter • Michel Redde, Domaine Saget, Château de Tracy
Fuller • Domaine Masson-Blondelet, Domaine Gitton, Roger Pabiot, J.D. Chatelain, Ladoucette

~~~~~~~~~~~~~~~~~~~~~~

WINE(s): Prosecco
COUNTRY: Italy
REGION: Veneto
SUB-REGION: N/A

COMPONENT(s): Moderate acidity, dry to off-dry

FLAVOR(s): Peach, pear, apricot, green apple, almond, straw

TEXTURE(s): Light to medium bodied, slightly sparkling to effervescent

VINTAGE CONSIDERATIONS: Drink the youngest vintage available

PRODUCER STYLES:
Lighter • Nino Franco, Cardinal, Santa Margherita, Zonin, Valdo
Fuller • Malvolti, Zardetto, Antica Quercia, Foss Marai

~~~~~~~~~~~~~~~~~~~~~~

WINE(s): Recioto della Valpolicella Amarone
COUNTRY: Italy

REGION: Veneto
SUB-REGION: N/A

COMPONENT(s): Moderate acidity

FLAVOR(s): Black cherry, plum, prune, red grape, cherry blossom, bitter almond

TEXTURE(s): Medium to full bodied, alcoholic

VINTAGE CONSIDERATIONS:
1979 • Rich; balanced
1980 • Fairly light; acidic
1981 • Fairly light; balanced
1982 • Moderately rich; balanced
1983 • Rich; balanced
1984 • Thin; acidic
1985 • Rich; balanced
1986 • Rich; balanced

PRODUCER STYLES:
Lighter • Aldegheri, Zeni Bolla, Santa Sofia, Tommasi
Fuller • Masi, Giuseppe Quintarelli, Tedeschi, Boscaini, Righetti, Santi, Allegrini, Bertani

~~~~~~~~~~~~~~~~~~~~~~

WINE(s): Ribera del Duero (Red)
COUNTRY: Spain
REGION: Valladolid
SUB-REGION: N/A

COMPONENT(s): Low to moderate acidity, dry

FLAVOR(s): Blackberry, blueberry, vanilla, cedar, earth, chocolate, tobacco, smoke, coffee, tar, game, roast nuts

TEXTURE(s): Medium to full bodied

VINTAGE CONSIDERATIONS:
1981 • Rich; balanced
1982 • Rich; alcoholic
1983 • Moderately rich; balanced
1984 • Moderately rich; balanced
1985 • Very rich; balanced
1986 • Moderately rich; balanced

PRODUCER STYLES:
Lighter • Vina Pedrosa, Victor Balbas, Protos, Ismael Arroyo
Fuller • Pesquera, Vega Sicilia, Penalba Lopez, Mauro

WINE(S): Retsina
COUNTRY: Greece
REGION: N/A
SUB-REGION: N/A

COMPONENT(S): Low to moderate acidity
FLAVOR(S): Pine, lemon, grapefruit
TEXTURE(S): Medium bodied

VINTAGE CONSIDERATIONS:
Drink the youngest available

PRODUCER STYLES:
Lighter • Boutari, Cambas, Logado, Boutrys, Vaeni
Fuller • Patraiki, Achaia Clauss

WINE(S): Riesling
COUNTRY: France
REGION: Alsace
SUB-REGION: N/A

COMPONENT(S): High acidity, dry to sweet
FLAVOR(S): Lemon, green apple, musk, honeysuckle, acacia, pear, apricot, petrol
TEXTURE(S): Light to medium bodied (Riesling), medium to full bodied (Vendange Tardive Riesling), full bodied (Selection des grains nobles Riesling)

VINTAGE CONSIDERATIONS:
1983 • Very rich; alcoholic
1984 • Fairly light; acidic
1985 • Rich; balanced
1986 • Fairly light; balanced
1987 • Fairly light; balanced

PRODUCER STYLES:
Lighter • Aussay, Hugel, Boeckel, Schmidt, Trimbach, Ostertag, Klug
Fuller • Josmeyer, Kuentz-Bas, Weinbach, Zind-Humbrecht, Schleret, Schaetzel, Sparr, G. Lorentz, Beyer, Schlumberger, Sipp, Dopff "au Moulin," Klack, Klipfel, Gisselbrecht, Dopff and Irion, Willm

---

WINE(S): Riesling
COUNTRY: USA
REGION: New York
SUB-REGION: Finger Lakes

COMPONENT(S): Moderate to high acidity, dry to off-dry
FLAVOR(S): Red apple, honeysuckle, pear, peach, petrol
TEXTURE(S): Light to medium bodied

VINTAGE CONSIDERATIONS:
1985 • Moderately rich; balanced
1986 • Fairly light; acidic
1987 • Moderately rich; balanced

PRODUCER STYLES:
Lighter • Casa Larga, Great Western, Vinifera Wine Cellars, Widmer's
Fuller • Heron Hill, Dr. Konstantin Frank, Hermann J. Weimer, Wagner

---

WINE(S): Riesling
COUNTRY: USA
REGION: Washington
SUB-REGION: Columbia Valley

COMPONENT(S): Moderate to high acidity, dry to off-dry
FLAVOR(S): Red apple, pear, apricot, peach, honeysuckle, orangeblossom, petrol
TEXTURE(S): Light to medium bodied

VINTAGE CONSIDERATIONS:
1983 • Moderately rich; balanced
1984 • Rich; balanced
1985 • Very rich; alcoholic
1986 • Very rich; balanced
1987 • Rich; balanced

PRODUCER STYLES:
Lighter • Ste. Michelle, Columbía, Pacifica, Hinzerling
Fuller • Hogue, Covey Run, Arbor Crest

〜〜〜〜〜〜〜〜〜〜〜〜〜〜〜〜〜〜

WINE(S): Riesling
COUNTRY: Germany
REGION: Mosel–Saar–Ruwer
SUB-REGION: N/A

COMPONENT(S): Moderate to high acidity, dry to sweet
FLAVOR(S): Green apple, pear, lemon, lime, peach, honey, spice, kerosene, honeysuckle, acacia, mint, rosewater
TEXTURE(S): Light bodied (QbA, Kabinett), medium bodied (Spätlese, Auslese), full bodied (Beerenauslese, Trockenbeerenauslese)

VINTAGE CONSIDERATIONS:
1983 • Rich; balanced
1984 • Fairly light; acidic
1985 • Rich; balanced
1986 • Moderately rich; low in acid
1987 • Light; acidic

PRODUCER STYLES:
Lighter • Bischöflichen Weingüter, Dr. Fischer, F. Wilhelm-Gymnasium, J. Lauerberg, S.A. Prüm, Selbach-Oster, von Landenberg, Wegeler-Deinhard
Fuller • F. Christoffel-Berres, F. Haag, Karthäuserhof, Geltz Zilliken, M. Grünhaus, J.J. Prüm, Max Ferd, Richter, Merkelbach, Milz Laurentiushof, Monchof, E. Müller, Dr. Loosen, Schloss Saarstein, Staati. Weinbaudomänen, Dr. H. Thanisch, van Volxem, Vereinigte Hospitien, von Hövel, von Kesselstatt, von Schubert

〜〜〜〜〜〜〜〜〜〜〜〜〜〜〜〜〜〜

WINE(S): Riesling
COUNTRY: Germany
REGION: Nahe
SUB-REGION: N/A

COMPONENT(S): Moderate to high acidity, dry to sweet
FLAVOR(S): Green apple, pear, lemon, lime, peach, honey, spice, kerosene, honeysuckle, acacia, mint, rosewater
TEXTURE(S): Light bodied (QbA, Kabinett), medium bodied (Spätlese, Auslese), full bodied (Beerenauslese, Trockenbeerenauslese)

VINTAGE CONSIDERATIONS:
1983 • Rich; balanced
1984 • Fairly light; acidic
1985 • Rich; balanced
1986 • Moderately rich; low in acid
1987 • Medium bodied; balanced

PRODUCER STYLES:
Lighter • von Plettenberg, W. Schweinhardt
Fuller • P. Anheuser, H. Crusius, Diel, H. Dönnhof, Staatl. Weinbaudomänen

〜〜〜〜〜〜〜〜〜〜〜〜〜〜〜〜〜〜

WINE(S): Riesling
COUNTRY: Germany
REGION: Rheingau
SUB-REGION: N/A

COMPONENT(S): Moderate to high acidity, dry to sweet

FLAVOR(S): Green apple, pear, lemon, lime, peach, honey, spice, kerosene, honeysuckle, acacia, mint, rosewater

TEXTURE(S): Light bodied (QbA, Kabinett), medium bodied (Spätlese, Auslese), full bodied (Beerenauslese, Trockenbeeren-auslese)

VINTAGE CONSIDERATIONS:
1983 • Rich; balanced
1984 • Fairly light; acidic
1985 • Rich; balanced
1986 • Moderately rich; balanced
1987 • Light; balanced

PRODUCER STYLES:
Lighter • Balthasar Ress, Graf von Kanitz, H. Hulbert, Landgräflich Hessisches, Schloss Groenesteyn, Schloss Vollrads, Staats. Eltville, Wegeler-Deinhard
Fuller • F. Altenkirch, J.B. Becker, J.F. Erben, Eser, Geheimrat Aschrott, Johannishof, Langwerth von Simmern, Riedel, Schloss Johannisberg, Schloss Reinhartshausen, Schloss Schönborn, G.M. Siftung, Staats. Bergstrasse, von Hessen, von Oetinger, Dr. R. Weil

~~~~~~~~~~~~~~~~~~~~~~~~~~~~~~~~

WINE(S): Riesling
COUNTRY: Germany
REGION: Rheinpfalz
SUB-REGION: N/A

COMPONENT(S): Low to moderate acidity, dry to sweet

FLAVOR(S): Green apple, pear, lemon, lime, peach, honey, spice, kerosene, honeysuckle, acacia, mint, rosewater

TEXTURE(S): Light bodied (QbA,) medium bodied (Kabinett, Spätlese, Auslese), full bodied (Beerenauslese, Trockenbeeren-auslese)

VINTAGE CONSIDERATIONS:
1983 • Rich; low in acid
1984 • Fairly light; balanced
1985 • Rich; balanced
1986 • Moderately rich; balanced
1987 • Moderately rich; balanced

PRODUCER STYLES:
Lighter • K. Schaefer, von Buhl, Wegeler-Deinhard
Fuller • J. Biffar, Dr. Bürklin-Wolf, G. Henninger, Knipser-Johannishof, Koehler-Ruprecht, Mosbacher, Müller-Catoir, Pfeffingen, E. Schuster, G. Siben, von Bassermann–Jordan, Werle

~~~~~~~~~~~~~~~~~~~~~~~~~~~~~~~~

WINE(S): Rioja (Red)
COUNTRY: Spain
REGION: Rioja
SUB-REGION: Rioja Alta, Rioja Baja, Rioja Alavesa

COMPONENT(S): Moderate acidity, dry

FLAVOR(S): Vanilla, black cherry, plum, coffee, smoke, earth, truffle (crianzas are the simplest and fruitiest, riserva are more complex and less fruity, and gran reservas are the most complex and least fruity)

TEXTURE(S): Light to medium bodied

VINTAGE CONSIDERATIONS:
1981 • Moderately rich; balanced
1982 • Very rich; alcoholic
1983 • Moderately rich; balanced
1984 • Fairly light; acidic
1985 • Rich; balanced
1986 • Fairly light; balanced

PRODUCER STYLES:
Lighter • Domecq, Gurpegui, Muerza, Riojanas, Marqués de Riscal, Montecillo, Muga, Campo Viejo
Fuller • Remelluri, Palacios Remondo, Beronia, Olarra, Marqués de Cáceres, Vina Tondonia, Cune, la Rioja Alta, Marqués de Murrieta

---

WINE(S): Rülander (Grauburgunder)
COUNTRY: Germany
REGION: Baden
SUB-REGION: N/A

COMPONENT(S): Low to moderate acidity, dry
FLAVOR(S): Red apple, grapefruit, melon, pear, spice, smoke
TEXTURE(S): Medium to full bodied

VINTAGE CONSIDERATIONS:
1983 • Rich; low in acid
1984 • Fairly light; balanced
1985 • Rich; low in acid
1986 • Moderately rich; low in acid
1987 • Moderately rich; balanced

PRODUCER STYLES:
Lighter • Badischer Winzergenossenschaften, H. Dörflinger, Winzergenossenschaft Auggen
Fuller • S. Adler, H. Männle, Staats. Meersburg, von Gleichenstein, Winzergenossenschaft Sasbachwalden

---

WINE(S): Sancerre (Red)
COUNTRY: France
REGION: Loire
SUB-REGION: Eastern Loire

COMPONENT(S): Moderate to high acidity, dry
FLAVOR(S): Tar, earth, raspberry, black cherry, violet, oak
TEXTURE(S): Light to medium bodied

VINTAGE CONSIDERATIONS:
1983 • Rich; alcoholic
1984 • Fairly light; acidic
1985 • Rich; balanced
1986 • Moderately rich; balanced
1987 • Moderately rich; balanced

PRODUCER STYLES:
Lighter • Alphonse Mellot, Jean-Max Roger, Domaine Chapuis
Fuller • Domaine Gitton, Bailly-Reverdy, Paul Prieur, Pierre Prieur, Christian Salmon, Jean Reverdy, Lucién Crochet, André Dezat, Jean Vacheron, Etienne Riffault

---

WINE(S): Sancerre (White)
COUNTRY: France
REGION: Loire
SUB-REGION: Eastern Loire

COMPONENT(S): Moderate to high acidity, dry
FLAVOR(S): Green apple, pears, earth, herbs, grass, straw
TEXTURE(S): Medium to full bodied

VINTAGE CONSIDERATIONS:
1983 • Rich; alcoholic
1984 • Fairly light; acidic
1985 • Rich; alcoholic
1986 • Rich; balanced
1987 • Moderately rich; balanced

PRODUCER STYLES:
Lighter • Château de Tracy, Guy Saget, Alphonse Mellot, Michel Redde
Fuller • Jean Reverdy, Hubert Reverdy, Jean-Max Roger, Vincent Delaporte, Lucién Crochet, Paul Cotat, Domaine Gitton, Château du Nozet

WINE(S): Santenay; Chassagne-
Montrachet (Red)
COUNTRY: France
REGION: Burgundy
SUB-REGION: Côte de Beaune

COMPONENT(S): Moderate acidity,
dry
FLAVOR(S): Cherry, raspberry,
blackberry, plum, smoke, violets,
game, earth, oak, spice, burning
leaves, licorice

TEXTURE(S): Light to medium bodied

VINTAGE CONSIDERATIONS:
1980 • Moderately rich; balanced
1981 • Fairly light; balanced
1982 • Fairly light; balanced
1983 • Very rich; alcoholic
1984 • Fairly light; acidic
1985 • Rich; balanced
1986 • Fairly light; acidic
1987 • Fairly light; balanced

PRODUCER STYLES:
Lighter • Gagnard, Prosper Mau-
foux, Prieur-Brunet, Roux
Fuller • Bouzereau, Girardin, L.
Latour, Lequin-Roussot, Leroy,
B. Morey, Pousse d'Or, Remois-
senet

WINE(S): Sauternes; Barsac
COUNTRY: France
REGION: Bordeaux
SUB-REGION: N/A

COMPONENT(S): Low to moderate
acidity, sweet, slightly bitter
FLAVOR(S): Honey, apricot, coconut,
pineapple, mango, melon, butterscotch, caramel, vanilla, oak,
spice
TEXTURE(S): Medium to full bodied

VINTAGE CONSIDERATIONS:
1982 • Fairly light; balanced

1983 • Very rich; balanced
1984 • Fairly light; balanced
1985 • Moderately rich; balanced
1986 • Very rich; balanced
1987 • Fairly light; balanced

PRODUCER STYLES:
Lighter • Doisy-Daëne, de Malle,
Filhot, la Tour Blanche,
Lafaurie-Peyraguey, Rayne-
Vigneau, Rabaud-Promis, Romer
du Hayot, Siglas Rabaud
Fuller • Climens, Coutet, Château
de Fargues, d'Arche, Doisy-
Védrines, Gilette, Guiraud,
Nairac, Rieussec, Raymond-
Lafon, Suduiraut, d'Yquem

WINE(S): Sauvignon Blanc
COUNTRY: New Zealand
REGION: North and South Islands
SUB-REGION: N/A

COMPONENT(S): Moderate to high
acidity, dry
FLAVOR(S): Green apple, lemon,
lime, herbs, asparagus, grass
TEXTURE(S): Light to medium bodied

VINTAGE CONSIDERATIONS:
1986 • Rich; balanced
1987 • Moderately rich; balanced
1988 • Moderately rich; forward

PRODUCER STYLES:
Lighter • Cook's, Montana, Selak's
Fuller • Cloudy Bay, Babich, Cor-
ban's, Hunter's, Kumeu River,
Morton Estate

WINE(S): Sauvignon Blanc
COUNTRY: USA
REGION: California
SUB-REGION: Mendocino–Lake

COMPONENT(S): Moderate acidity,
dry

FLAVOR(s): Lemon, grass, herbs, green apple, hay, lima bean, asparagus
TEXTURE(s): Light to medium bodied

VINTAGE CONSIDERATIONS:
1984 • Moderately rich; balanced
1985 • Rich; balanced
1986 • Moderately rich; balanced
1987 • Rich; balanced

PRODUCER STYLES:
Lighter • Fetzer, Milano, Husch, McDowell Valley
Fuller • Kalin, Parducci, Kendall-Jackson, Guenoc

~~~~~~~~~~~~~~~~~~~~~~~

WINE(s): Sauvignon Blanc
COUNTRY: USA
REGION: California
SUB-REGION: Napa

COMPONENT(s): Moderate acidity, dry
FLAVOR(s): Lemon, grass, herbs, green apple, hay, lima bean, asparagus
TEXTURE(s): Light to medium bodied

VINTAGE CONSIDERATIONS:
1984 • Moderately rich; balanced
1985 • Moderately rich; balanced
1986 • Moderately rich; balanced
1987 • Rich; balanced

PRODUCER STYLES:
Lighter • Beringer, Chateau Bouchaine, Frog's Leap, Beaulieu, Spottswoode, Sterling, Robert Pecota, Stag's Leap, Stratford, Cakebread, Flora Springs
Fuller • Joseph Phelps, St. Clement, Robert Mondavi-Reserve, Duckhorn

~~~~~~~~~~~~~~~~~~~~~~~

WINE(s): Sauvignon Blanc

COUNTRY: USA
REGION: California
SUB-REGION: Sonoma

COMPONENT(s): Moderate acidity, dry
FLAVOR(s): Lemon, grass, herbs, green apple, hay, lima bean, asparagus
TEXTURE(s): Light to medium bodied

VINTAGE CONSIDERATIONS:
1984 • Moderately rich; balanced
1985 • Rich; balanced
1986 • Moderately rich; balanced
1987 • Rich; balanced

PRODUCER STYLES:
Lighter • Alderbrook, Chateau St. Jean, Carmenet, Dry Creek, Fritz, Glen Ellen, Preston-Cuvée de Fumé, Simi
Fuller • Kenwood, Lyeth Vineyard, Clos du Bois-Alexander Valley, Matanzas Creek

~~~~~~~~~~~~~~~~~~~~~~~

WINE(s): Sauvignon Blanc, Sémillon
COUNTRY: USA
REGION: Washington
SUB-REGION: Columbia Valley

COMPONENT(s): Moderate to high acidity, dry
FLAVOR(s): Green apple, grass, herbs, straw, citrus fruit, candle wax
TEXTURE(s): Light to medium bodied

VINTAGE CONSIDERATIONS:
1983 • Rich; balanced
1984 • Light; acidic
1985 • Moderately rich; fruity
1986 • Fairly light; balanced
1987 • Rich; alcoholic

PRODUCER STYLES:
Lighter • Ste. Michelle, Griffin,

Columbía, Snoqualmie, Preston, Covey Run
Fuller • Hogue, Arbor Crest

WINE(S): Savennières
COUNTRY: France
REGION: Loire
SUB-REGION: Anjou-Saumur

COMPONENT(S): Moderate to high acidity, dry
FLAVOR(S): Melon, green apple, quince, honey, pear, earth, acacia
TEXTURE(S): Medium bodied

VINTAGE CONSIDERATIONS:
1983 • Rich; balanced
1984 • Fairly light; acidic
1985 • Rich; alcoholic
1986 • Moderately rich; balanced
1987 • Moderately rich; balanced

PRODUCER STYLES:
Lighter • Domaine du Closel, Château de la Bizolière, Château d'Epiré
Fuller • Coulée de Serrant, Château de Chamboureau, Clos de Coulaine

---

WINE(S): Cream Sherry, Pedro Ximenez
COUNTRY: Spain
REGION: Andalusia
SUB-REGION: Jerez

COMPONENT(S): Moderate acidity, sweet
FLAVOR(S): Raisin, fig, chocolate, coffee, toffee, spice
TEXTURE(S): Full bodied, alcoholic

VINTAGE CONSIDERATIONS:
Blended from many different vintages by the solera system (casks triangularly stacked and connected)

PRODUCER STYLES:
Lighter • Osborne, Croft, Gonzalez Byass, Duff Gordon, Williams and Humbert
Fuller • Harvey and Sons, Sandeman, Domecq, Lustau, Díez-Merito

---

WINE(S): Shiraz and blends of primarily Shiraz
COUNTRY: Australia
REGION: New South Wales
SUB-REGION: Hunter Valley

COMPONENT(S): Low to moderate acidity, dry
FLAVOR(S): Black cherry, plum, black pepper, earth
TEXTURE(S): Medium to full bodied, alcoholic

VINTAGE CONSIDERATIONS:
1983 • Rich; balanced
1984 • Light
1985 • Rich; fruity
1986 • Very rich; balanced
1987 • Moderately rich; balanced

PRODUCER STYLES:
Lighter • Rothbury, Sutherland
Fuller • Tulloch, Lindeman's, Elliott's, Tyrrells, Robson, Hungerford Hill, Rosemount

---

WINE(S): Shiraz and blends of primarily Shiraz
COUNTRY: Australia
REGION: New South Wales
SUB-REGION: Mudgee–Griffith

COMPONENT(S): Low to moderate acidity, dry
FLAVOR(S): Black cherry, plum, black pepper, earth

TEXTURE(S): Medium to full bodied, alcoholic

VINTAGE CONSIDERATIONS:
1983 • Rich; balanced
1984 • Very rich; balanced
1985 • Rich; fruity
1986 • Very rich; balanced
1987 • Moderately rich; balanced

PRODUCER STYLES:
Lighter • Craigmoor, Huntington, McWilliams
Fuller • Miramar, Botobolar, de Bortoli, Montrose

WINE(S): Shiraz and blends of primarily Shiraz
COUNTRY: Australia
REGION: South Australia
SUB-REGION: Barossa, Clare, Riverland and Southern Vale

COMPONENT(S): Low to moderate acidity, dry
FLAVOR(S): Black cherry, plum, black pepper, earth
TEXTURE(S): Medium to full bodied, alcoholic

VINTAGE CONSIDERATIONS:
1983 • Moderately rich; balanced
1984 • Very rich; balanced
1985 • Rich; balanced
1986 • Very rich; balanced
1987 • Moderately rich; balanced

PRODUCER STYLES:
Lighter • Henschke-Mount Edelstone, Thomas Hardy, Seppelt, Hill Smith, Berri Estate
Fuller • Henschke, Wolf Blass, Basedows, Bleasdale, Penfold's, Wirra Wirra

WINE(S): Shiraz and blends of primarily Shiraz

COUNTRY: Australia
REGION: South Australia
SUB-REGION: Coonawarra

COMPONENT(S): Moderate acidity, dry
FLAVOR(S): Black cherry, plum, black pepper, earth
TEXTURE(S): Light to medium bodied

VINTAGE CONSIDERATIONS:
1983 • Fairly light; acidic
1984 • Very rich; balanced
1985 • Very rich; fruity
1986 • Rich; balanced
1987 • Rich; balanced

PRODUCER STYLES:
Lighter • Wynn, Mildara
Fuller • Bowen Estate, Brand's Laira, Lindeman's, Coriole, Katnook

WINE(S): Shiraz and blends of primarily Shiraz
COUNTRY: Australia
REGION: Victoria
SUB-REGION: Central and Western Victoria

COMPONENT(S): Low to moderate acidity, dry
FLAVOR(S): Black cherry, plum, black pepper, earth
TEXTURE(S): Medium to full bodied

VINTAGE CONSIDERATIONS:
1982 • Rich; balanced
1983 • Very rich; balanced
1984 • Moderately rich; fruity
1985 • Very rich; balanced

PRODUCER STYLES:
Lighter • Chateau le Amon, Mitchelton, Redbank
Fuller • Chateau Tahbilk, Best's Concongella, Campbells, Balgownie, Mt. Avoca, Taltarni

WINE(S): Shiraz and blends of primarily Shiraz
COUNTRY: Australia
REGION: Victoria
SUB-REGION: Yarra Yarra Valley and Northeast

COMPONENT(S): Moderate acidity, dry
FLAVOR(S): Black cherry, plum, black pepper, earth
TEXTURE(S): Light to medium bodied

VINTAGE CONSIDERATIONS:
1983 • Moderately rich; balanced
1984 • Rich; balanced
1985 • Rich; balanced
1986 • Very rich; tannic
1987 • Moderately rich; balanced

PRODUCER STYLES:
Lighter • Chateau Yarrinya, Campbells, Seville Estate
Fuller • St. Huberts, Yarra Yering, Bannockburn, Brown Brothers

WINE(S): Silvaner
COUNTRY: Germany
REGION: Franconia
SUB-REGION: N/A

COMPONENT(S): Moderate acidity, dry
FLAVOR(S): Green apple, lemon, melon, peach, earth, honeysuckle
TEXTURE(S): Light bodied

VINTAGE CONSIDERATIONS:
Drink within two years of vintage.
1987 • Moderately rich; balanced

PRODUCER STYLES:
Lighter • Bürgerspital, Juliusspital, H. Wirsching
Fuller • Fürst Castell, Staatl. Hofkeller, P. Schmitt, R. Schmitt

WINE(S): Silvaner
COUNTRY: Germany
REGION: Rheinhessen
SUB-REGION: N/A

COMPONENT(S): Moderate acidity, dry
FLAVOR(S): Green apple, lemon, melon, peach, earth, honeysuckle
TEXTURE(S): Light to medium bodied

VINTAGE CONSIDERATIONS:
Drink within two years of vintage.
1987 • Moderately rich; balanced

PRODUCER STYLES:
Lighter • H. Braun, A.B. Erben, C.K. Erben, Kappellenhof, Rappenhof, F. Schmitt, C. Sittmann
Fuller • G. Gessert, L. Guntrum, Gunderloch-Usinger, Heyl Zu Herrnsheim, Dr. R. Muth, Dr. A. Senfter, J. and H.A. Strub, Villa Sachsen

WINE(S): Soave
COUNTRY: Italy
REGION: Veneto
SUB-REGION: N/A

COMPONENT(S): Moderate to high acidity, dry
FLAVOR(S): Citrus fruit, almond, green apple
TEXTURE(S): Light to medium bodied

VINTAGE CONSIDERATIONS:
Drink the youngest vintage possible

PRODUCER STYLES:
Lighter • Bertani, Bolla, Folonari, Tommasi, Zonin, Zenato, Aldegheri, Santa Sofia
Fuller • Pieropan, Tedeschi, Anselmi, Masi, Boscaini, Mirafiore

WINE(S): Sparkling (Vouvray)
COUNTRY: France
REGION: Loire
SUB-REGION: Touraine

COMPONENT(S): Moderate to high
acidity, dry to off-dry
FLAVOR(S): Melon, lemon, pear,
peach, apricot, honeysuckle,
apple
TEXTURE(S): Light to medium bodied, effervescent

VINTAGE CONSIDERATIONS:
Drink the youngest available vintage, or freshest nonvintage
blend

PRODUCER STYLES:
Lighter • Bernard Avignon, Alain
Ferrand, Chevreau Vigneau,
Viticulteurs de Vouvray, Marc
Bredif
Fuller • Pierre Foreau, Prince
Poniatowski, Jean-Pierre Freslier,
Daniel Jarry

WINE(S): Sparkling wine (Spumante)
COUNTRY: Italy
REGION: Lombardy
SUB-REGION: N/A

COMPONENT(S): Moderate to high
acidity, dry
FLAVOR(S): Lemon, wheat biscuit,
straw, yeast, toast, vanilla,
dough
TEXTURE(S): Light to medium bodied, effervescent

VINTAGE CONSIDERATIONS:
Drink the youngest available vintage, or the freshest nonvintage
blend

PRODUCER STYLES:
Lighter • Bellavista-Cuvée Brut,
Villa Mazzucchelli, Prandell

Fuller • Bellavista-Franciacorta
Cuvée Brut, Ca' del Bosco-Brut

WINE(S): Sparkling (Cava)
COUNTRY: Spain
REGION: Catalonia
SUB-REGION: N/A

COMPONENT(S): Moderate to high
acidity, dry (extra brut and brut)
to off-dry (extra seco and seco) to
sweet (demi-seco and dulce)
FLAVOR(S): Toast, wheat biscuit,
vanilla, lemon, grapefruit, green
apple
TEXTURE(S): Light to medium bodied, effervescent

VINTAGE CONSIDERATIONS:
Though some cava are vintage-
dated, most wines are blended
from several vintages for consis-
tency of style; purchase the
freshest cava you can find

PRODUCER STYLES:
Lighter • Juvé y Camps, Paul
Cheneau, Mascaro,
Castellblanch, Segura Viudas
Fuller • Codorníu, Freixenet,
Raïmat

WINE(S): Sparkling
COUNTRY: USA
REGION: California
SUB-REGION: Napa

COMPONENT(S): Moderate to high
acidity, dry
FLAVOR(S): Green apple, toast, vanilla, lemon, yeast, wheat biscuit
TEXTURE(S): Light to full bodied,
effervescent

VINTAGE CONSIDERATIONS:
1982 • Moderately rich; balanced
1983 • Rich; fruity

1984 • Very rich; balanced
1985 • Moderately rich; fruity
1986 • Rich; balanced
1987 • Rich; balanced

PRODUCER STYLES:
Lighter • Domaine Chandon,
Christian Brothers, Beaulieu,
Hanns Kornell
Fuller • S. Anderson, Domaine
Mumm, Schramsberg

WINE(S): Sparkling
COUNTRY: USA
REGION: California
SUB-REGION: Sonoma–Mendocino

COMPONENT(S): Moderate to high
acidity, dry to off-dry
FLAVOR(S): Green apple, toast, vanilla, lemon, yeast, wheat biscuit
TEXTURE(S): Light to full bodied,
effervescent

VINTAGE CONSIDERATIONS:
1982 • Rich; balanced
1983 • Moderately rich; fruity
1984 • Rich; forward
1985 • Very rich; balanced
1986 • Moderately rich; balanced
1987 • Rich; balanced

PRODUCER STYLES:
Lighter • Gloria Ferrer, Korbel,
Robert Hunter, van der Kamp,
Tijsseling, Piper-Sonoma,
Shadow Creek
Fuller • Iron Horse, Chateau St.
Jean

WINE(S): St.-Estèphe
COUNTRY: France
REGION: Bordeaux
SUB-REGION: Northern Médoc

COMPONENT(S): Moderate acidity,
dry

FLAVOR(S): Blackberry, cassis, black
cherry, earth, smoke, chocolate,
tobacco, vanilla, oak, cedar,
spice, leather, minerals, herbs
TEXTURE(S): Medium to full bodied

VINTAGE CONSIDERATIONS:
1980 • Fairly light; balanced
1981 • Moderately rich; balanced
1982 • Very rich; balanced
1983 • Rich; balanced
1984 • Fairly light; tannic
1985 • Rich; balanced
1986 • Very rich; tannic
1987 • Fairly light; fruity

PRODUCER STYLES:
Lighter • Cos Labory, Marbuzet,
Meyney, Phélan-Ségur
Fuller • Calon-Ségur, Cos d'Es-
tournel, de Pez, Lafon-Rochet,
les-Ormes-de-Pez, Montrose,
Tronquoy-Lalande

WINE(S): St.-Julien
COUNTRY: France
REGION: Bordeaux
SUB-REGION: Northern Médoc

COMPONENT(S): Moderate acidity,
dry to off-dry
FLAVOR(S): Blackberry, cassis, black
cherry, earth, smoke, chocolate,
tobacco, vanilla, oak, cedar,
spice, leather, minerals, herbs
TEXTURE(S): Medium to full bodied

VINTAGE CONSIDERATIONS:
1980 • Fairly light; balanced
1981 • Moderately rich; balanced
1982 • Very rich; balanced
1983 • Rich; balanced
1984 • Fairly light; tannic
1985 • Rich; balanced
1986 • Very rich; tannic
1987 • Fairly light; fruity

PRODUCER STYLES:
Lighter • Beychevelle, du Glana,

Gloria
Fuller • Branaire-Ducru, Ducru-Beaucaillou, Gruaud-Larose, Lagrange, Lalande Borie, Langoa-Barton, Léoville-Barton, Léoville-las Cases, Léoville-Poyferré, Talbot

~~~~~~~~~~~~~~~~~~~~~~~~~~~~~~~

WINE(S): Tocai
COUNTRY: Italy
REGION: Friuli-Venezia Giulia
SUB-REGION: N/A

COMPONENT(S): Moderate acidity, dry, slightly bitter
FLAVOR(S): Honeysuckle, orange blossom, almond toast, herbs, melon
TEXTURE(S): Medium bodied

VINTAGE CONSIDERATIONS:
1986 • Very rich; balanced
1987 • Moderately rich; balanced

PRODUCER STYLES:
Lighter • Badoglio, Cantoni, Villa Ronche
Fuller • Pighin, Buzzinelli, Ca' Ronesca, Formentini, Villa Russiz, Masut, Ronco del Gnemiz, Doro Princic

~~~~~~~~~~~~~~~~~~~~~~~~~~~~~~~

WINE(S): Valpolicella
COUNTRY: Italy
REGION: Veneto
SUB-REGION: N/A

COMPONENT(S): Moderate to high acidity, dry
FLAVOR(S): Black cherry, plum, red grape, cherry blossom, bitter almond
TEXTURE(S): Light to medium bodied

VINTAGE CONSIDERATIONS:
1985 • Moderately rich; balanced

1986 • Moderately rich; balanced
1987 • Fairly light; acidic

PRODUCER STYLES:
Lighter • Bolla, Bertani, Santa Sofia, Aldegheri, Tommasi, Fratelli Fabiano
Fuller • Allegrini, Bolla, le Ragose, Giuseppe Quintarelli, Tedeschi, Masi, Zeni, Righetti, Boscaini, Anselmi

~~~~~~~~~~~~~~~~~~~~~~~~~~~~~~~

WINE(S): Vinho Verde (White)
COUNTRY: Portugal
REGION: Minho
SUB-REGION: N/A

COMPONENT(S): Moderate to high acidity, dry to off-dry
FLAVOR(S): Green apple, lemon, grapefruit, orange blossom, straw
TEXTURE(S): Light bodied

VINTAGE CONSIDERATIONS:
Drink the youngest available

PRODUCER STYLES:
Lighter • Caves Messias, Caves Aliança, Carvalho, Ribiero and Ferreira
Fuller • Quinta da Aveleda, Paço de Teixeiro, Casa de Sezim, Palacio da Brejoeira, Alvarinho de Monção

~~~~~~~~~~~~~~~~~~~~~~~~~~~~~~~

WINE(S): Vino Nobile di Montepulciano
COUNTRY: Italy
REGION: Tuscany
SUB-REGION: Montepulciano

COMPONENT(S): Moderate acidity, dry
FLAVOR(S): Black cherry, plum, oak, cedar, smoke, spice, leather, violets, tobacco, orange peel (riservas have less fruit and more

complexity than nonriservas)
TEXTURE(S): Medium to full bodied

VINTAGE CONSIDERATIONS:
1982 • Very rich; balanced
1983 • Rich; alcoholic
1984 • Thin; acidic
1985 • Very rich; balanced
1986 • Moderately rich; fruity
1987 • Fairly light; balanced

PRODUCER STYLES:
Lighter • Bologna Buonsignori,
  Sant'Agnese
Fuller • Avignonesi, Fassati, Bos-
  carelli, Poggio alla Sala,
  Fognano, il Macchione

WINE(S): Vin Santo (White)
COUNTRY: Italy
REGION: Tuscany
SUB-REGION: N/A

COMPONENT(S): Moderate acidity,
  semi-sweet to sweet
FLAVOR(S): Orange peel, lemon,
  straw, honey
TEXTURE(S): Medium to full bodied,
  alcoholic

VINTAGE CONSIDERATIONS:
Vin santo is made from semi-dried
grapes, which make vintage distinctions difficult; purchase the
freshest bottles you can find

PRODUCER STYLES:
Lighter • Antinori, Brolio, Cap-
  pelli, Falchini, Frescobaldi
Fuller • Avignonesi, Badia a Colti-
  buono, Castellare di Castellina,
  Castello di Volpaia, Barbi,
  Strozzi, il Poggione

WINE(S): Vosne Romanée,
  Flagey-Echézeaux
COUNTRY: France

REGION: Burgundy
SUB-REGION: Côte de Nuits

COMPONENT(S): Moderate acidity,
  dry
FLAVOR(S): Black cherry, raspberry,
  blackberry, plum, smoke, violets,
  game, earth, oak, spice, burning
  leaves, licorice
TEXTURE(S): Medium bodied

VINTAGE CONSIDERATIONS:
1980 • Moderately rich; balanced
1981 • Fairly light; acidic
1982 • Fairly light; balanced
1983 • Very rich; alcoholic
1984 • Fairly light; acidic
1985 • Rich; balanced
1986 • Moderately rich; balanced
1987 • Fairly light; balanced

PRODUCER STYLES:
Lighter • Drouhin
Fuller • Dujac, Engel, Faiveley,
  Forey, H. Jayer, J. Jayer, L.
  Jayer, Jayer-Gilles, Hudelot-
  Noëllat, L. Latour, Moillard, G.
  Mugneret, Mongeard-Mugneret,
  Rion, Domaine de la Romanée
  Conti, Sirugue

WINE(S): Vougeot
COUNTRY: France
REGION: Burgundy
SUB-REGION: Côte de Nuits

COMPONENT(S): Moderate acidity,
  dry
FLAVOR(S): Black cherry, raspberry,
  blackberry, plum, smoke, violets,
  game, earth, oak, spice, burning
  leaves, licorice
TEXTURE(S): Medium bodied

VINTAGE CONSIDERATIONS:
1980 • Moderately rich; balanced
1981 • Fairly light; acidic
1982 • Fairly light, balanced
1983 • Very rich; alcoholic

1984 • Fairly light; acidic
1985 • Rich; balanced
1986 • Moderately rich; balanced
1987 • Fairly light, balanced

PRODUCER STYLES:
Lighter • Bertagna, Drouhin,
Drouhin-Laroze, Grivot
Fuller • Arnoux, Gros, Leroy,
Moillard, G. Mugneret,
Mongeard-Mugneret, Rion,
Roumier, Domaines des Varoilles

WINE(S): Vouvray (still)
COUNTRY: France
REGION: Loire
SUB-REGION: Touraine

COMPONENT(S): Moderate to high
acidity, dry to sweet
FLAVOR(S): Melon, lemon, pear,
peach, apricot, honeysuckle,
apple
TEXTURE(S): Medium to full bodied

VINTAGE CONSIDERATIONS:
1983 • Rich; balanced
1984 • Fairly light; acidic
1985 • Rich; alcoholic
1986 • Moderately rich; balanced
1987 • Moderately rich; balanced

PRODUCER STYLES:
Lighter • J.M. Monmousseau,
Château Moncontour, Marc
Bredif, Domaine Debreuil,
Deuplessis-Mornay
Fuller • Gaston Huet, Pierre
Foreau, Prince Poniatowski

WINE(S): Zinfandel
COUNTRY: USA
REGION: California
SUB-REGION: Mendocino

COMPONENT(S): Low to moderate
acidity, dry

FLAVOR(S): Berry-fruit, spice, red
cherry, plum, prune, rose petal,
nasturtium, papaya seed, briar,
coffee, cedar
TEXTURE(S): Medium to full bodied

VINTAGE CONSIDERATIONS:
1982 • Rich; tannic
1983 • Moderately rich; fruity
1984 • Rich
1985 • Very rich; balanced
1986 • Rich; balanced

PRODUCER STYLES:
Lighter • Fetzer-Ricetti, Milano,
Tyland, Willow Creek
Fuller • Fetzer-Special Reserve,
Kendall-Jackson, Edmeades,
Hidden Cellars

WINE(S): Zinfandel
COUNTRY: USA
REGION: California
SUB-REGION: Napa

COMPONENT(S): Low to moderate
acidity, dry
FLAVOR(S): Berry-fruit, spice, red
cherry, plum, prune, rose petal,
nasturtium, papaya seed, briar,
coffee, cedar

TEXTURE(S): Medium to full bodied

VINTAGE CONSIDERATIONS:
1982 • Moderately rich; balanced
1983 • Fairly light; acidic
1984 • Very rich; alcoholic
1985 • Moderately rich; balanced
1986 • Rich; fruity

PRODUCER STYLES:
Lighter • Louis M. Martini, Clos
du Val, Christian Brothers, Joseph Phelps, Cuvaison, Green
and Red
Fuller • Ridge-York Creek and
Howell Mountain, Chateau Montelena, Storybook Mountain,

Buehler, Deer Park, la Jota,
Lamborn, Rosenblum-Napa

WINE(S): Zinfandel
COUNTRY: USA
REGION: California
SUB-REGION: Sierra Foothills

COMPONENT(S): Low to moderate
acidity, dry
FLAVOR(S): Berry-fruit, spice, red
cherry, plum, prune, rose petal,
nasturtium, papaya seed, briar,
coffee, cedar
TEXTURE(S): Light to full bodied,
light to heavy tannin

VINTAGE CONSIDERATIONS:
1982 • Fairly light; balanced
1983 • Moderately rich; tannic
1984 • Very rich; alcoholic
1985 • Rich; balanced
1986 • Moderately rich; fruity

PRODUCER STYLES:
Lighter • Baldinelli, Monteviña,
Granite Springs, Story, Mon-
tino, Boeger
Fuller • Sutter Home, Amador
Foothill, Monteviña-Winemaker's
Choice, Santino, Shenandoah,
Madrona

WINE(S): Zinfandel
COUNTRY: USA
REGION: California
SUB-REGION: Sonoma

COMPONENT(S): Low to moderate
acidity, dry
FLAVOR(S): Berry-fruit, spice, red
cherry, plum, prune, rose petal,
nasturtium, papaya seed, briar,
coffee, cedar
TEXTURE(S): Medium to full bodied

VINTAGE CONSIDERATIONS:
1982 • Moderately rich; balanced
1983 • Fairly light; fruity
1984 • Rich; alcoholic
1985 • Very rich; balanced
1986 • Rich; fruity

PRODUCER STYLES:
Lighter • Fritz, Meeker, Nalle,
Pedroncelli, Sausal, Rafanelli
Fuller • Grgich Hills, Alexander
Valley, Ravenswood-Dry Creek
and Old Hill, Ridge-Geyserville
and Lytton Springs, Coturri,
Lytton Springs, DeLoach, Dry
Creek, Haywood, Hop Kiln,
Quivera, Rosenblum-Sonoma

In addition to the normal functions of an index, the following listings enable you to use this book in a completely new way. We feel, of course, that the best way to match wine and food is to familiarize yourself with the principles in the book, and then to make your own creative choices. However, if you need a quick fix, you can always look up a food or wine item in the index and get an instant recommendation. For example: company's due, you haven't finished the book, and you need a wine selection for lamb. Simply look up lamb in the index, where you'll see page references for six different lamb preparations. By turning to those pages, you'll get a quick idea of what we like to serve with lamb. You can do the same with a wine ("What should I serve with Sancerre?"), or with an ethnic cuisine ("What should I serve with Italian food?").

[Page numbers in *italic* refer to dishes for which recipes appear in text.
Page numbers in **boldface** refer to entries for wines in "The Big List."]

ABOUT THE AUTHORS

DAVID ROSENGARTEN is copublisher and coeditor of *The Wine &
Food Companion*. He has contributed dozens of recipe and wine articles
to such publications as *Food & Wine, Bon Appétit, The Wine Spectator,
Harper's Bazaar, House Beautiful*, and *Business Week*. He collaborated
with Hugh Johnson on the computer food and wine program, "Hugh
Johnson's Wine Cellar," and frequently teaches cooking classes on a
wide range of culinary subjects. He lives with his wife, Connie, in
New York City.

JOSHUA WESSON is copublisher and coeditor of *The Wine & Food
Companion*. In 1984, he was named "Best Sommelier in America," and
in 1986 he was selected as one of the top five sommeliers in the world.
He has consulted to many of America's finest restaurants and
contributed articles to *Food & Wine* and *House Beautiful*. His wine
recommendations can also be found in Anne Rosenzweig's *Arcadia
Cookbook* (Abrams, 1986) and Betty Fussell's *Eating In* (Ecco, 1986).
He lives with his moderately large nose in New York City.

Many of the ideas in this book are given ongoing attention by David Rosengarten and Joshua Wesson in *The Wine & Food Companion*, a bi-monthly, independent newsletter devoted to bringing wine and food together. A one-year subscription is $36 for delivery in the United States. Subscriptions can be obtained by sending a check for $36, or an American Express card number, to The Wine & Food Companion, 250 East 73th St., Suite 14H, New York, NY 10021, or by dialing the toll-free subscription line, 1-800-888-1961.